**YOU CAN ASTONISH** your friends with trick billiard shots—but first you must master the fundamentals of the game. You'll learn the basics as well as trick set-ups in the authoritative article on billiards, page 274

**TWO CHILDREN, ONE ROOM?** Try the attractive set-up shown here. Check page 225 for complete plans. And even the smallest bathroom can be modernized into a glamor spot (below). For unique ideas, see page 197

**IT'S NOT THE STRIKES,** but the spares that build a solid bowling score. You'll find the precise aiming spot to pick up every spare on page 366

**A SMALL ROOM** can be a headache with the clutter of two boys. Try building an attractive bedroom that folds away for play. See page 220

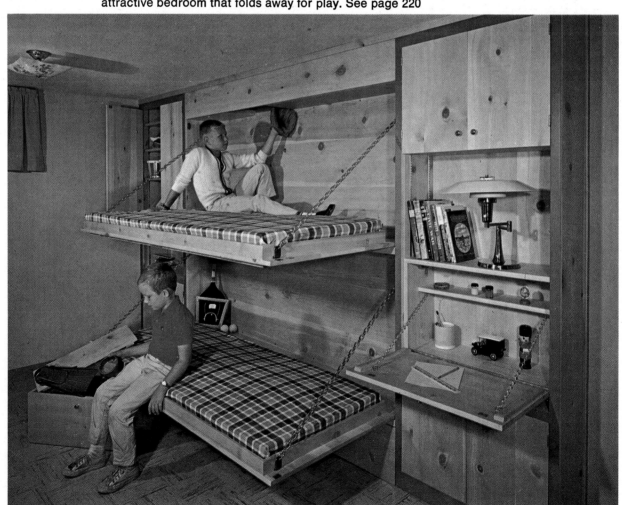

**BUYING YOUR FIRST BOAT?** It's a major investment, whether you plan to use it for skindiving (above), skiing, fishing or just pure enjoyment (below). You'll find tips for buying the boat that's exactly right for you on page 331

# Popular Mechanics
# Do-It-Yourself Encyclopedia

## in 16 volumes

## A complete guide to

- home maintenance
- home improvement
- hand-tool skills
- craft projects
- power-tool know-how
- hobbies
- automotive upkeep
- automotive repair
- shop shortcuts
- boating
- fishing
- hunting
- model making
- outdoor living
- radio, TV and electronics

## Volume 2

Book Division, Hearst Magazines, New York, N.Y. 10019

Printed in the United States of America

# VOLUME 2

# How to use your Encyclopedia

*Browse*. Glance through this volume, or any other volume of the Encyclopedia. Likely you will find the solution to a particular home-maintenance problem that has been bothering you, or a shop project so appealing that you will immediately head for your bench. Browsing not only is enjoyable, but is a source of ideas.

*Seek specific information*. Perhaps you want to find out how to cure that leak in your basement, how to keep the exterior paint from peeling, or how to tune and set the carburetor on your car.

Four reader aids, all cross-referenced, will enable you to find specific information:

**1.** *Alphabetical headings*. Located at the top of the page, these headings cover broad classifications of information. If you are looking for information on how to keep paint from peeling, for example, look up "Paints" alphabetically, then find the particular section dealing with peeling paint.

**2.** *Alphabetical cross-references*. These are shown in a box at the bottom of the page. Some material can logically be classified under more than one alphabetical heading, so if you don't find what you are seeking alphabetically (as described above), be sure to check the *alphabetical cross-references* at the bottom of the page; there you may find precisely the classification you are seeking. For example, you and your son decide to build a model airplane, and are looking for plans. You look up "Model airplanes" and find nothing under that alphabetical heading. However, if you glance at the bottom *of that same page* you will find an alphabetical cross-reference that reads: **model airplanes,** see airplane models.

**3.** *See also references*. These are shown at the end of many articles. They refer you to related articles which may also be of interest.

**4.** *Instant index*. Located at the end of Volume 16, it is thoroughly cross-referenced to help you find information under any heading.

# Deluxe bathroom for a modest home

### BY AL LEES

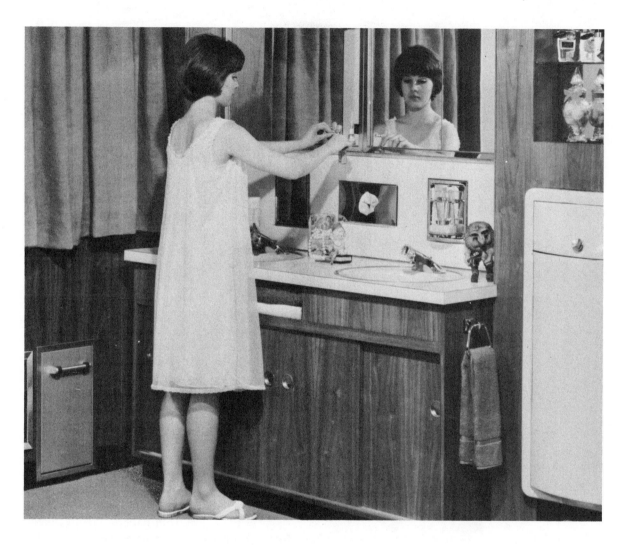

WHAT ROOM IN YOUR HOME is the mood setter? We'll wager it's your bathroom—the room that greets you in the morning and sends you off to bed at night. Small wonder, then, that many of us start and end the day glumly. Most bathrooms are cursed with clutter: The family toothbrushes bristle at you from exposed racks—the wife's lingerie droops soggily from the shower rod—and the general atmosphere is as chilly and antiseptic as a hospital.

What we wanted to create was a *cheerful* bathroom—one that exploited the warmth of

Beauty on a budget
was our goal when we tackled
the updating of an outmoded bathroom.
You might try these ideas in your home

bath, sauna: see sauna

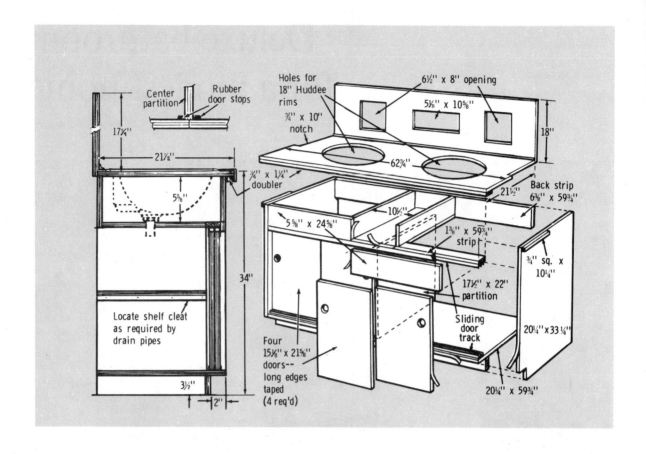

Center partition
Rubber door stops

17¼"

21½"

5⅝"

Locate shelf cleat as required by drain pipes

34"

3½"

2"

Holes for 18" Huddee rims

¾" x 10" notch

6½" x 8" opening

5⅛" x 10⅝"

18"

62¾"

¾" x 1¼" doubler

21½"

Back strip 6⅜" x 59¾"

10½"

5⅝" x 24⅝"

1⅜" x 59¾" strip

¾" sq. x 10¼"

17½" x 22" partition

Sliding door track

Four 15⅛" x 21⅝" doors-- long edges taped (4 req'd)

20¼"x33¼"

20¼" x 59¾"

*deluxe bathroom, continued*

natural wood and sunny colors, tucked unsightly necessities into the wall when they weren't in use, promised easy maintenance—*and* offered the do-it-yourselfer maximum opportunity to cut outside labor costs.

To keep our feet on the ground, we hunted up an actual bathroom in a home—one that presented a grim challenge, as you can see from our "before" photo. Neglect and hard use from a succession of owners had left this bath the ugliest room in the house, with battered fixtures dating from an era that wasn't noted for good design. An exposed radiator added another age wrinkle, as did a naked shower rod and a tiled backsplash with crumbling mortar.

We asked designer Franklyn Jacoby to give this room a major facelift, replacing the fixtures but keeping their present locations to simplify plumbing. We then researched the accessories field to select a wealth of commercial units that could be built into our bathroom—including the tub-alcove clothesline and let-down scale.

We decided to be different by using plywood in our bathroom. This was an heretical decision, since home designers have a long established convention that only ceramics, glass and plastics

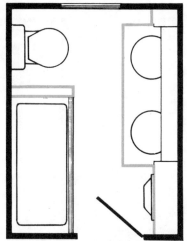

The floor plan was basically unchanged in transforming this old bathroom into a deluxe room. This avoided any major plumbing revision and kept costs down. The color outlines on the plan indicate new construction

are appropriate for "wet rooms." But our design puts these watershedders where they count: We've wrapped the tub alcove and surrounded the flush double basins with them. Then to protect adjacent veneer surfaces from splash spotting, we finished the plywood with a primer and two coats of a top-quality plywood finish. There are a number of excellent brands available at most building supply dealers.

If you prefer a softer sheen than the plywood finish gives, rub down the final coat with fine steel wool. With this moisture seal, you should have no problem—unless your bathroom is the Dismal Swamp, without air circulation.

All construction involving a visible face was done in ¾-in. walnut plywood. The exposed edges were covered with matching walnut veneer. The window wall was covered with a sheet of ¼-in. walnut, applied with a contact adhesive.

If you want to save time, you can go to a prefinished paneling, both on the window wall and on the toilet side of the stub partition. Standard black rubber baseboard contributes a finished look to the floor line and masks the wall from wet mopping.

You'll note that the back wall between these two alcove faces is surfaced with vinyl sheeting, covered right up from the floor. This not only creates a striking effect but eliminates the bathroom's most unsanitary corner. (The wall-hung bowl makes cleaning even easier.)

The flooring is a vinyl with a foam vinyl backing that "gives" underfoot, then springs back as you lift your foot. Many flooring materials are labeled "resilient," but these foam-layer types really are. Such resilience offers two bonuses besides foot comfort: Because it cushions impact, the sheet is protected from puncture and wear; and the foam's insulating quality creates a warmer floor—ideal for barefoot standing. The bonded-on surface vinyl features a deep pebbled texture that tends to slip-proof a wet floor.

This type of flooring comes in sheets and most manufacturers don't recommend do-it-yourself installation of sheet flooring—and particularly of so novel a floor as this, which requires two special adhesives.

The other installation you may wish to leave to a pro is the tiling of the tub alcove, although you can do it yourself. We chose a light yellow tile to match the fixtures and the countertop.

In the counter construction detail, you'll note

*deluxe bathroom, continued*

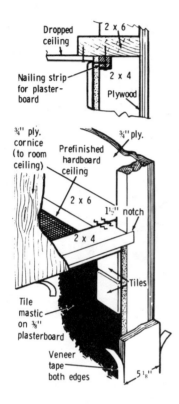

that we have made the backsplash panel optional. If the wall between the countertop and the recesses for the medicine cabinets is sound, you'll doubtless want to apply a plastic laminate directly to the wall (after cutting three holes for the dispensing fixtures, as indicated). A full back has been omitted from the cabinet to facilitate the plumbing hook-up. The basins hang from special rims and require no support blocking. The countertop is made of any smooth-faced ¾-in. panel with forward edges doubled to present a greater thickness for edge-banding.

The two mirror-backed shelf shadow-boxes are easily custom-made, utilizing a standard-sized chrome-framed mirror set against back cleats and "locked" in place with the adjustable L brackets that support the plate-glass shelves. The shadow-box above the hamper is identical to the one in the stub partition, except for its greater depth. Each 24-in. lighting fixture is simply wall-mounted so its bottom panel is flush with the top of the recess.

The old-fashioned radiator was replaced with

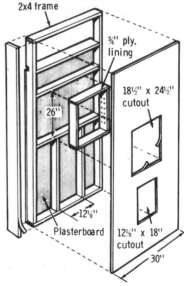

an efficient electric wall heater with its own circulating fan, but we could have converted to one of the modern baseboard radiators instead.

**See also:** ceramic tile; condensation; drains; measurements; remodeling; remodeling ideas; sauna; tile, floor.

200

Check the polarity of the battery with the tester. With the clip to the positive terminal and the case to the negative, the bulb will light. Tape the tester to a cable to keep it handy

# Polarity tester

BY RAY SHOBERG

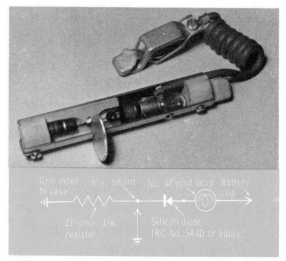

Cutaway and schematic are shown oriented

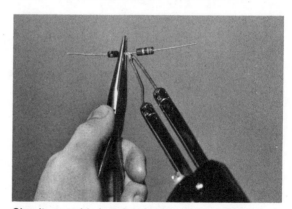

Circuit assembly is quite simple and the parts are inexpensive, but the diode must be protected from excessive heat in soldering. Pliers do the trick

THE WEATHER IS BLUSTERY and getting colder. You hop into the car and turn the key, hoping for a quick warmup to get the heater going. But the battery is colder than you are. All you get is a low moan. You have your neighbor pull his car over to yours as you ready the jumper cables . . . but, whoa? Which side of the battery is which? A wrong clamp and you could burn up your alternator!

Save the worry. You can build a simple polarity indicator in a jiffy, at a cost of about $2. The parts (see schematic) include a diode that can handle at least 2 amps. steady state and at least 24 PIV.

The resistor permits operation of the 6-v. bulb on 12 v., while the diode will block the tester's operation if hooked to the battery in reverse.

Solder the components in series as close together as practical. Use a heat sink or pliers between the soldering gun and the diode to prevent damage to the heat-sensitive diode. If the diode's polarity is not marked, determine it with a 12-v. battery of known polarity before soldering. The diode's positive terminal is then soldered to the center contact of the bulb. Tape the battery-clip junction on the shell of the bulb to avoid contact with the case.

Cut the case from ½-in. thinwall conduit about 1 in. longer than from the tip of the bulb to the end of the resistor, excluding the free lead. The ends of the case are plugged with ½-in. dowels.

At the bulb end, whittle the dowel so as to leave a flat blade on which to clip the positive lead for storage. Groove the plug's side to pass this lead. Drill a series of holes around the case where the bulb will rest so the light can be seen.

For the other end of the case, use a dowel that will reach past the diode. Leaving ½ in. of it to form a plug, cut away a half-round section and gouge the flat side to form individual cradles for

the resistor and diode. Drill a hole through the dowel's center to pass the resistor's free lead, which hooks under one of the ¼-in. No. 4 panhead sheet-metal screws that secure the plugs.

In line with the soldered junction between the resistor and diode, hacksaw a slot wide and deep enough to admit a coin to contact the junction. This will bypass the resistor to light the bulb on a 6-v. battery or when a 12-v. is weak.

Finally, mark the positive terminal and tape the tester to a jumper cable.

**See also:** batteries, dry cell; battery chargers; electrical system, auto; starting, auto, cold weather.

# Winter battery care

BY MORTON J. SCHULTZ

Special attention during the winter won't help much—unless you give the battery its due all year round. But if you follow all the rules, you get extra starts

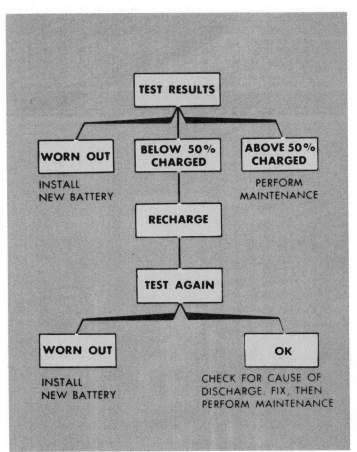

This chart sums up the sequence you should follow to decide whether careful maintenance will help your battery get you through the winter

A BLEAK WINTER NIGHT, and you've just paid a visit to your mother-in-law. It's late, you're miles from home, but you've finally succeeded in prying your wife loose and she's followed you out to the snow-heaped car. You're anxious to make a fast getaway before her mother thinks up some ruse to coax you both back for another hour's chat. But when you turn the ignition key, all you get is that heart-sinking sound of an exhausted battery struggling—in vain—to crank the cold engine.

Would special winter maintenance have spared you this sad little scene? Not likely. No amount of once-a-year battery care is going to avert the inevitable. It's a waste of time and effort unless your battery is in a healthy state to begin with. Winter care might coax a few extra starts from a worn battery, but in the end you're only going to replace it anyway.

Looking at it practically, maintenance of a weak battery may carry you into January or February—right to the heart of winter. In other words, this care will provide just the time you

need to experience the inconvenience, discomfort and road expense of a dead battery on a cold day when you're in a rush to get to work— or *away* from your mother-in-law's.

Battery maintenance is a year-round task. Without it, your battery will probably last some 30,000 miles. With it, you can increase this figure to some 40,000 and even 50,000 miles.

How can you tell if your battery will last the winter? You invest about $2 for a battery hydrometer and test the battery's condition (its ability to store and deliver power) and its state of charge (the amount of electrical power in the battery). Then take the necessary action, as shown in the chart above.

A hydrometer records the strength of the electrolyte in the battery's cells by measuring the acid's specific gravity, the weight of the electrolyte as compared to the weight of pure water.

As a battery's failure point is approached, there is a widening range in the specific gravities of electrolyte taken from the various cells. In a completely discharged battery, for example, the

A hydrometer offers the best inexpensive way to check battery condition and state of charge. Squeeze the bulb, insert the nozzle into the cell, and release the nozzle slowly to draw electrolyte into the transparent barrel around the float

Cover the nozzle with a finger to prevent dripping electrolyte and hold the barrel vertical. With the float hovering free of the top as well as the bottom, read its scale at the electrolyte level. Then return the fluid to the cell from which it came

specific gravity of a cell's electrolyte may be close to that of pure water, which is 1.000. When specific gravity readings vary significantly from cell to cell, your battery has outlived its usefulness and should be replaced.

There is a knack to using a hydrometer. Employed the right way, it is an accurate tool—as accurate as a voltmeter (and less expensive), and almost as accurate as a load tester, which mechanics use to determine the serviceability of batteries.

When reading a hydrometer, be sure the float rides free. Record the reading from the scale and return all the electrolyte to the cell from which it was drawn. Proceed to the next cell.

Hydrometer readings are affected by the temperature of the electrolyte. Many hydrometers have a built-in thermometer and are capable of recording temperature as well as specific gravity. If yours doesn't, use a separate thermometer to determine the temperature of the electrolyte. Simply insert the thermometer into the cell from which you are drawing electrolyte and record the temperature reading.

For precise specific gravity readings, you should make the following corrections for temperature: *add* .004 to the specific gravity reading for each 10 deg. that battery temperature exceeds 90 deg. F; *subtract* .004 from the specific gravity reading for each 10 deg. that battery temperature is below 80 deg. F.

For example, suppose the hydrometer reads 1.260, but the thermometer records the temperature of the electrolyte as 65 deg. The true hydrometer reading, then, would be 1.260 minus .006, or 1.254.

Now, what do you do with the readings once you have them? You determine battery condition and the state of charge.

To find the condition of your battery, compare the difference between the highest-reading and lowest-reading cells. If this difference is .050 or more, the battery is nearing the end of its life and should be replaced before the coldest weather.

For example, suppose you get readings of 1.230, 1.220 and 1.220 from the three cells of a 6-v. battery (for a 12-v. battery, you will have six readings from six cells). The difference between the high-reading and low-reading cells is only .010, indicating that the battery's ability to store and deliver power is okay.

However, if the readings between the cells are

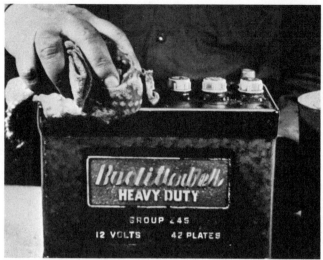

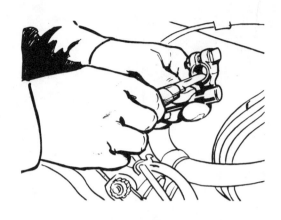

A dirty, fouled battery case can provide a current path around the outside of the battery and let it discharge. To prevent this, dissolve half a pound of baking soda in water and wipe the mixture over the entire battery, guarding against getting any into the cells (above). To insure good contacts, scrape cable terminals clean with a knife (top right) and brighten the battery posts with emery cloth or fine sandpaper (right). A petroleum jelly coat on the posts will control corrosion

1.250, 1.180 and 1.240, the difference between high-reading and low-reading cells is .070. This indicates that one cell of the battery is extremely weak and that the battery as a whole will soon fail—especially if used in cold weather.

A battery's state of charge—the amount of electrical energy it is storing—is usually expressed as a percentage of full charge. Thus, a battery that is 50 percent charged has about one-half the power it's capable of storing.

To determine the state of charge of your battery, you should know the full-charge capacity of your brand of battery. To get this information, write the battery's manufacturer or consult a battery reference book at your local battery dealer's shop.

Most American batteries are full-charge rated at from 1.260 to 1.280 specific gravity. European batteries, however, are rated at about 1.240.

To find your battery's state of charge, add up the specific gravity readings of all cells and divide by the number of cells to get an average. If all cells read 1.260 and the battery is rated at 1.260, state of charge is 100 percent.

An average of 1.225 indicates the battery's state of charge is 75 percent; an average of 1.190 means a 50 percent charge; 1.155 indicates 25 percent, and 1.110 means the battery is discharged.

If the battery shows a state of charge of less than 50 percent, have it recharged and test it again. Recharging should be done with a low output charger and should take at least 24 hours.

If the recharged battery still doesn't exceed a 50 percent charge, the battery is worn out and should be replaced. However, if it recharges to more than 50 percent, there might be a mechanical cause for its discharging in the first place. Before the coldest months arrive you should track down and correct this cause.

Keep in mind, though, that no battery holds a charge indefinitely—there will be a constant loss of charge although no useful electrical power is being delivered. This standing loss is due to internal chemical action. There is nothing you can do about it, except keep checking specific gravity every month or so, recharging as needed.

Recharging is extremely important to prevent battery sulphation, which is the hardening of the lead sulphate that forms on the positive and negative plates. It occurs more quickly in a battery that is not up to full charge. When a discharged battery is finally charged, the hardened

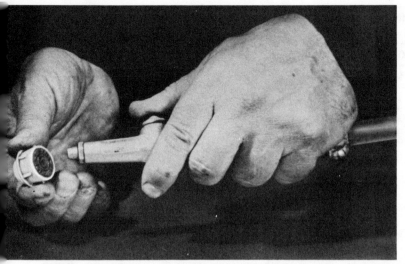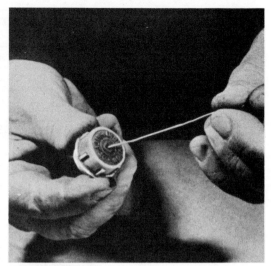

Battery vent caps must be kept free of dirt. If they become clogged, gas built up inside the battery has no way to escape and could bulge the case. The best way to clean out caps is with an air hose as at left. If none is available, dig dirt out of the holes with a wire. Battery vent caps have holes on both the top and underside. Both, of course, must be clean

lead sulphate prevents conversion of the plates back to lead and lead peroxide, causing a loss of battery capacity and leading to faster battery wear-out.

Sulphation is also hastened by lack of water inside the cells. For this reason, always maintain the electrolyte level.

A common cause of discharge that you *can* do something about is external leakage of current. Dirt, foreign matter and spilled electrolyte on a battery's case provide a conducting path through which the battery can discharge itself, even while standing still. With a 12-v. battery, the percentage of charge lost because of current leakage is four times greater than with six-volt batteries under the same condition.

To guard against current loss, the battery should be cleaned about once every three months. Give it a baking soda bath (see photos). If your battery has much acid on it from spilled electrolyte or from vent-cap fumes, you will notice that the baking soda will foam. When foaming stops, flush the battery with clean water. Repeat the process until a fresh application of baking soda fails to produce foaming, thus indicating that all acid on the battery has been neutralized.

As important as it is to keep the battery case clean, it's just as important to keep battery cables clean, tight and in good condition. These cables must pass current to the starter and the rest of the electrical system. They're connected to the battery by means of terminals which clamp to battery posts, making a solid electrical connec-tion. One cable terminates in the ground of the electrical system, usually the frame or engine block, and the other hooks to a live connection, usually the starter switch.

The battery is unable to deliver power to the electrical system unless cables are capable of carrying the full electrical load. You should, therefore, inspect cables for wear and cracks in the insulation—particularly cables in contact with parts of the car, since these are more subject to chafing. The insulation covering the cables may wear through, creating the possibility of short circuits.

Cable terminals that are heavily corroded reduce the effectiveness of the electrical connection between terminals and battery posts.

To do away with corrosion on cable terminals, scrape off as much as you can with a knife, wash the terminal with baking soda solution, rinse with clean water and dry with a rag.

Prevent further corrosion by applying a protective coating of non-metallic grease to the terminals. Petroleum jelly will do the job. When reconnecting terminals, make sure they are tight.

The battery hold-down compartment should receive the same baking soda treatment, since a battery can discharge across its bottom if the compartment is dirty. Also, clean corrosion from battery hold-down bolts. When tightening these, however, just turn the bolts up snugly.

There are several other reasons why a battery loses its charge. These can be broken down into mechanical and operational causes. If the battery

| STATE OF CHARGE | SPECIFIC GRAVITY | FREEZING POINT—F.° |
|---|---|---|
| 100% | 1.260 | -70° |
| 75% | 1.225 | -36° |
| 50% | 1.190 | -12° |
| 25% | 1.155 | + 3° (PLUS) |
| DISCHARGED | 1.110 | +16° |

*winter battery care, continued*

keeps discharging for no apparent reason—and it is clean—look into these possibilities:

- Faulty regulator or one out of adjustment
- Short circuit in the wiring (may go unnoticed except for effect on battery)
- Stuck stop-light or trunk compartment switch that causes lights to burn constantly at partial or full brilliance
- Hard starting, which drains a battery while the engine cranks
- Worn, stretched fan belt that slips and won't turn generator at proper speed
- Faulty generator
- Insufficient driving to maintain proper battery charge.
- Operational errors, such as forgetting to turn off lights, radio or ignition

The most important consideration you can give your battery during the winter is to keep in mind the temperature at which electrolyte freezes. This depends upon the specific gravity of the electrolyte.

From the chart you can see that a fully charged battery stands very little chance of freezing, no matter where you live. A battery only 50 percent charged, however, has a specific gravity of about 1.190. Electrolyte at such a low specific gravity freezes at about minus 12 deg. F., common in many northern states.

Sulphuric acid, or electrolyte, acts as a battery antifreeze. The more acid in solution in the cells, the safer the battery from freezing. To obtain this greater concentration of sulphuric acid, keep the battery as fully charged as possible.

An important point to remember: In freezing weather, don't add water unless you're going to drive enough to mix it well with the electrolyte. Newly added water tends to remain at the tops of cells and will begin freezing at 32 deg. F.—

the freezing point of water. Either wait for a thaw to add water or take the battery to a warm place and add water. Then, have it charged before returning it to the car.

What happens when a battery freezes? If you are lucky, the electrolyte will get only semi-hard. You will find some ice forced out the vent holes in the battery caps. Most likely, the car won't start.

Put the battery in a warm place for about 12 hours until it thaws out. Fill the cells with water and charge the battery before putting it back into the car.

If you aren't lucky, a hard freeze can occur. This will cause the battery case to crack or plates to buckle. Either way, you'll need a new battery.

Another important factor to consider during the winter is the battery's ability to provide power. A starting motor places the heaviest demands on a battery although, if it is in good condition and starts properly, this demand is relatively short.

**cold starts are tough**

Difficulties of starting in cold weather can be seen in the fact that a fully charged battery at 32 deg. F. delivers 65 percent of the cranking power available at 80 deg. F. At 0 deg. F., the cranking power is reduced to a mere 40 percent.

A car's engine at 32 deg. F. requires about 65 percent more starting power than the same engine at 80 deg. F. At 0 deg. F., it needs about 150 percent more starting power. In other words, a partly discharged or nearly worn-out battery might start a car satisfactorily in warm weather. In cold, however, it will leave you stranded.

You should be particularly wary if you have a foreign battery in your car and live in a cold section. In temperatures of 20 deg. F. or colder, a foreign battery with its lower specific gravity of about 1.240 may not have sufficient capacity to start the car, although it may be fully charged. In such case, you can either change to an American battery or have the specific gravity of the battery increased. Your local garage can do this by adding stronger electrolyte.

From these facts, the only conclusion that can be drawn is this: During the winter, you must keep a close watch on your battery's state of charge. Take a hydrometer reading often—during a really bad cold snap, once a day wouldn't be too much. At the slightest indication that specific gravity is falling below the allowable temperature limits for your area, get the battery recharged—pronto!

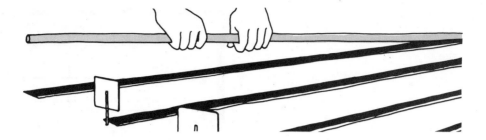

When planting in fine soil, make the rows by pressing a length of pipe into the earth.

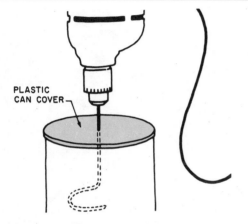

PLASTIC
CAN COVER

Use a plastic coffee-can lid to make a
splash guard for your drill-powered
paint mixer. Be sure the hole in the
lid is a snug fit on the shaft.

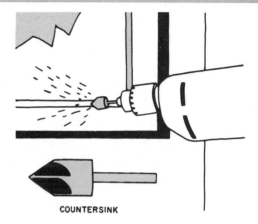

COUNTERSINK

The countersinking tool for your drill
is perfect for removing old putty when
you replace a broken pane of glass.

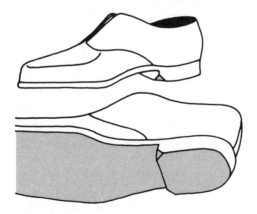

If you bevel the heels of a new pair
of shoes with a file or sharp knife,
they won't catch on your trouser cuffs.

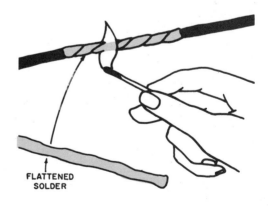

FLATTENED
SOLDER

To solder without a soldering iron,
flatten a length of rosin-core solder,
wrap it around the joint, and melt
it with a candle or a match.

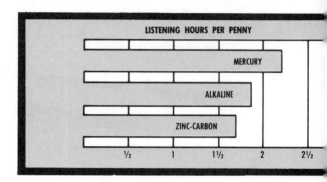

LISTENING HOURS PER PENNY

MERCURY

ALKALINE

ZINC-CARBON

½   1   1½   2   2½

# Which battery is best?

BY  LARRY  STECKLER

There are specialists among the batteries
      you use, too. When your radio goes
dead or your flashlight fades, it
            might be that you've selected the
wrong type of battery to do the job

New sealed lead-acid wet-cell may soon replace
more costly nickel-cadmium types. The rechargeable battery holds more power

BATTERIES ARE an important part of everyday
life. You'll find them in your electric toothbrush,
the emergency flashlight in the car, powering the
motor in your movie camera, giving life to your
transistor radio or portable TV, and keeping the
kids' toys going. But when it's time to replace a
set of run-down batteries, your problems are just
beginning.

Take the "standard" D cells that fit your flashlight—there are endless types to choose from.
There are high, low and medium output zinc-
carbon cells. There are steel-jacketed leakproof
types, cardboard-jacketed leakproof types and
no-jacket, not-leakproof types. Then there are
alkaline, mercury and rechargeable nickel-cadmium batteries. Prices in this assortment of types
vary from a low of seven cents for the imported,

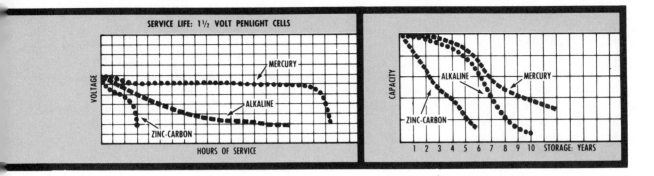

SERVICE LIFE: 1½ VOLT PENLIGHT CELLS

VOLTAGE / HOURS OF SERVICE — MERCURY, ALKALINE, ZINC-CARBON

CAPACITY / STORAGE: YEARS — 1 2 3 4 5 6 7 8 9 10 — ALKALINE, MERCURY, ZINC-CARBON

not-leakproof battery to six dollars or so for the rechargeable ones.

There are three basic demands we make on batteries: The amount of power needed, the length of time the power is required and the storage life of the battery. For example, we may want a little power for a prolonged period of time as in transistor radios. We may need medium power for continuous use in toys, movie cameras or other motor-driven devices. Or we may require high power for short intervals, as for firing flashbulbs. We also want standby time. We want to be able to store batteries, leave them standing idle, and still have them deliver full power.

These are factors that determine the best battery for a particular job. The charts above show what happens in a transistor radio. You'll note that the mercury battery gives the lowest cost of operation. And this is true even though the mercury type costs as much as an alkaline dry cell and three times the zinc-carbon dry cell.

However, if the same chart were drawn for a flashlight that is used every day, the zinc carbon cell would come out ahead. Draw a similar chart for flashguns and the alkaline cell would lead.

As a general rule, mercury batteries are excellent where low power is required for prolonged periods of time. This is why mercury types are found in hearing aids, electric watches and transistor radios. They also have the ability to pack a lot of electricity into a small package and are used in almost all subminiature electronic devices. For extra power capacity, special silver-mercury cells are made.

Alkaline cells are at their best where high power is required for intermittent short periods of time. The cell recuperates rapidly. This makes them extremely useful in motorized devices or for firing flashbulbs or strobe lights.

Zinc carbon cells have a moderate life, but are available almost anywhere. They are made

in three basic categories—general purpose, photoflash, and transistor applications. Each should be used for the purpose specified. Do otherwise and you shorten their life.

In the charts above, we compare the hours of service various types of batteries can be expected to deliver. Again the application illustrated is a transistor radio. If long life in a low-power circuit is required, mercury batteries are best.

If we change the application and draw this same chart for a high-current motor, the alkaline cell would take the lead.

Try to draw high current from a mercury cell and you shorten its life drastically. Zinc-carbon cells don't stand a chance here—the high power drain kills them fast. They may be inexpensive, but for high power use, alkaline is best.

The charts above also compare the shelf or standby life of various batteries. Again the mercury cell comes out on top. It can stand idle up to eight years and still deliver 50% of its original power. In less than two years a zinc carbon cell is almost dead. So, if standby power in an emergency radio is required, mercury is best. Note too that alkaline cells have a good shelf life. For this reason they make good standby power for the flashlight in your car.

Note that the Service Life chart also shows the comparative voltage stability of the battery over its useful life. Both the zinc-carbon and the alkaline drop steadily. However, mercury cell voltage remains relatively constant until it reaches its final hours. Here's another reason why mercury batteries are used in watches and clocks and in the new cadmium-sulfide light meters.

What about leakage? We've all seen what happens when an over-aged zinc-carbon cell splits and corrosive electrolyte oozes out all over the inside of a flashlight. You usually end up throwing out the flashlight. Leakproof cells help, but I can show you many a leakproof cell that has split and oozed. In a transistor radio this can be fatal; electrolyte can ruin the copper-printed circuit board.

Alkaline cells are much more resistant to leakage and mercury cells almost never leak. However, it's a good policy to remove the batteries from any equipment that will stand idle.

The rechargeable nickel-cadmium cells are a world to themselves. They keep you tied to an a.c. outlet for recharging, but if you recharge after each use, they last indefinitely. Be sure not to let the battery go completely dead. If it does, it can never be fully charged again.

Zinc-carbon, alkaline, and mercury batteries are rechargeable, too. Several rechargers for these units are on the market. Also a new re-

## WHERE TO USE THEM

| Use | Battery Type | Pros and Cons |
|---|---|---|
| Clocks, Watches | Mercury | Long, constant-voltage life gives accurate timekeeping with minimum of battery changing. Excellent resistance to leakage |
| | Alkaline | Voltage curve not constant, could affect timekeeping accuracy. Not available in subminiature sizes used in watches |
| | Zinc-carbon | Voltage curve not constant. Not available in subminiature sizes. Tendency to leak which could damage mechanism |
| | Nickel-cadmium | Not suitable. Life too short before recharging |
| Flashlights | Zinc-carbon | Excellent for everyday watchman-type service where it can give lowest-cost operation. Replacements are readily available |
| | Alkaline | Good for rarely-used emergency flashlight in car or home. Long shelf life (see Fig. 3). High current output. Little chance of leakage |
| | Nickel-cadmium | Very useful around the house where a.c. line voltage available for recharging. Needs recharge after using |
| | Mercury | Use when long standby life is mandatory. Comparatively high current drain of flashlight will rapidly run down battery |
| Hearing Aids | Mercury | Best bet. Provides long-term power in these low-current circuits. Minimum replacement |
| | Alkaline | Not available in subminiature button-type sizes often used |
| | Zinc-carbon | Not available in subminiature sizes. Short useful life. Leakage may damage device |
| | Nickel-cadmium | Not practical. Short useful life before recharging. Might not last eight hours |
| Cadmium-sulphide light meters | Mercury | Long, constant-voltage characteristic with minimum battery changing makes this best |
| | Alkaline | Voltage does not remain constant. Not available in subminiature sizes |
| | Zinc-carbon | Not available in subminiature sizes. Voltage does not remain constant. Tends to leak |
| | Nickel-cadmium | Voltage does not remain constant. Short useful life before recharging |
| Flashbulbs | Alkaline | High power keeps firing bulbs in sync. Long shelf life ideal. Leakage not a problem |
| | Zinc-carbon | Shorter life but readily available. Change every eight months no matter how much or how little used. Leakage can damage equipment |
| | Nickel-cadmium | Short life before recharging |
| | Mercury | Not recommended. Lacks high-current capability. Life short and erratic in this application |
| Movie camera | Alkaline | Excellent choice. Provides high, fairly constant power. Good storage life. Little leakage |

chargeable alkaline battery has been announced.

When recharging these batteries, remember that a battery that has gone dead from sitting around cannot be recharged and you shouldn't let a battery go completely dead before recharging. When recharging, you'll be able to use that zinc-carbon cell about two more lifetimes, the alkaline five to ten lifetimes, and the mercury 50 lifetimes. Charging must be slow and steady (usually overnight). A fast or overlong charge may cause the cell to explode.

Now for some final tips. If you want to extend the life of zinc-carbon batteries during storage, keep them cold. The colder the better. This slows down the electro-chemical action, prolonging shelf life.

Wherever you keep or use zinc-carbon cells, replace them every eight months whether they

## WHERE TO USE THEM

| Use | Battery Type | Pros and Cons |
|---|---|---|
| Movie camera (cont.) | Mercury | Second choice. High current required by some motors can reduce life. Much better voltage stability than alkaline (see Fig. 3). Practically no leakage |
| | Zinc-carbon | Can be used, but leakage can damage camera. Short life, rapid voltage drop, readily available |
| | Nickel-cadmium | Short life before recharging needed. Rapid voltage drop. Ties user to a.c. outlet |
| Strobe | Nickel-cadmium | Permits a.c. and battery operation. Indefinite life if recharged after each use |
| | Alkaline | High power. Little leakage possibility. Rapid recycling. Long storage life |
| | Zinc-carbon | Short life. Leakage may damage equipment. Rapid voltage available in emergency |
| | Mercury | Not recommended. High power drains can reduce life of battery |
| Tape recorder | Alkaline | High current for motors. Fairly stable voltage output. Reasonably long shelf life |
| | Mercury | Long flat voltage output means better speed regulation. However, high current drain from motor may shorten life |
| | Zinc-carbon | Short life. Leakage may damage recorder. Rapid voltage drop. Easily available |
| | Nickel-cadmium | Good only for short periods of operation before recharging |
| Toys | Alkaline | Longer life and better performance because of high-current potential |
| | Zinc-carbon | Low cost per unit, but life can be very short. Leakage can damage toy. Readily available |
| | Mercury | Not recommended. High current drain can shorten battery life |
| | Nickel-cadmium | High cost can be prohibitive in this use |
| Transistor radios | Mercury | Longest life, best performance and lowest end cost. (see Fig. 1) |
| | Alkaline | Good in sets requiring high power (e.g. table models). In pocket sets won't last as long as mercury, but costs as much |
| | Zinc-carbon | Readily available, but life is short and end cost high. Leakage can damage receiver |
| | Nickel-cadmium | Very costly. Practical if only short periods of operation are required before recharging |
| Transistor portable TV | Nickel-cadmium | Permits battery or a.c. operation. Indefinite life if recharged after each use. Usable life after recharging may be as little as 2 or 3 hours. Light weight for size |
| | Mercury Alkaline Zinc-carbon | All three expensive, non-chargeable and heavy for this application |

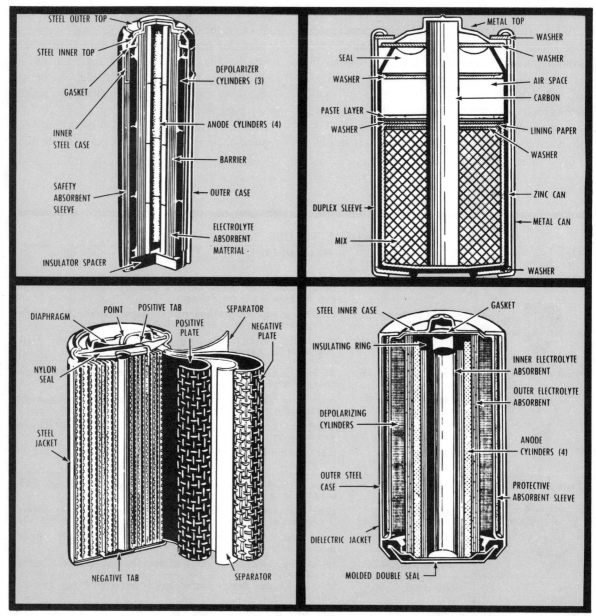

Cutaway views of the four major battery types showing their internal structure. Cylindrical mercury cell is in the upper left. To its right is a standard zinc-carbon battery. On the lower left is a rechargeable nickel-cadmium type and to its right an alkaline battery

*battery selection, continued*

have been used or not. This will insure you against dead or weak batteries when you need them. This is especially true for your flashgun. Weak batteries may fire the flash, but the firing time may be late and the bulb won't sync with the shutter.

Looking into the future, there's a new battery coming that won't have a storage problem. It is not even charged until you are ready to use it. You'll turn a thumbscrew before use to release the electrolyte and activate the cell. But it's experimental as of this writing.

For more battery data, you can purchase detailed manuals from the major battery manufacturers.

In the "Where to Use Them" charts, you'll find that there are simply some batteries that are not suitable for certain jobs. For example, the high cost of nickel-cadmium is prohibitive for powering toys; yet they are perfect for powering a transistor portable TV. Looking ahead, the new sealed lead-acid wet cell may soon replace the more costly nickel-cadmium.

**See also:** batteries, auto; battery chargers.

# Transistor battery recharger

BY FRANK GREENWALD

Batteries last 5 to 10 times longer with a simple recharger you can adapt to your set

Once the radio has been modified, the recharger plugs into what used to be its earphone jack (left). Add a miniature phone jack to the recharger output (bottom left) and make changes as in schematic

■ TRANSISTOR RADIOS are portable, handy— and battery eaters if operated continuously. Many of the sets use little 9-v. batteries that have a fairly short life to start with. These sets can be rewired so you can plug in a recharger to rejuvenate a worn battery, or to use the set directly off the 115-v. line.

The only changes made are in wiring the earphone jack (below right). Then pick out a little 9-v. recharger (you can get one from most of the electronic mail-order houses). Attach a miniature phone jack to the recharger output leads (below left) and you're all set to take advantage of longer battery life.

To recharge the battery, plug the charger into the wall outlet, and the jack into the radio.

**See also:** batteries, auto; batteries, dry cell; electrical system, auto; transistor radios.

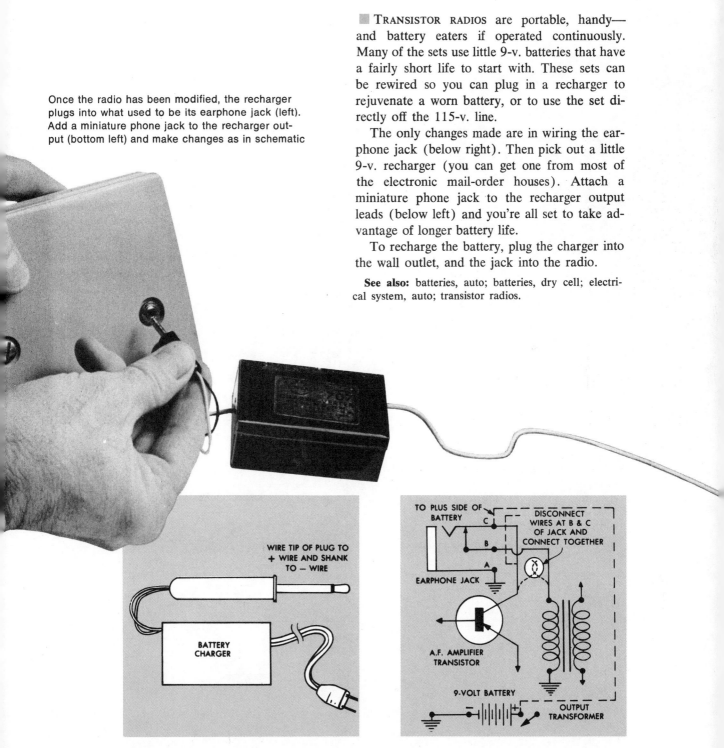

WIRE TIP OF PLUG TO + WIRE AND SHANK TO − WIRE

BATTERY CHARGER

TO PLUS SIDE OF BATTERY

DISCONNECT WIRES AT B & C OF JACK AND CONNECT TOGETHER

EARPHONE JACK

A.F. AMPLIFIER TRANSISTOR

9-VOLT BATTERY

OUTPUT TRANSFORMER

# Get longer battery life

### BY THOMAS W. SIKES

Don't throw away toys and portable
appliances or relegate them to the
storage closet just because you're
always running out of batteries.
Here's an inexpensive charger unit
you can build easily

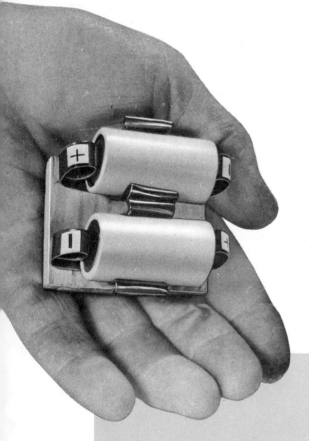

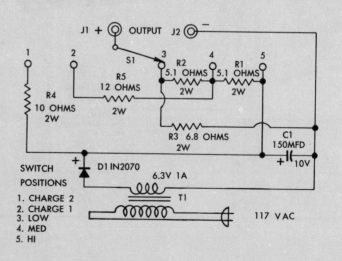

Slip two nickel-cadmium batteries into a homemade holder
and you're ready to insert them into the battery compartment
of your child's favorite toy or a portable appliance

**PARTS LIST**
C1—150 MFD, 10 volts, electrolytic capacitor
D1—1N2070 (Texas Instruments)
J1—Banana jack, red
J2—Banana jack, black
R1, R2—5.1 ohms, 2 watts, 5% resistors
R3—6.8 ohms, 2 watts, 10% resistor
R4—10 ohms, 2 watts, 10% resistor
R5—12 ohms, 2 watts, 10% resistor
S1—1 pole, 5 position, rotary switch (Mallory 3215J)
T1—Filament transformer (Lafayette 33C3702)
Case, 2¾ x 2⅛ x 1⅝ in. (Premier AMC type 1000 or equiv.)

SWITCH
POSITIONS

1. CHARGE 2
2. CHARGE 1
3. LOW
4. MED
5. HI

214

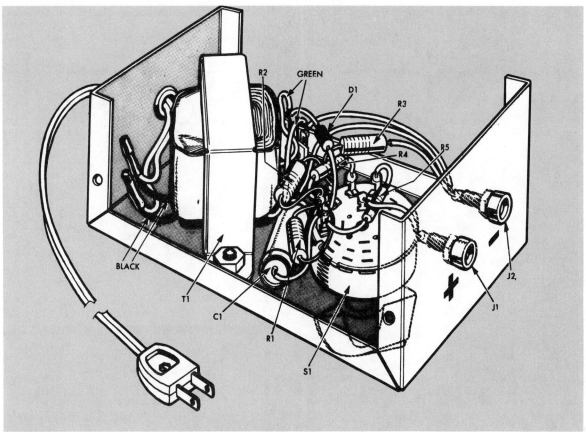

Pictorial diagram shows all wiring in the charger-power unit. Wherever bare leads get too close to each other or to the case, use lengths of insulating spaghetti for protection

■ IF YOU SCOUT around your home, you are likely to find several toys which aren't being used because they require frequent battery replacement. Nor should you relegate those small appliances to the storage closet just for want of a few batteries.

One way you can continue to make use of expensive toys and gadgets is to use rechargeable batteries and the battery charger described here.

It is best to use the CD-12 nickel-cadmium battery which is somewhat smaller than a size-C cell, and you will have to build a little adapter so it will fit into the battery compartment of the toy. The adapter shown is made from ¼-in. plywood and scrap copper. Cut the metal into strips ¼-in. wide to form the end contacts. A bracket made from ½-in. strips holds the batteries in place.

Begin construction following the pictorial diagram. Cut the transformer primary leads (black) down to 1½ in., strip the insulation, and solder to the power cord leads. Now cut the secondary leads (green) to 1½ in. Then complete the wiring following the diagrams.

Any place that wiring happens to run close to the chassis or that the bare leads get too close to one another, use lengths of insulating spaghetti to protect against short circuits in the unit's system.

To charge a single cell, set the charger to *Charge 1* and connect the red lead from J1 to the positive battery terminal and the black lead from J2 to the negative battery terminal. To charge two cells in series, switch to *Charge 2. Never charge nickel-cadmium batteries in parallel.*

A battery is fully charged when its voltage reads 1.4 volts. It will normally take 12 hours to recharge a battery.

The charger-power supply can also be used for direct powering of toys and some appliances. Simply connect the charger to the toy and turn it on. Start with the power supply switch in the low position and switch up in voltage until the toy operates normally.

Connect the battery, flip on the power, and go back in for breakfast. Within half an hour, the battery will be charged and ready to fire up your car's engine

Above is the completed charger. Below is the simple circuit for a trickle charger for 6- or 12-volt batteries. Assembly takes only a couple of hours

# Car battery charger

BY MORTON J. SCHULTZ

This easily built unit can provide a hard, half-hour jolt or an effective, overnight trickle charge

WITHOUT FAIL, WHEN WINTER WEATHER comes, car batteries will become a problem. If yours is weak, it won't have the power to crank and fire a cold, sluggish engine. The best way to avoid this frustration is to keep the battery fully charged at all times. You can do this by hooking up a trickle charger in the evening and disconnecting it in the morning. But should you forget, and the battery is low when you get up, you'll need a quick charger to strengthen your battery if you intend to get to work on time.

The unit described here provides four different charging rates ranging from a slow trickle charge to a rapid 8-amp half-hour jolt.

The circuit is not critical and the builder can

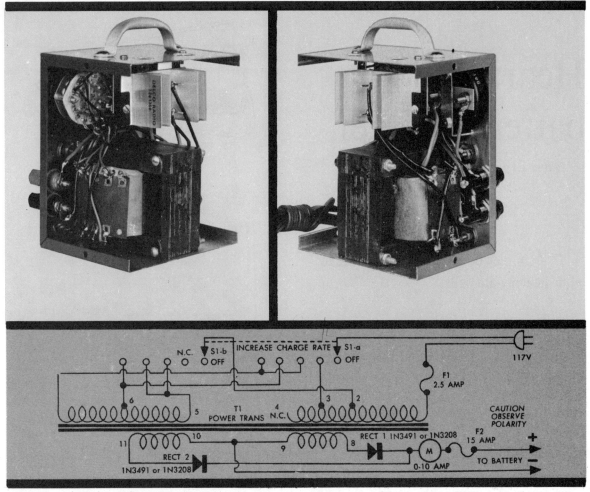

Two views of the charger interior are shown above. Below is the circuit for the full four-speed charger. To boost the charging rate, pick a high-voltage transformer tap with the rotary switch

use nearly any parts layout desired. Drill the Delco heat sink to take a 1N3491 or 1N3208 rectifier. Use a $^{31}/_{64}$-in. hole with a .01″ x 45° chamfer for the 1N3491. The 1N3208 requires only an ordinary ¼-in. mounting hole.

A few precautions should be observed: Make sure that the heat sink is completely insulated from the main chassis, and allow for as much ventilation as possible. If the heat sink is mounted inside the case, as shown here, drill several holes in the top and sides or back to allow air flow through the heat sink fins. Without proper ventilation, you can burn out the rectifier.

When using the charger connect it to the car battery with less than 8 to 10 ft. of No. 12 wire.

If all you need is a trickle charger use the circuit on page 216. It is easy to build and forms a neat compact package. Overnight, it will charge a weak battery.

### PARTS LIST

T1—transformer, Stancor RT-204
RECT 1, RECT 2—Delco 1N3491 or 1N3208
Heat Sink—Delco 7281360
M—Ammeter, 0-10 amps (Emico RF-2C)
S1—2-pole 5-position rotary switch (Mallory 173C)
F1—2.5 amp slow-blow fuse with holder
F2—15 amp fuse with holder

# Hearing-aid battery charger

BY PHILLIP WILSON

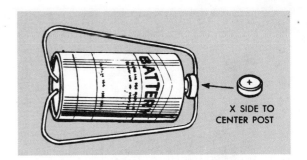

X SIDE TO CENTER POST

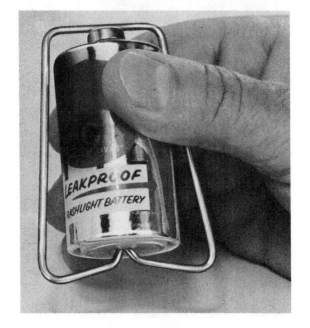

This simple "booster" adds extra life to your hearing-aid cells

OWNERS OF HEARING-AIDS using mercury-cell batteries will welcome this "booster" which extends the life of the cells by as much as 75 percent, provided the cells are not allowed to become completely dead. Dead cells cannot be charged when the chemicals have dried out, but weak cells can be partially rejuvenated. There is no danger of damaging the hearing aid with this booster, as the voltages of the mercury cell and the booster are equal. The booster merely drains current from a high-capacity flashlight cell into the smaller mercury cell.

Purchase an ordinary flashlight cell, size "D," Eveready No. 950 or its equal, and make a wire holder, as shown in the drawing. Use brass or bronze wire or ³⁄₃₂-in. brazing rod. Adjust the wire legs of the holder so a mercury cell will fit snugly between the wire and the center (positive) post of the flashlight cell. The mercury cells have a number and an "X" on one side and it is important to insert the cell so that the "X" side is in contact with the center post. If your mercury cell is not marked, try one side on the post at a time until you can determine which side takes the charge. Eveready mercury cells 312, 400, 520, 625, 630 and 675, as well as others, can be recharged by this method.

For best results, start with a new flashlight cell and two new mercury cells. Use one cell in the hearing aid for one day only. Remove it and apply the booster for four hours while you wear the second cell. If you alternately change and use the cells every other day, they will last about two months, by which time the flashlight cell will have to be replaced. If you notice a slight hum which can't be tuned out with the volume control after charging, just put the cell aside for a few hours before using it again.

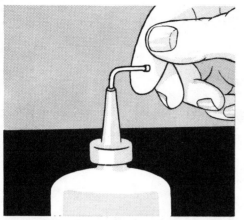

Bend an aluminum nail to a right angle and use it to seal glue containers which don't have push-pull tops.

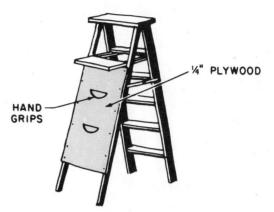

A ¼-in. plywood panel replacement for the regular cross braces makes your ladder more rigid and easier to carry.

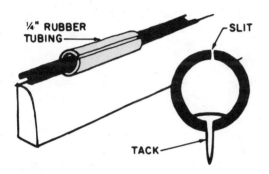

To keep lamp cords off the floor, slit a piece of rubber tubing and tack it to the baseboard.

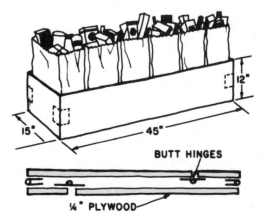

A child's flying saucer sled can be used in the summer as a cover for your portable barbecue grill.

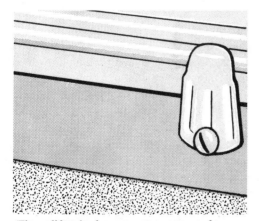

Those lift tabs from pop-top cans make good cleats for holding windows and screens in place.

Prevent your grocery bags from toppling in your car with a folding fence of ¼-in. plywood.

# Fold-away bedroom

Double-deck bunks, a desk,
bookshelves, five cupboards, and two
roll-out toy chests—all packed
into a foot-deep built-in
that solves your kids' bedroom
problem in one fell swoop

■ PUT A GROWING FAMILY into one of today's small homes and *something's* gotta give! When the youngsters pass the crib stage and need their own rooms, space has a way of shrinking. That "extra" room you press into service is apt to be the smallest in the house. If *two* children must share it, you'll probably have to resort to double-deck bunks—and nothing crowds a small room more. Even if the room's to be used by only one child, he or she will want an extra bed so a chum can stay over sometimes.

And the sleeping problem is only the start. School-age children need a study desk and a place for books—plus lots of storage space for games and hobby equipment. And if the room wasn't originally a bedroom, it probably won't even have a closet for extra sheets and blankets.

Imagine the full solution to so knotty a problem being tucked neatly behind a knotty-pine wall! The ingenious design shown on these pages can be adapted to any problem room. As

Bunk section is made first by nailing 1 x 12 frame to the glued-up back panel. This panel is then anchored to the wall by driving 2½-in. screws into the studs. Because of the panel weight, use 18 screws. A secret storage compartment is formed at the top under the nailed-on cornice

Bar clamps, or a substitute wedging system, are a necessity when you glue up the drop panels for the bunks. Two hours of clamping should do it

The inner edge of the mitered 2 x 6 frame is rabbeted to make a nailing recess for the springs. Burlap stapled to the frame covers the springs

Cork panel is glued to the underside of the top bunk panel, then framed with rabbeted molding. The two center strips prevent warping

Support chains are installed after the spring frame is fastened to the bunk panel. The bunk panel is attached to the bunk section with piano hinge

Who'd suspect an entire sleep-study-play room was waiting behind this attractive wall? Note that the underside of the bottom bunk has trim of mitered molding to match bulletin board frame above it. Borders outside of these frames are painted a bright accent color

To prevent tumbles, note two points that are not detailed at the right. The top end of the bed chains must be anchored to U-bolts passed through the back panel and a steel plate mortised into the rear face  Slip-fit dowels are pushed in after desk is in place

The door bin unit is treated like other doors, hung after assembly. One leaf of both hinges is secured to the door first, then the door is held in place while the positions of the other leaves are marked for drilling. Only the front of the bin is angled for clearance

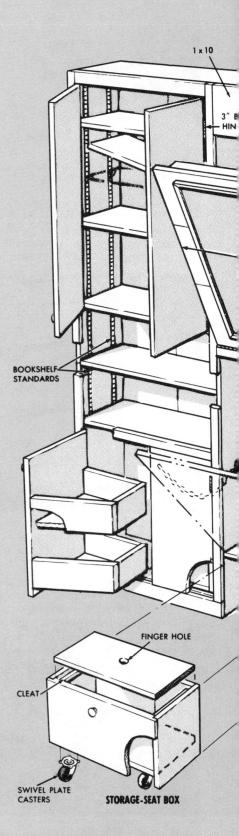

1 x 10

3" B
HIN

BOOKSHELF
STANDARDS

FINGER HOLE

CLEAT

SWIVEL PLATE
CASTERS

**STORAGE-SEAT BOX**

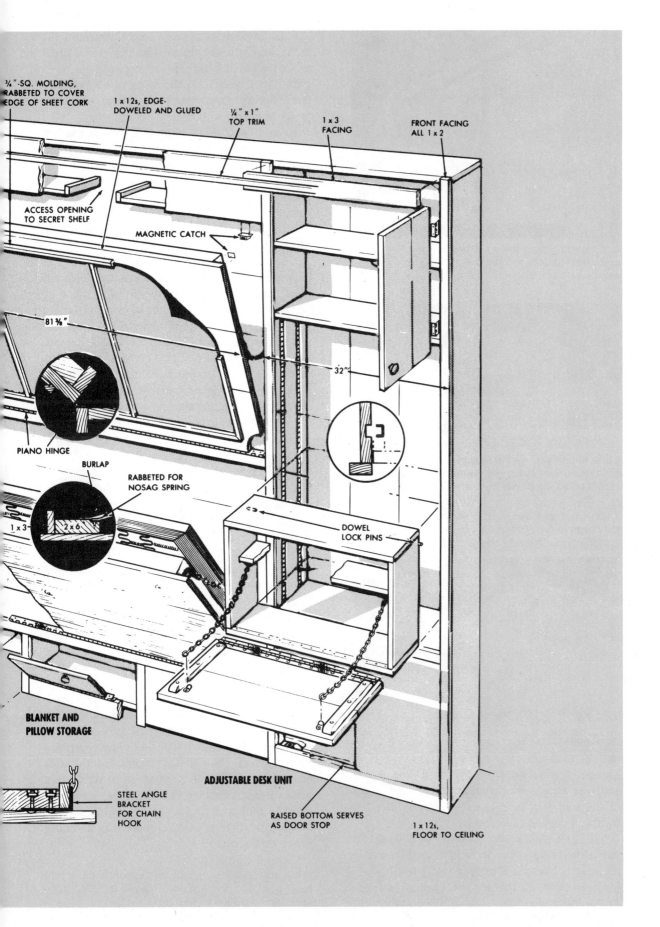

¾"-SQ. MOLDING, RABBETED TO COVER EDGE OF SHEET CORK

1 x 12s, EDGE-DOWELED AND GLUED

¼" x 1" TOP TRIM

1 x 3 FACING

FRONT FACING ALL 1 x 2

ACCESS OPENING TO SECRET SHELF

MAGNETIC CATCH

81 ⅜"

PIANO HINGE

BURLAP

RABBETED FOR NOSAG SPRING

1 x 3    2 x 6

32"

DOWEL LOCK PINS

BLANKET AND PILLOW STORAGE

STEEL ANGLE BRACKET FOR CHAIN HOOK

ADJUSTABLE DESK UNIT

RAISED BOTTOM SERVES AS DOOR STOP

1 x 12s, FLOOR TO CEILING

A flat molding hides the crack between the top of the built-in units and the ceiling. If a splice is necessary, bevel the ends 45 degrees

Optional bins replace the shelves in the left-hand cabinet for swing-out storage of bulky gear. Screws are driven from rear of the door

The bin bottom is recessed ¼ in. less than the height of the plate casters so, when bin is flipped over, the sides don't touch the floor

Solid Ponderosa pine is used throughout the room, and you can finish it natural for a boy's room, or tint it with a pastel wiping stain for a girl's. Or, if you build the room of a wood that lacks knotty Ponderosa's character, you may prefer to coat it with enamel.

Even if you don't copy this design exactly, you'll find it boasts a number of novel features you'll want to incorporate into your own version. Starting at the top: Behind that center cornice is a secret storage area for those private treasures that mean so much to kids. What a spot to stow the gang's code messages—or hide that Mother's Day gift.

The built-in desk really *isn't* built in. The drop leaf—hung on sturdy chains to match the bunk supports—is merely the lid of a tipped-up box; it's attached (by means of a piano hinge) to the edge of the bottom side of this box, and the whole unit nests inside the larger cabinet, resting on clips inserted in shelf brackets that are recessed into the inner face of the cabinet's side walls. This arrangement makes the height of the drop-leaf fully adjustable. You can mount it low for a child's chair, to start, then keep raising it as the child grows.

**storage bins swing out**

The base cabinet on the left side gives up its shelves in favor of swing-out bins for easy access to bulky equipment. These bins are screwed directly to the back of the doors, and since the doors were to have a natural finish that precluded countersinking and plugging the screw heads, the screws were "toenailed" in from the back as shown, left, by sinking them in screw pockets.

The three storage sections under the bottom bunk are novel, too. The stationary one, at the center, has a drop-down door (again attached with a piano hinge) that gives access to a cupboard designed to store extra bedding. This is flanked by two berthed-but-unattached toy chests. A tug on the drawer pull rolls each chest completely free of the wall unit. The chests are simple boxes (butt-joined except for the rabbeted front) with a bottom set in to recess four plate casters, as shown at left. A cleat across the inner face of each end provides a lip to support a loose lid that turns the chest into a mobile bench and scooter.

presented, it requires a 12-ft. wall, but it can easily be expanded or contracted to fit the length of the wall you have in mind. Simply alter the widths of the end cabinets.

The unit stands about 7½ ft. tall, to fit today's low ceilings, but its height, too, is readily adjustable. The one thing you won't want to adjust is the slimness that lets you pack a roomful of furniture into one foot of floor space!

**See also:** children's furniture; closets; finishes, furniture; legs, furniture; mirror; refinishing; remodeling; upholstery; vacation homes.

Pulling the wall of ganged doors across the bedroom divides it
in half to create two separate areas for both sleeping and study

# Two rooms from one

An accordion wall down the middle
of a room can solve your space
problem when two youngsters want
—and need—areas of their own

WHAT CAN YOU DO when two youngsters, who
occupy the same bedroom, need semiprivate
places to study? If this is your problem, perhaps
you can solve it by taking an idea from Bill
Baker's 100-year-old dream home in Westport,
Conn.

Faced with such a problem, Baker cleverly
split a bedroom down the middle with an ac-
cordion-fold wall of flush doors which made it
possible to divide the room into two separate
study areas by merely pulling the track-hung
panels away from the wall.

Whereas this created (and would, in most
cases) areas too small to accept a regular-size
bed, chest and desk for each youngster, simple
wall-hung units were designed and built to solve
the space problem and still provide the three
pieces.

The result was twin "bedrooms" which per-
mitted one youngster to burn the midnight oil

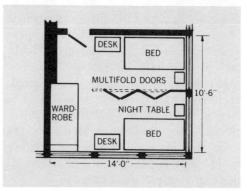

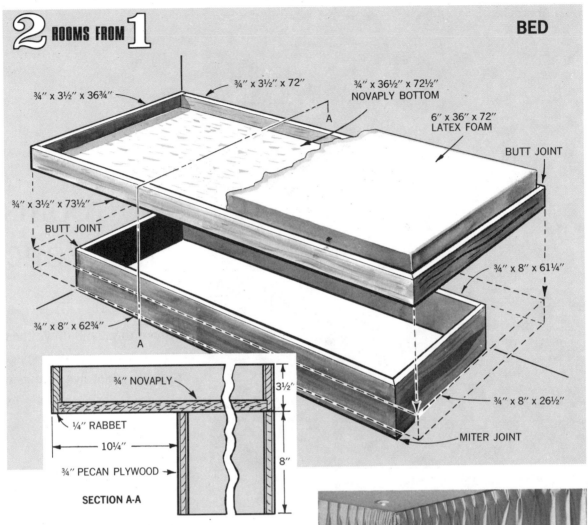

## 2 ROOMS FROM 1       BED

¾″ x 3½″ x 36¾″

¾″ x 3½″ x 72″

A

¾″ x 36½″ x 72½″
NOVAPLY BOTTOM

6″ x 36″ x 72″
LATEX FOAM

BUTT JOINT

¾″ x 3½″ x 73½″

BUTT JOINT

¾″ x 8″ x 61¼″

¾″ x 8″ x 62¾″

A

¾″ x 8″ x 26½″

MITER JOINT

¾″ NOVAPLY

¼″ RABBET

10¼″

3½″

8″

¾″ PECAN PLYWOOD

### SECTION A-A

Thick latex-foam slabs provide comfortable mattresses for the cantilever beds.
Allow 1 in. of clearance all around

*two rooms, continued*

without disturbing a younger brother or sister
should he be ill or have different sleeping habits.
Of course, to revert back to one large open room,
a push on the piano-hinged doors folds them
back on their track and against the wall.

In completely remodeling the original dated
bedroom, Baker had space to include a built-in,
floor-to-ceiling cabinet with chest to provide additional wardrobe storage. Details for building
it are given on page 230. Whether you have room
to include this too, depends upon the size and
shape of your particular room.

ALL EXPOSED EDGES CONCEALED
WITH MATCHING VENEER TAPE

LIGHT VERMILLION LAMINATE

¾" x 16" x 30"

¾" x 1⅝" x 30" PECAN RAILS

¾" x 6" x 30"

WHITE LAMINATE

¾" x 3" x 30"

¾" x 3" x 29⅞"

¾" x 14¼" x 29⅞"

FULL EXTENSION SLIDES

¾" x 6" x 29⅞"

¾" DURAPLY BOTTOM

¾" x 16" x 18"
CHARTER PECAN
PLYWOOD

2½"
2"
4⅞"
2"
4⅞"

3"
6"
6"

18"

½" CLEARANCE
FOR SLIDE

16"

8"

**END SECTION**

WALL     FLOOR

**DRAWER CORNER**
(TOP VIEW)

As you can see from the photo of the completed room, shown on page 229, and the "before" picture on page 225, the original double-hung windows were replaced with clerestory ones and fitted with bright lemon-yellow draw drapes. The walls were faced with prefinished, charter-pecan paneling after they were soundproofed with sound-deadening board; a recessed-ceiling spotlight was installed over each bed for reading, and the room was wired for an AM-FM intercom system.

The old floor was renewed with Swedish oak parquet flooring.

As for furniture, each "room" has identical units, consisting of a cantilever-type bed fitted with a 6-in. slab of latex foam rubber, a wall-hung night table and a wall-hung desk-dresser that has a slick pull-out writing surface. The tops of both the night tables and the desk-dressers were surfaced with plastic laminate.

Construction of the three basic pieces is extremely simple and the use of full-extension,

Top "drawer" of wall-hung dresser pulls out to serve as a handy writing desk for homework

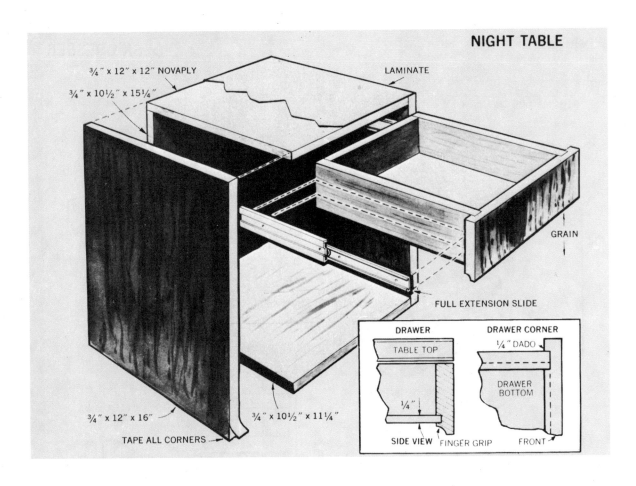

**NIGHT TABLE**

¾" x 12" x 12" NOVAPLY

¾" x 10½" x 15¼"

LAMINATE

GRAIN

FULL EXTENSION SLIDE

¾" x 12" x 16"

TAPE ALL CORNERS

¾" x 10½" x 11¼"

DRAWER

TABLE TOP

¼"

SIDE VIEW   FINGER GRIP

DRAWER CORNER

¼" DADO

DRAWER BOTTOM

FRONT

*two rooms, continued*

metal drawer slides simplifies building even more. There's nothing to making the single beds. The top is little more than a tray supported 8 in. off the floor by a simple base of four boards.

Since the beds are designed to fit snug in a corner, the top overhangs the base 10 in. at the front and one end and ¾ in. along the back to clear the room's baseboards. Only the outer corner of each assembly requires mitering; all the others are merely butted, glued and nailed with finishing nails. Since two of the side members are actually hidden against the walls, these parts can be made of less expensive wood. Exposed edges of the plywood numbers are covered with a matching trim. In the case of pecan plywood, oak trim is the nearest match. The top is attached to the base with glue and nails driven

Temporary support placed under wall-hung units helps to hold them in place for attaching and leveling

228

through the bottom, and the completed beds are screwed in place to wall studs with 2½-in. #12 flathead screws.

In ordering foam for the mattresses, allow 1-in. clearance all around.

The desk and table units are open boxes which are fitted with drawers that roll freely on standard metal extension slides. The construction of both pieces is clearly shown in the pull-apart drawings on pages 227 and 228. In each case, the side members lap the edges of the top so the exposed end grain will later be covered by the laminate which is bonded to the tops with contact cement. The desk-dresser looks as if it has three drawers, but the top one is actually a pull-out writing shelf which, like the drawers, is fitted with the same metal slides. Laminate also covers the writing surface, and exposed plywood edges are covered with wood trim.

In mounting both units to the wall, they must be located so that the mounting screws can be driven into studs to assure rigid support. This is particularly important in the case of the desk-dresser. Pilot holes for the screws are made in the mounting strips provided across the backs of the cabinets. A temporary support placed on the floor under the units will facilitate fastening them to the wall and checking to see that they are

mounted level. The desk-dresser is mounted 8 in. off the floor, whereas the night table is 12 in. Stain and finish before hanging.

The accordion wall is made of 18-in. flush doors which are ganged together to hang from a ceiling track mounted in the center of the room. Your room will determine the number of doors required to extend from wall to wall. The doors are hinged together at alternate edges so they'll fold, and equipped with multiple folding-door hardware. One basic set takes care of four doors. The track in which the pivoting hangers ride is not a part of the basic set but is ordered separately in 2 and 4-ft. lengths.

All doors collect at one side of the room, and while the hardware is designed to allow the first door of the group to be located at the edge of an opening, such as a doorway, here it is hinged to a separate fixed door which juts out from the wall. This was necessary for the collection of doors to clear the night stands. Complete instructions for adding the hangers, top and bottom pivot sockets, as well as the spring-and-stud assemblies, come with the hardware.

Your own variations of these basic plans, again adjusted to the size of your own room, can include all manner of ideas. Perhaps an extra room can be converted to a combination study

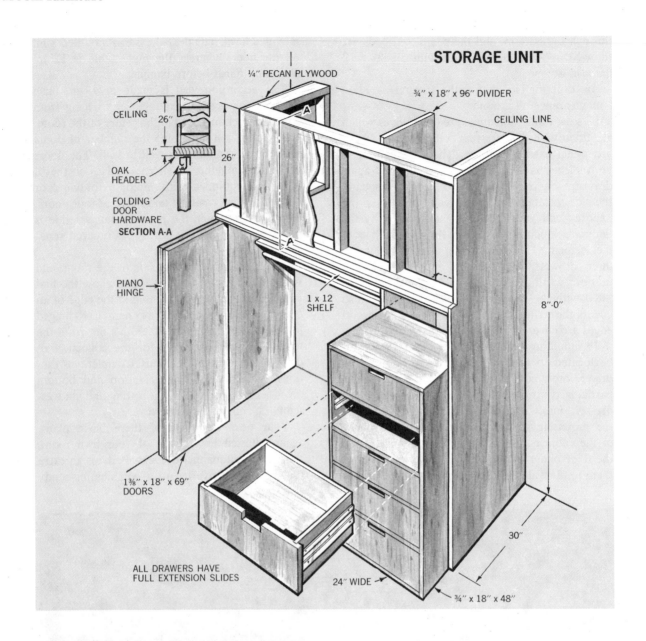

## STORAGE UNIT

¼" PECAN PLYWOOD

¾" x 18" x 96" DIVIDER

CEILING LINE

CEILING

26"

1"

OAK HEADER

FOLDING DOOR HARDWARE

**SECTION A-A**

26"

26"

A

A

PIANO HINGE

1 x 12 SHELF

8"-0"

1⅜" x 18" x 69" DOORS

30"

ALL DRAWERS HAVE FULL EXTENSION SLIDES

24" WIDE

¾" x 18" x 48"

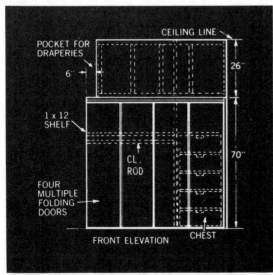

POCKET FOR DRAPERIES

CEILING LINE

6"

26"

1 x 12 SHELF

CL. ROD

70"

FOUR MULTIPLE FOLDING DOORS

CHEST

FRONT ELEVATION

and guest room, or a nursery and sewing room. If the room has two doors, as those in many older houses do, you can even arrange to build the multifold doors so they'll run completely across the room, dividing it so that each section can have its own doorway.

The wood panels of the multifold doors are shown with a natural wood finish. To save money, or tailor color schemes to fit individual preferences or personalities, less expensive panels can be used and then painted.

No matter how you decide to adapt these plans, prepare a detailed sketch, with accurate dimensions, before you begin.

The hour or two you spend at this task will help to visualize the finished room and save many hours of work.

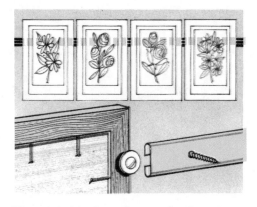

Pictures can be hung from a curtain rod attached to the wall, if screws with washers are fastened to the frames.

A footrest of ⅛ x ¾-in. steel bolted to your mower will help you get started when it bogs down in the high grass.

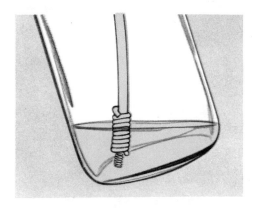

A few turns of solder around the tube inside your garden-hose sprayer keeps it in the deepest part of the liquid.

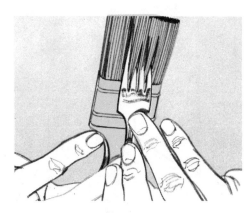

An old kitchen fork is a handy tool for cleaning paint brushes.

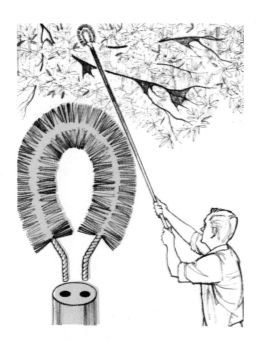

Use the bristles from a fiber kitchen brush attached to a pole to sweep caterpillar nests off trees.

# Table stores a guest bed

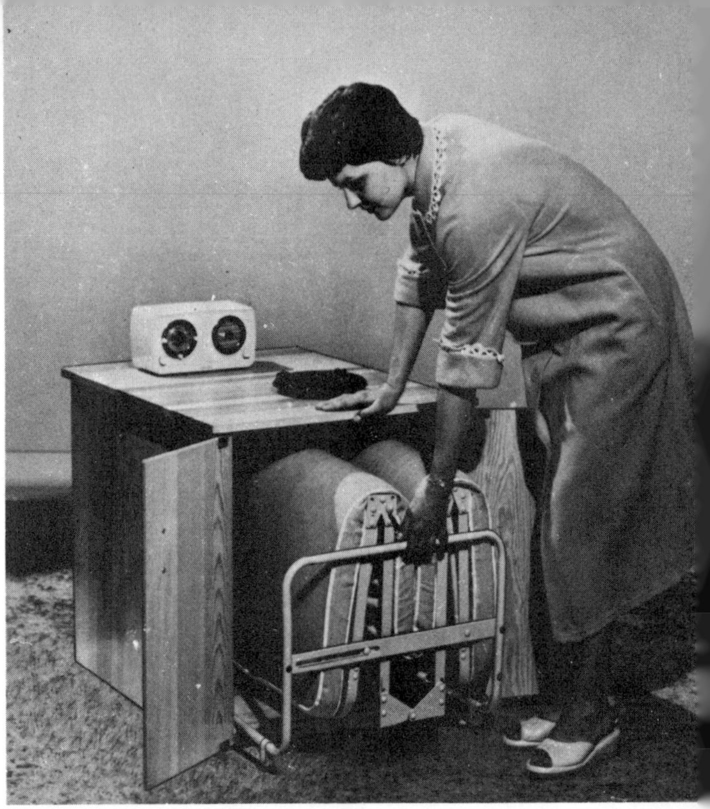

Hide a rollaway bed inside this table and you'll be ready for unexpected guests, even in a small apartment

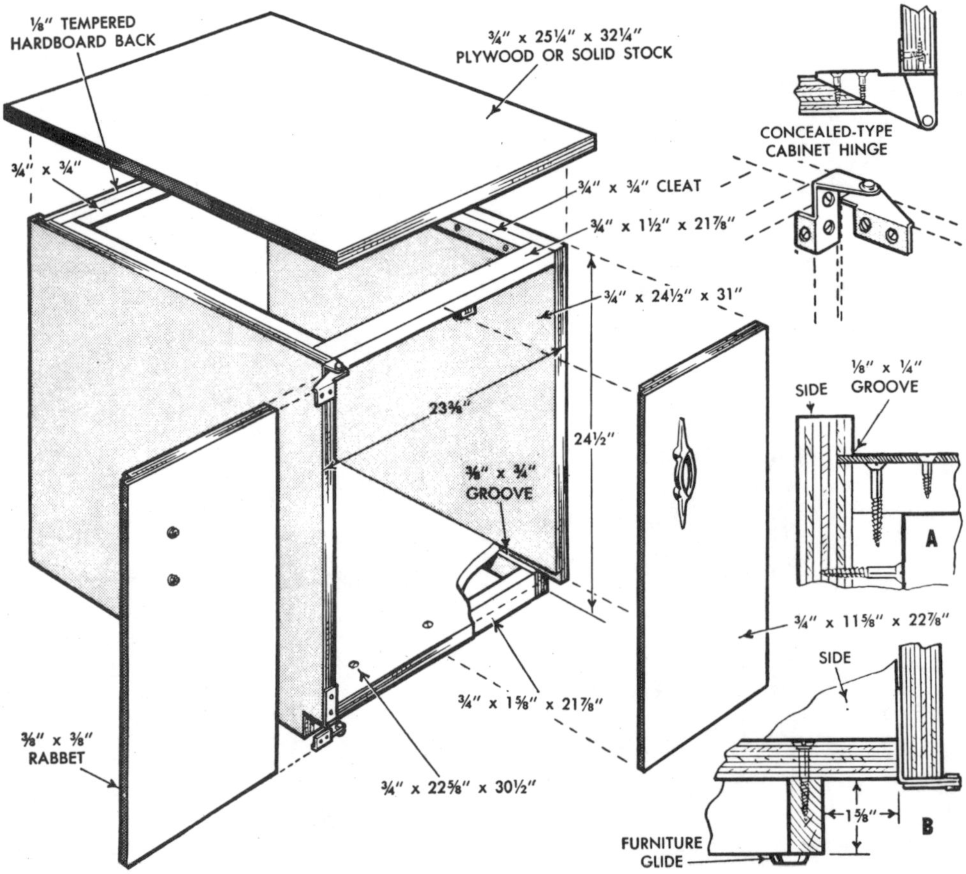
1/8" TEMPERED HARDBOARD BACK
3/4" x 25 1/4" x 32 1/4" PLYWOOD OR SOLID STOCK
CONCEALED-TYPE CABINET HINGE
3/4" x 3/4"
3/4" x 3/4" CLEAT
3/4" x 1 1/2" x 21 7/8"
3/4" x 24 1/2" x 31"
23 3/8"
24 1/2"
3/8" x 3/4" GROOVE
1/8" x 1/4" GROOVE
SIDE
A
3/4" x 11 5/8" x 22 7/8"
SIDE
3/4" x 1 5/8" x 21 7/8"
3/8" x 3/8" RABBET
3/4" x 22 5/8" x 30 1/2"
1 5/8"
B
FURNITURE GLIDE

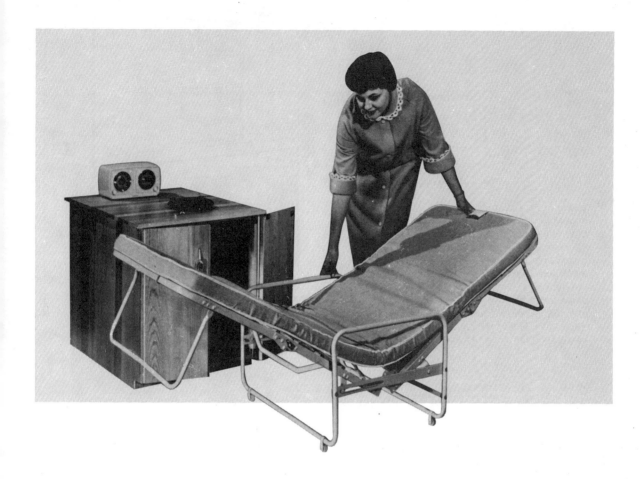

PROVIDING accommodations for overnight guests is always a problem in small homes and apartments. Since most housewives don't want to allot precious closet space to a rollaway bed, the unexpected guest is likely to find himself spending the night curled up on a short sofa which was definitely not made for sleeping. If you're faced with the problem of where to park a stand-by bed here's the perfect solution— simply park it in this dual-purpose cabinet table.

The table can be used in your family room, doing double duty as a game table, TV stand or end table. Two such end tables placed at the ends of your sofa will provide sleeping accommodations for a visiting couple, and you can make up the sofa as a bed for one child. Used as a night stand in the guest room (if you are lucky enough to have one), it will give the room sleeping space for three. In a vacation home, such an arrangement will come in especially handy for those last-minute guests who drop in for a Friday-evening swim and stay the week end.

The table may be constructed of ¾-in. plywood or solid stock, from pine or hardwood. If you plan to locate the table with its back to a wall, you may use ⅛-in. tempered hardboard for the back. However, should you decide to use it as an end table where all four sides will show, make the back of the same material used for the sides and top. Assemble the table according to the plan on the opposite page, securing all joints with both screws and glue. The top is attached from the underside with screws which run through ¾-in. cleats.

Finish and hardware will depend on the decor of the room where you plan to use the table. If made of cabinet wood, you may wish to stain it to match other pieces in the room. If made of pine, the table can be enameled. You might even add a colorful decalcomania or stenciled design on the side panels. As for the handles, either brass or aluminum will blend well with a modern room. For an early-American look, try using hammered-iron handles or plain white porcelain knobs.

Before beginning construction, double-check the dimensions of your own rollaway bed and alter the ones shown here to fit.

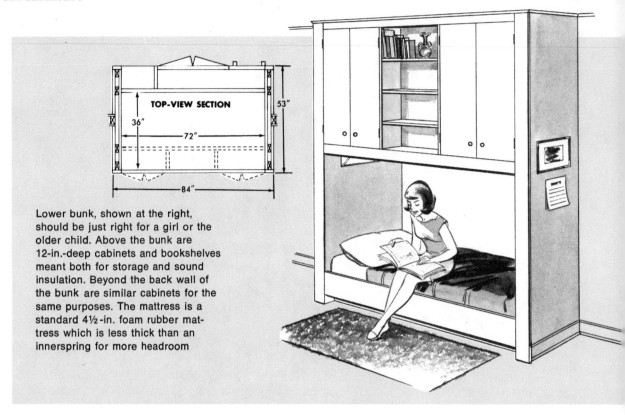

TOP-VIEW SECTION

53"

36"

72"

84"

Lower bunk, shown at the right, should be just right for a girl or the older child. Above the bunk are 12-in.-deep cabinets and bookshelves meant both for storage and sound insulation. Beyond the back wall of the bunk are similar cabinets for the same purposes. The mattress is a standard 4½-in. foam rubber mattress which is less thick than an innerspring for more headroom

# Room-dividing bunks

When you need a room separator,
and additional sleeping quarters
too, here is the perfect
solution. You can cut a room
down the middle with built-in
bunks that form a partition

MOST FAMILIES live in a two-bedroom or three-bedroom house that—when the family is young—seems to offer space to spare. But, all too soon, it's outgrown.

After a few short years brothers have to be separated from sisters, and the older children (who must stay up later to study) from the younger fry who "have to go to bed by day." In addition, sick children must occasionally be separated from healthy ones. And teenagers will probably want to have overnight guests.

To solve these problems, you can, of course, build extra bedrooms. Or you can finish the attic —expensive solutions, both.

Here is a much simpler and cheaper means of solving sleeping problems—build a double bunk with the upper bunk in one bedroom and the lower bunk in the adjoining room. This is a space-saving method, too: when you stack the beds, you get two for the space of one. The floor plans at the right show just four of many ways in which the bunks can be located. Note how closets can be built at one or both ends to serve either or both rooms.

The section and plan views above show a lower bunk for older sister and an upper bunk for younger brother in separate rooms. Shelves for books and storage are built beside each bunk to sound-insulate one bedroom from the other as

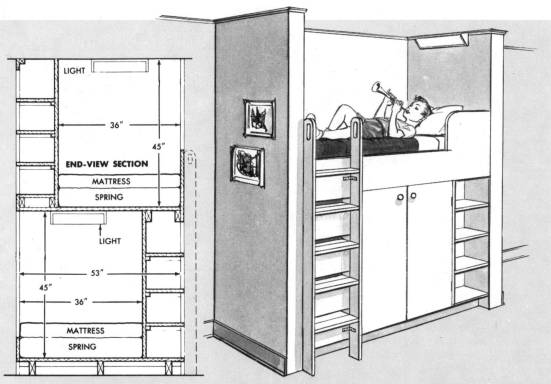

LIGHT

36"

45"

**END-VIEW SECTION**

MATTRESS

SPRING

LIGHT

53"

45"

36"

MATTRESS

SPRING

Climb to top bunk is adventure for young child. Note optional toe recess behind each rung. High sideboard beside pillow—and projecting ladder at foot—guard against tumbles

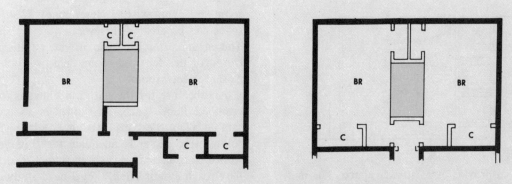

This unit adapts to almost any layout, and thus provides a multitude of floor-plan possibilities. Samples here show three ways to split an existing room into two useful bedrooms. Two at left involve cutting new access door while those at right do not

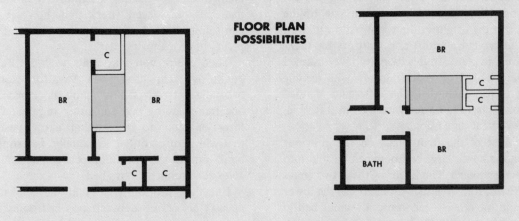

**FLOOR PLAN POSSIBILITIES**

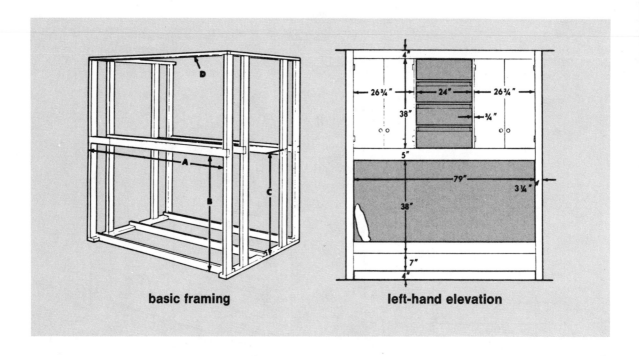

**basic framing**          **left-hand elevation**

*room-dividing bunks, continued*

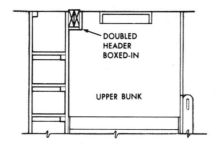

DOUBLED
HEADER
BOXED-IN

UPPER BUNK

well as to provide extra storage space. The mattress and spring of the upper bunk sound-insulate this bunk from the one below.

The dimensions are given only as suggestions. The controlling dimensions are the size of the spring and the height of the room. Allow at least ½ in. all around a spring and mattress for tucking covers in place. In this case we have assumed a ceiling height of 8 ft.-0 in. If your ceiling height is less than that, the difference divided by two will have to be subtracted from 3 ft. 9 in. —our vertical dimension.

The first of the floor plans on the previous page shows how a large bedroom can be split into two smaller rooms. The larger of these two could be, perhaps, for two sisters—one to use the lower bunk and the other sister to use a regular bed in the opposite corner. Their brother then uses the upper bunk in the smaller room.

Where the room to be split is smaller (as in the second and third floor plans) it should be divided evenly. But this may cut one of the new rooms off from existing closet space. If so, such space can be created in several ways, as shown. The partition unit itself can provide a full walk-in closet for the deprived room, or a two-foot-deep closet for *each* room.

Another use for the partition bunks is to free cramped floor space, as shown in the fourth sample plan. Perhaps two tiny adjacent bedrooms were perfectly adequate for your youngsters during their first years in school. But when they reach Junior High, they'll need study desks —and you can't squeeze them in because the beds take up too much room. If you knock out enough of the existing partition to accommodate this "two-faced" bunk unit, however, you can sell or store the free-standing beds and have plenty of space for the desks.

Then again, you may only need the built-in bunks as extra guest beds. Say, for example, two adjacent rooms have ample floor space for one free-standing bed and other required furniture—but none to spare for an extra guest bed that will be used only occasionally. Inserting the bunk unit into the partition between such rooms gives *each* room an extra bed.

But the partition you build the bunks into needn't always be between two bedrooms. Perhaps you have a small room next to a family room or den. Insert a bunk unit into the sepa-

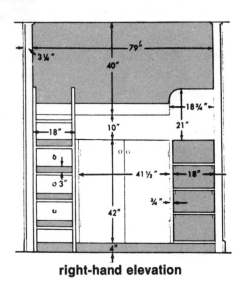

**right-hand elevation**

rating wall and you've got a private bedroom on one side and a guest bed on the other. The lower bunk would, in this case, face into the family room, and would serve as a built-in sofa when not made up as a bed.

In the drawings of the two different treatments of the upper bunk (pages 235 and 238) note the toe-space beyond each tread of the ladder, to make climbing easier and safer. While not an essential feature of the construction, these little pockets will also make it more comfortable for the child's mother when she has to stand on the ladder to make his bed. The space above these recessed steps can be shelves, or drawers as seen in the elevation above. The ladder itself is made of 1 x 4s, and should be fastened to the bed above and the cabinet below with 1-in. steel angles.

In studying the framework drawing at upper left, remember that dimension A—the space between the end frames—is the mattress length plus 1 in., plus the thickness at both ends of the ½-in. plywood inner facing—a total of two inches. Dimension B, based on an 8 ft.-0 in. ceiling, should be 4 ft.-1¾ in. Dimension C, which is the distance from the floor to the *top* of the far horizontal pair of 2 x 4s, would be ¾ in. less than B, or 4 ft.-1 in. You can see from the section drawing that this framework is designed to slip pieces of ¾ in. plywood under the higher horizontal 2 x 4s, and over the lower ones.

Piece D is a horizontal 2 x 2 member fastened to the ceiling as a nailing strip for the fascia over

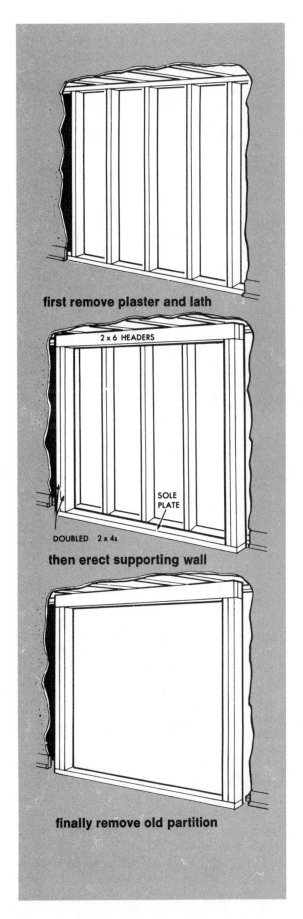

**first remove plaster and lath**

**then erect supporting wall**

**finally remove old partition**

If the child to occupy the upper bunk is of school age, a drop-leaf desk can be built into the space below the bunk. To the left are bookcases for school books. The section below gives suggested dimensions. For teen-agers increase desk height to 30 in. for greater kneeroom

18″
28″

*room-dividing bunks, continued*

the cabinets. It should be about 3½ in. longer than dimension A.

Exact plywood cutting diagrams cannot be given because the bunks will vary in size with each particular installation. With judicious planning, you should get by with eight 4 x 8 panels. Use ¾-in. plywood except for the inner and outer facing of the end walls. This could be ½-in. ply, ¼-in. hardboard, or even plasterboard, if these panels are to be wallpapered to match the room. For economy, it is suggested that A-B or even A-C plywood be used instead of A-A grade since, with the exception of the cabinet doors, only one side of the plywood is exposed.

In removing a partition, if such is necessary, be sure that it isn't a bearing partition. Climb up in the attic to see if the joists run parallel or at right angles to the wall you are about to remove. Almost always when the joists are at right angles to the partition in question, it is a load-bearing wall. In that case, remove the plaster and lath from both sides of the section of the partition to be removed, as shown in the sketches on the previous page. Then, right beside it, build a new partition with a 2 x 4 sole, double studs at

both ends, and double 2 x 6s for the header beam. It's easier to toenail the doubled studs to this beam working flat on the floor; then raise this assembly onto the spiked-down sole plate and nail it to both the sole and the ceiling joists. This new partition must fit tight against the joists and as close to the old partition as possible. Once it's securely in place, remove the old partition. If you're working on the second floor, above a first-floor bearing partition, this new, relatively short section will be no more than 4 in. to one side of the partition below. The factor of safety being adequate, this new wall will not materially weaken the structure of the house. But before tackling this job, be sure that you are complying with all local building regulations. A sketch of what you propose to do may be required, and a building permit.

The new lintel with casing would extend down below the ceiling about 6½ in., so it would be better to build these bunks in such a way that the lintel would not interfere with the child's headroom. Thus the new lintel should come in the corner formed by the bunk's rear wall and the ceiling (sketch, page 236).

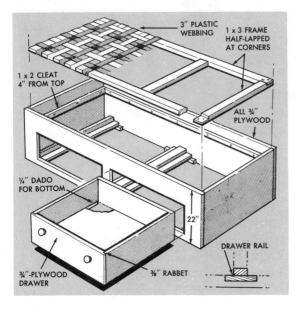

3" PLASTIC WEBBING

1 x 3 FRAME HALF-LAPPED AT CORNERS

1 x 2 CLEAT 4" FROM TOP

ALL ¾" PLYWOOD

¼" DADO FOR BOTTOM

22"

DRAWER RAIL

¾"-PLYWOOD DRAWER

⅜" RABBET

Taking advantage of the manner in which bi-fold doors open, you can have a handy two-way dressing mirror by using wood-and-mirror doors

# Spare bunks

ORDINARILY, there's not much one can do with the dead space under the slanting roof of a second floor other than use it for storage. But you can take advantage of the low head room required and build twin bunks under the eaves. Closed off when not in use by louvered bifold doors, they appear to be regular closet doors. Swung open, two extra standby beds are always available when accommodations get tight.

Four drawers allow ample storage for a supply of sheets and blankets. At the head of each bunk is a small shelf for holding such things as books, clock and radio.

The mattress is supported by a frame laced with plastic webbing. If you prefer, a spring of suitable size may be used instead of the webbed frame. Another option is to dustproof the drawers by installing a sheet of ½-in. plywood, using the 1 x 2-in. cleats as support. The spring can then be rested directly on the plywood.

Exact dimensions depend on space available.

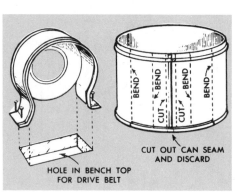

CUT OUT CAN SEAM
AND DISCARD

HOLE IN BENCH TOP
FOR DRIVE BELT

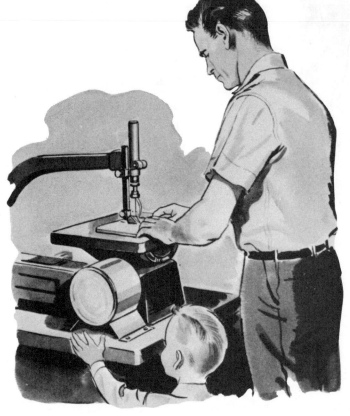

# Belt guard from a coffee can

BY MANLY BANISTER

AN UNGUARDED V-pulley on a power tool is an open invitation to a painful injury or permanent disability, especially when there are likely to be small children in the vicinity of the workshop. To safeguard little fingers as well as your own, it will pay you to take the time to cover open pulleys. Here is an easy and quick way to provide this protection.

For a small pulley such as that on a jigsaw, use a 1-lb. coffee can which measures about 3¼ in. high and is 5 in. in diameter. The newer type of coffee can which is 5½ in. high and only 4 in. in diameter—also a 1-lb. can—is not suitable for many pulleys. Using the larger 1-lb. can, you should first remove the loose ring from the top of the can and cut out the soldered seam. Then make a cut along the bottom flange as shown in the drawing at the upper left. Bend the two ends outward to form brackets. Then paint the completed guard to closely match the finish of the machine. Position the guard so that it clears the pulley when mounted over the belt opening in the bench top. Use screws to fasten it in place so it can be removed easily should this be necessary.

Such a guard can be used on a horizontal drive by attaching it to a vertical mounting bracket and cutting a suitable opening in the can for the belt.

This easy and quick method of providing welcome protection is an "insurance policy" well worth the effort.

**See also:** ellipsograph; indexer; maintenance center; saber saws; workshops.

For shaping, deburring,
sharpening or sanding,
build this . . .

# Combination sander

BY HOWARD R. CLARK

■ IF YOU OWN a portable electric drill, you not only have the tool you'll need to help *build* this versatile little machine but you have the motor to drive it. Cradled in a stand, the drill is coupled directly to drive the belt, then backed away and swung around to operate a 4-in. disc.

The belt-disc sander is one of those easy-to-produce projects that can be assembled during a leisurely after-work evening.

Make the drill stand first so you can accurately spot the location of the centerline of the drive shaft. Wherever possible, shape and drill matching parts as a unit to insure accuracy. For instance, the three pulleys should be turned simultaneously from a single block of wood, leaving a slight crown to assure correct tracking of the belt. Once shaped, they can be cut apart

and drilled. Holes in the idler pulleys may have to be enlarged slightly to receive the outer bearing races. These should be a snug press fit.

In the case of the drive-shaft bearings, it's the inner races that rotate. The $\frac{5}{16}$-in. threaded rod is a rather loose fit in these bearings, so it should be centered with two $\frac{5}{16}$-in. compression sleeves (one on each side) of the type used in making joints in copper tubing. The inner bearing races are already countersunk, and you may have to countersink the lock nuts slightly also.

When assembling the idler pulleys in the idler arm, tighten the nuts only enough to prevent

**belt massager:** see exercise equipment

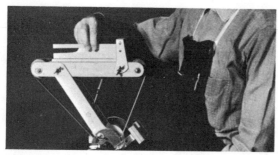

For edge sanding, bring the sanding platen up to a horizontal position and attach the stop block

the inner races from rotating. Then stake the nuts in place with a center punch. Bearings (Standard Conveyor Co. No. 100FC) and compression sleeves are available from industrial supply firms.

Belts for the sander are custom made from cloth-backed lathe sanding tape which comes in ½ and ¾-in.-width rolls. In cementing the lapped ends, the ends are first cut at an angle and the abrasive scraped off for about 1 in. before clamping together with a small C-clamp.

**See also:** band grinder; band sander; belt sanders; drum sanders; lathe accessories; pad sander; sanding jig; spindle sander.

*combination sander, continued*

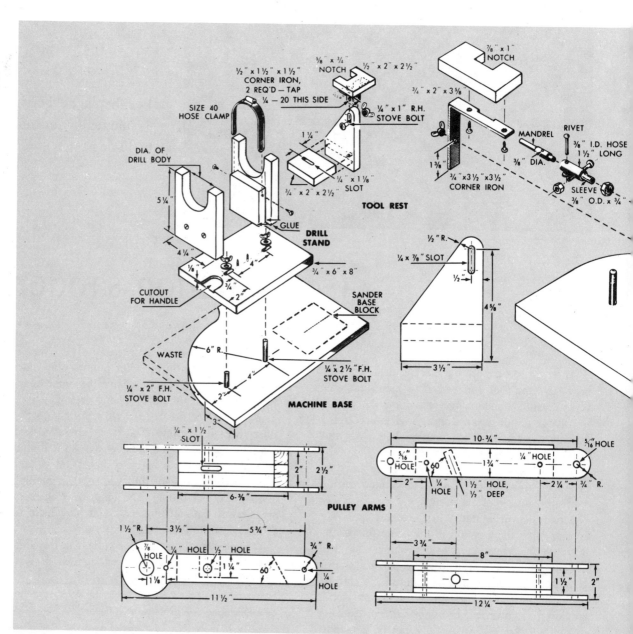

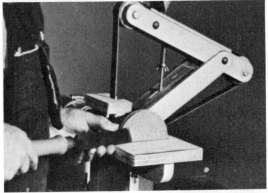

When using small grinding wheels with the sander, swing the drill stand 90 degrees and attach the tool rest

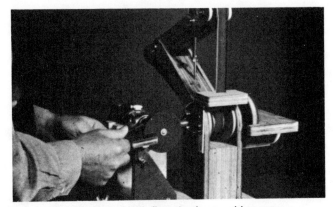

To put a sharp edge on tools, use a sanding disc faced with fine aluminum-oxide paper

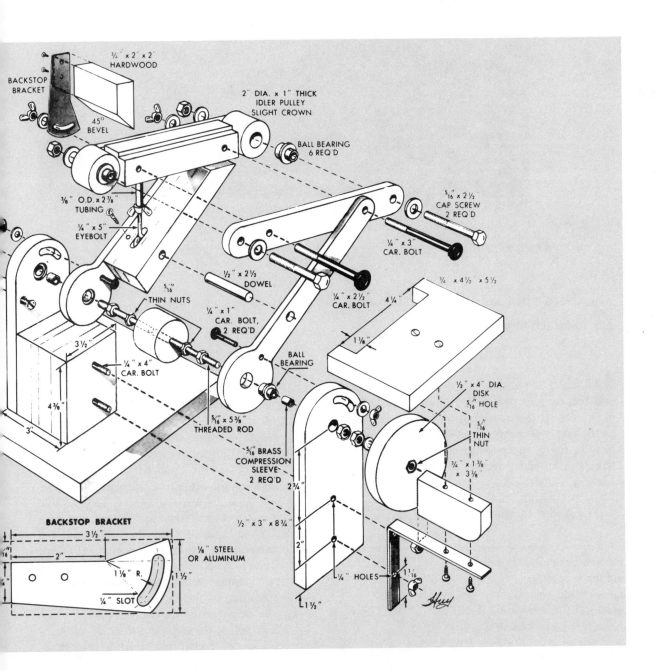

BACKSTOP BRACKET

3/8" x 2" x 2" HARDWOOD

BACKSTOP BRACKET

45° BEVEL

2" DIA. x 1" THICK IDLER PULLEY SLIGHT CROWN

BALL BEARING 6 REQ'D

5/16" x 2 1/2" CAP SCREW 2 REQ'D

3/8" O.D. x 2 7/8" TUBING

1/4" x 5" EYEBOLT

1/4" x 3" CAR. BOLT

1/2" x 2 1/2" DOWEL

THIN NUTS

5/16"

1/4" x 1" CAR. BOLT, 2 REQ'D

1/4" x 2 1/2" CAR. BOLT

3/4" x 4 1/2" x 5 1/2"

4 1/4"

1 1/8"

3 1/2"

1/4" x 4" CAR. BOLT

BALL BEARING

1/2" x 4" DIA. DISK 5/16" HOLE

4 3/8"

3"

5/16" x 5 3/8" THREADED ROD

5/16" BRASS COMPRESSION SLEEVE 2 REQ'D

5/16" THIN NUT

3/4" x 1 3/8" x 3 3/8"

2 3/4"

1/2" x 3 x 8 3/4"

2"

1/4" HOLES

1 1/16"

1 1/2"

**BACKSTOP BRACKET**

3 1/2"

2"

1/8" STEEL OR ALUMINUM

1 1/8" R.

1 1/2"

1/4" SLOT

243

# Belt sander for a lathe

This little belt sander, which is practically dust-free, clamps on the lathe bed

BY HOWARD R. CLARK

Need a belt sander in your shop occasionally? Here's an inexpensive one to attach to your lathe

■ QUICKLY ATTACHED to a wood-turning lathe, this belt sander, measuring about 6 by 8 by 18 in. in size, is just the thing for occasional jobs in the home workshop. It costs only a few dollars, is sturdy in construction and accurate in tracking. An added feature is the provision for using a vacuum-cleaner hose so that you can enjoy belt sanding that is practically dustless.

The sander illustrated here was made to fit in a 12-in. Delta lathe, and uses 4 by 36-in. belts. Some of the dimensions may have to be altered to fit other makes. The driving drum is screwed onto a 3-in. faceplate which turns onto the lathe spindle. The faceplate should be an extra one so it can be left on the drum permanently. If you have to fasten the drum to a faceplate every time that you want to use the sander, considerable time is lost in assembling even though you have marked both drum and faceplate, and have the same attachment screws conveniently at hand. The drum is held entirely by the lathe spindle and is not supported by a bearing on the sander.

The housing of the sander consists of a bottom, ends or access doors, two sides and a sanding table. All of these parts are made of ¾-in. plywood except the left side, which is ⅛-in. hardboard as it serves only to enclose the housing and does not support other parts. A T-shaped clamping block slips under the lathe bed and holds the sander firmly in position. Two bolts passing through the clamping block fit slots in the bottom and are tightened by means of wing nuts. The slots permit adjustment of the sander for belt tension and tracking. This adjustment is obtained by means of an aligning bar which is rigidly attached to the underside of the bottom. Two eyebolts that turn in nuts recessed in the aligning bar bear against the side of the lathe bed to pull the belt tight. The bed should be spot drilled to provide seats for the eyebolt ends.

Both ends or access doors are hinged at the bottom so that they can be swung open. The rear access door must be opened when the sander is being attached to the lathe. This door is held in the closed position securely with a spring latch, detail A. It is merely a pin made from an eyebolt and provided with a coil spring and a small plate screwed to the side of the housing. The pin enters a hole in the door edge thus locking it, but allows instant release by pulling the head. The front access door has a different locking arrangement as shown in detail C. It is a simple pivoted catch having a notch that slips over a screw projecting from the side. The end of the catch is bent at right angles to form a finger hold. Both doors are provided with de-

Accurate right-angle sanding is assured by using fence held firmly by tool-rest support on lathe bed, and holding work against stop at end of fence

flectors or shields of No. 18-ga. sheet aluminum projecting inwards as shown, almost up to the surface of the belt where it passes over the sanding table.

Both the drive and idler drums are turned from hardwood and should be slightly crowned to keep the belt tracking centrally over them. In turning the idler drum, a true-running job is assured if the stock is first mounted on a ⅜-in. shaft and then turned to finish size. The shaft projects through two brass or bronze bearing sleeves as shown in details B and C, or through ball-bearing races, which are held in the housing side and a

The idler drum is first drilled and pressed on a steel shaft which is mounted in the lathe as shown here so that the drum surface will be concentric and true-running

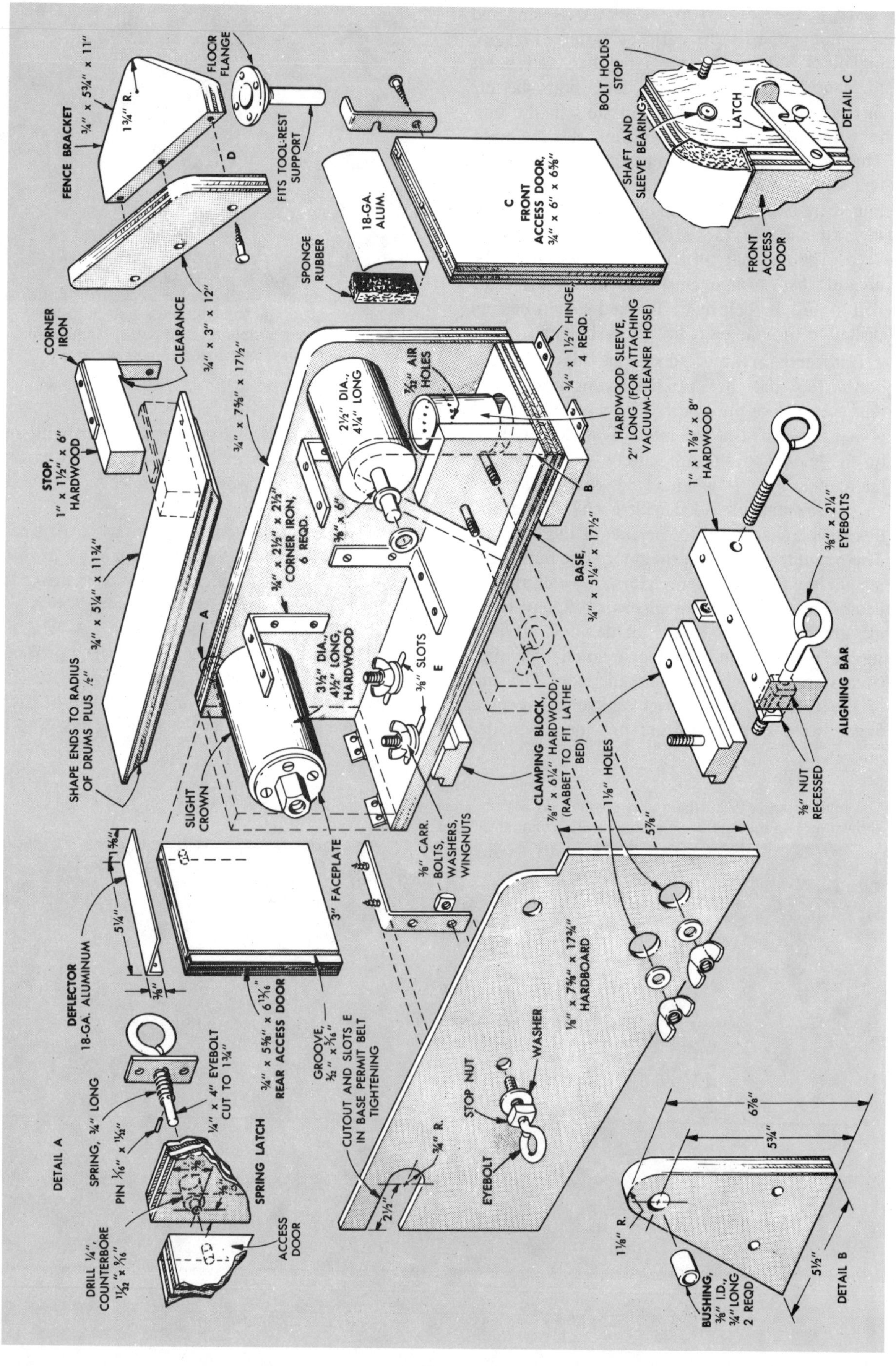
DETAIL A
SPRING, ¾" LONG
PIN 1/16" x 1½"
DRILL ¼", COUNTERBORE 11/32" x 9/16"
¼" x 4" EYEBOLT CUT TO 1¾"
SPRING LATCH
ACCESS DOOR
DEFLECTOR 18-GA. ALUMINUM
5¼"
1⅝"
⅜"
¾" x 5⅝" x 6 13/16" REAR ACCESS DOOR
GROOVE, 3/32" x 3/16"
CUTOUT AND SLOTS E IN BASE PERMIT BELT TIGHTENING
3" FACEPLATE
⅜" CARR. BOLTS, WASHERS, WINGNUTS
SLIGHT CROWN
SHAPE ENDS TO RADIUS OF DRUMS PLUS ½"
¾" x 5¼" x 11¾"
STOP, 1" x 1½" x 6" HARDWOOD
CORNER IRON
CLEARANCE
¾" x 3" x 12"
FENCE BRACKET
¾" x 5¾" x 11"
1¾" R.
D
FLOCR FLANGE
FITS TOOL-REST SUPPORT
SPONGE RUBBER
18-GA. ALUM.
C FRONT ACCESS DOOR, ¾" x 6" x 6⅝"
¾" x 7⅝" x 17½"
A
¾" x 2½" x 2½" CORNER IRON, 6 REQD.
3½" DIA., 4½" LONG, HARDWOOD
2½" DIA., 4¼" LONG
⅜" x 6"
3/32" AIR HOLES
¾" x 1½" HINGE, 4 REQD.
HARDWOOD SLEEVE, 2" LONG (FOR ATTACHING VACUUM-CLEANER HOSE)
B
BASE, ¾" x 5¼" x 17½"
⅜" SLOTS E
CLAMPING BLOCK, ⅞" x 6¼" HARDWOOD (RABBET TO FIT LATHE BED)
1⅛" HOLES
5⅞"
⅛" x 7⅝" x 17¾" HARDBOARD
WASHER
STOP NUT
EYEBOLT
¾" R.
2½"
6⅞"
5¾"
1⅛" R.
BUSHING, ⅜" I.D., ¾" LONG 2 REQD
5½"
DETAIL B
1" x 1⅞" x 8" HARDWOOD
⅜" x 2¼" EYEBOLTS
ALIGNING BAR
⅜" NUT RECESSED
BOLT HOLDS STOP
SHAFT AND SLEEVE BEARING
LATCH
FRONT ACCESS DOOR
DETAIL C

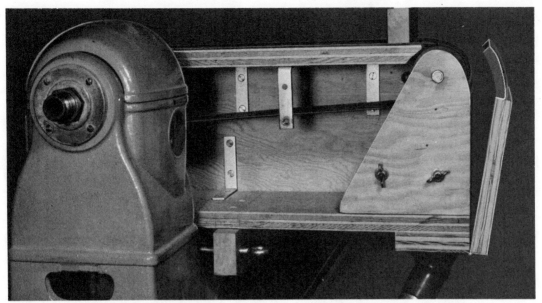

A view of the sander with the hardboard side removed to show the belt and sanding table

bearing support block. To assure boring the bearing holes in these pieces so that they will be in perfect alignment, they are first carefully stacked together in alignment, clamped in this position and then bored. The bearings should be a press fit in the plywood, and are locked with setscrews if they tend to rotate with the shaft. The bearing-support block is removable to permit installing sanding belts, and is held with bolts and wing nuts to another block which is permanently attached to the bottom.

The ends of the sanding table are shaped to a radius of ⅛ in. more than the radius of the drums. The table is held by angle brackets and has an angle bracket (with nut soldered on) for holding the ⅛-in. hardboard side. The top surface of the sanding table comes slightly above the top line of the drums. When the table is in place the location of the hole in the hardboard side is marked from the inside after dropping down one of the access doors. In the arrangement shown, the end of a vacuum-cleaner hose was slipped up through a hole in the bottom, just below the idler drum, and a tapered wooden cylinder was used to wedge the hose in place. However, the exact method of attachment varies with the type of hose used.

A hardwood work stop is also shown. This attaches to a bolt projecting through the side (detail C) and rests firmly on the edge of the side so there is clearance between the stop and belt. This is handy for sanding end grain, in which case the work is held vertically against a

fence to assure accurate 90-deg. sanding. The fence is provided with a bracket, floor flange and pipe nipple that fits the tool rest support.

One each of 40, 60 and 100-grit aluminum-oxide sanding belts will provide a good assortment for most types of work in the home shop. The belts are marked with a directional arrow, and should be installed in the sander to run in this direction.

**See also:** band sander; belt-disc sander; drum sander; pad sander; sanding jig; spindle sander.

Attached to a pipe floor flange and nipple that fits into the tool rest support, this sturdy fence provides a firm guide and helps to keep work square

# Big table for a small saw

What's a big saw got that a small one hasn't? A big table.

Now your little saw can have a big table, too

■ WISH YOUR SAW had a bigger table? Set flush in the top of this cabinet base, any pint-size saw becomes king size, with a table measuring almost 24 x 27 in. All it takes is one sheet of plywood which, when finished with several coats of gray enamel, looks as sleek as the steel cabinets of the big commercial models.

You can adapt these plans to suit any small rear-drive bench saw by changing the dimensions. The door-fitted compartment in the base can be used as tool storage or as a bin to catch sawdust. In the latter case, an opening would be cut in the shelf directly under the saw.

The conversion lets you use the original miter gauge but you'll need to replace the rip fence with a longer one. This part usually is available as an accessory, along with the front track to which it clamps. The layout diagram shows how parts can

be nested on a sheet of ¾-in. fir plywood.

If your miniature saw is the only power tool you own, it can build its own house—that's why the design was kept simple. It would be easier, of course, to cut the miter-gauge grooves with a portable router, but you can even manage these cuts by fastening another piece of the plywood to the saw as a temporary table and making repeated passes until the grooves are wide enough to provide a slip fit for the gauge tongue. Don't lay out these grooves until you've cut the center opening, so you can set the table panel over the saw's table.

In converting some saws, you will find it necessary to bore a ¾-in. hole in the left side of the cabinet to insert the rod.

**See also:** band sander; radial-arm saws; saber saws; slitting saws; woodworking.

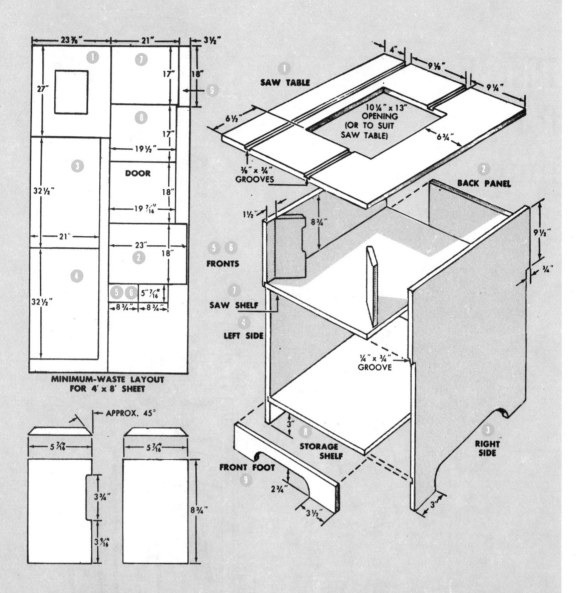

**MINIMUM-WASTE LAYOUT FOR 4' x 8' SHEET**

APPROX. 45°

SAW TABLE

10¼" x 13" OPENING (OR TO SUIT SAW TABLE)

⅜" x ¾" GROOVES

BACK PANEL

FRONTS

SAW SHELF

LEFT SIDE

¼" x ¾" GROOVE

RIGHT SIDE

STORAGE SHELF

FRONT FOOT

You have a choice of fitting top and bottom shelves in dadoes or batting the members and reinforcing with glue cleats. With butt joints, the shelves are cut ½-in. shorter. Glue and nail the sides to the shelves first, then add the back. Use the plywood top to position the saw on its shelf, but attach the top last

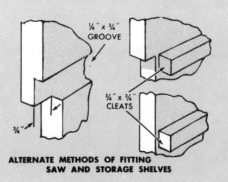

¼" x ¾" GROOVE

¾" x ¾" CLEATS

**ALTERNATE METHODS OF FITTING SAW AND STORAGE SHELVES**

# Pistol grip for your miter gauge

BY HOWARD R. CLARK

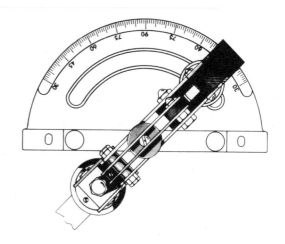

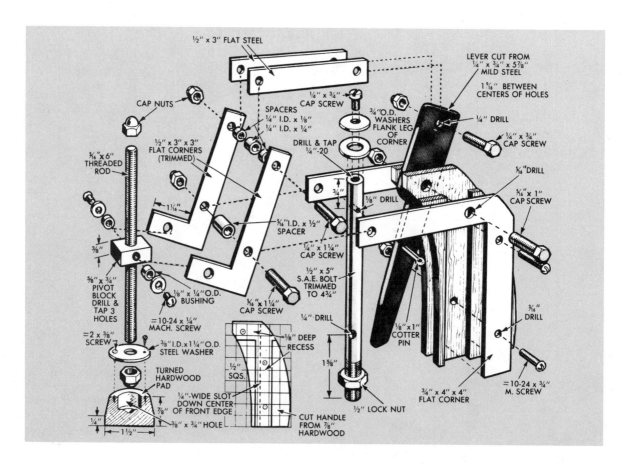

Making mitered cuts on your bench saw
can be tiring. Here's a
positive hold-down with a pistol grip
that's easy on your hands

HOLDING STOCK FIRMLY against both saw table and miter gauge while you feed it through
your bench saw can be tiring on the hands. Yet if
you don't, the stock will creep enough to ruin
the cut—particularly when you're cutting miters.

Here's a quick-acting, positive hold-down that
screws on top the miter gauge. A squeeze of the
pistol grip provides compound leverage that
presses the hardwood pad firmly against the face
of the stock. The long threaded rod lets you ad-

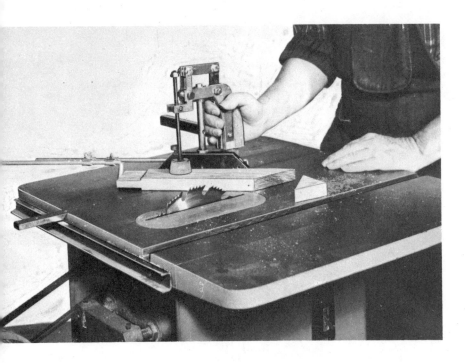

just the pad to any stock thickness. After you've made your pass, you just release the pad with thumb pressure on the top of the lever and the work is free.

Used with a stop rod, as shown, the hold-down makes fast work of production cutting. Identical pieces can be quickly and accurately positioned for mitering or trimming to size.

You can assemble this unit in a short time and at very small cost, from parts available at any hardware store. The two sizes of flat corners are used just as you buy them, except for trimming off unwanted portions and enlarging the holes for the cap screws. The bushings and spacers may be found at radio supply stores—or cut from copper tubing. The ½-in. S.A.E. bolt should be the type stocked by hardware stores—not the double-heat-treated type, sold at auto supply stores, which are much harder to drill and tap. The ¼-in. hole near the lower end is merely for the insertion of a rod or large nail to permit easy turning of this shaft into (and out of) a tapped hole at the top of the miter gauge.

The hold-down is shown on my miter gauge which comes already tapped with ½-in. S.A.E. threads. Other makes may require a different-size shaft and some change in the handle dimensions so that the butt will rest on the clamping knob (photo right). If there's no hole on your gauge, and no way to drill and tap one, you could braze a nut on the top edge.

Cut the T-shaped recess in both sides of the hardwood block and drill the three holes (using the larger flat corner as a template) before you saw the handle to shape. The only other wooden piece is the hold-down pad which can be turned on a lathe or cut out on a jigsaw and bored.

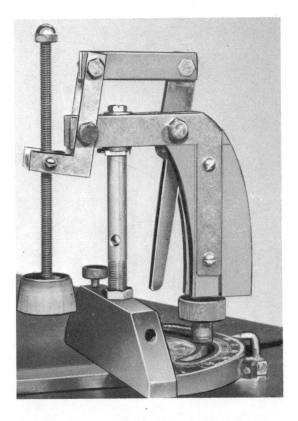

# Sliding tabletop improves saw accuracy

BY R. J. DeCRISTOFORO

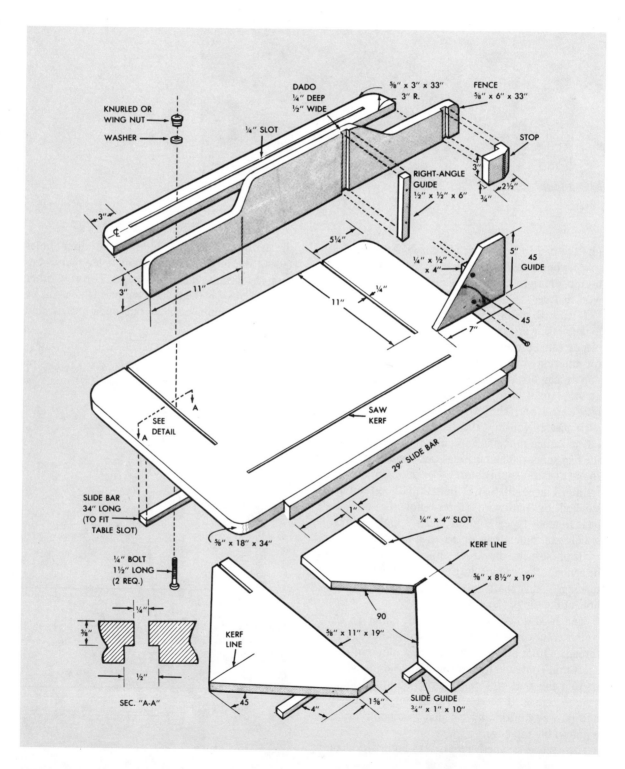

KNURLED OR WING NUT

WASHER

DADO
¼" DEEP
½" WIDE

⅝" x 3" x 33"
3" R.

FENCE
⅝" x 6" x 33"

STOP

¼" SLOT

RIGHT-ANGLE GUIDE
½" x ½" x 6"

3"

¾"

2½"

5¼"

¼"

¼" x ½" x 4"

5"

45 GUIDE

3"

11"

3"

11"

45

7"

45

SAW KERF

SEE DETAIL

29" SLIDE BAR

SLIDE BAR 34" LONG (TO FIT TABLE SLOT)

⅝" x 18" x 34"

1"

¼" x 4" SLOT

KERF LINE

⅝" x 8½" x 19"

¼" BOLT 1½" LONG (2 REQ.)

90

¼"

⅝" x 11" x 19"

SLIDE GUIDE
¾" x 1" x 10"

⅜"

KERF LINE

KERF LINE

1⅝"

½"

45

4"

SEC. "A-A"

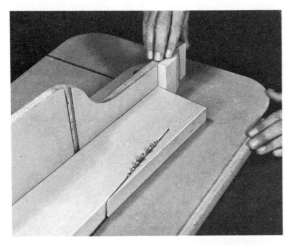

Taper cuts require only the stop block and fence set at an angle to the jig's blade slot. The entire jig moves to make the cut, with slide bars moving in the miter-gauge grooves in the saw table

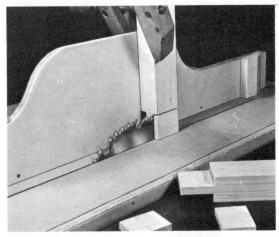

To make a tenon, add a right-angle guide in the dado provided, and clamp the work upright against it. What might be a dangerous cut to make free-hand now becomes safe when the entire jig moves forward

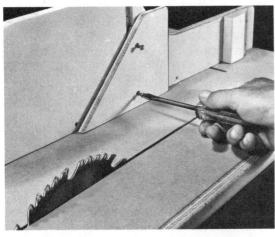

A cleat on the 45-deg. guide sets into the same dado as the right-angle guide. It creates a shoulder to rest mitered pieces against for cutting angled tenons. The work stays steady during the pass

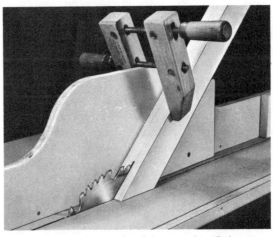

To spline or feather a miter joint, use the 45-deg. guide to position the work. For any cut where the fence and the blade must be parallel, be sure distance from the blade kerf to each end of the fence is equal

■ SOME HOMEMADE ACCESSORIES for power tools have such limited use that it's a tossup whether they'll earn their space in your shop. Not this one: It increases the accuracy and safety of your table saw in so many ways you'll never regret the evening you invest in making it.

For many jobs, it's superior to the saw's miter gauge and ripping fence, since it combines the function of both in a single unit, and completely eliminates friction between the work and the machine. It's ideal for making taper cuts, straight-faced or angled tenons, kerfs for splined miter joints and grooves in small work. Fasten on a shaped, flat panel (instead of the jig's fence) and it's an accurate miter jig.

Basically, this accessory is an auxiliary table that drops over the blade and slides back and forth on top of the saw table. The blade projects through a long slot. Attached along one edge and to the bottom face are slide bars, spaced to match the miter-gauge grooves to the right and left of the saw blade. These keep the jig positioned as you push it forward. The jig's fence can be set parallel to, and at any desired distance from, the blade. Unlike the standard ripping fence, it may also be set at an *angle* to the blade path, for taper cuts.

The jig also provides a clamping platform so you can advance small or awkwardly-shaped pieces into a blade set high for deep cuts—an

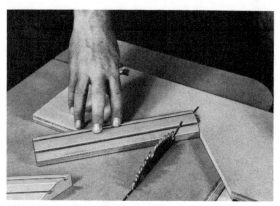

Accurate miters are quickly made by cutting the frame pieces to overall length, then trimming them in the V-guide attached to the sliding table. Held against this guide, the work can't shift or creep

You can make two mitered ends with one cut, without waste, when the stock's edges are interchangeable. By using the reverse V-guide above, you can cut at any point along a strip of any length

*sliding tabletop, continued*

action that can be dangerous, free-hand. Creep —that spoiler of miter cuts—is no longer a problem when work and table move together. In short, this jig incorporates a number of essential but usually separate jigs, and adds the advantage of the sliding action to each one.

The jig shown was cut from ⅝-in. plywood to fit a particular 10-in. circular saw. You will have to adjust the dimensions for your saw. The jig may prove too large for smaller table saws, but it is wise to make it as large as possible. Dimension the slide bars to fit snugly in the miter gauge—but not tight enough to bind. A smooth sanding and heavy waxing are essential.

After attaching the slide bars, you can cut the blade kerf by lowering the saw blade beneath the throat plate and setting the jig in place. Start the saw and raise the blade slowly to its full height, so that it slices through the jig table from beneath. Slide the jig forward and back to complete the kerf, taking care not to cut closer than 3 in. to either end of the jig table.

The slots for the fence lock-bolts may also be cut on the saw. Use a very high blade projection to minimize the arc at the end of the cut. To recess the bolt head, lower the blade so it projects about ¼ in. above the throat plate and enlarge the original slot by making repeat passes. This work is done with the slide bars removed, using the saw rip fence as a guide.

When making the jig's own fence, it's very important that the groove for the right-angle guide is cut accurately at 90 degrees to the base edge. Fuss a little to get this and other vital cuts exactly right.

The ¼-in slot through the fence flange can be cut with a saw blade, or you may prefer to rout it out on a drill press. Assemble this flange to the fence with glue and flathead wood screws, making sure the two pieces are at right angles.

Use extra care, again, when making the two miter-cut guides. Check the angles carefully, and make several trial cuts with each guide positioned temporarily on the jig table. If the results are accurate, attach the stop strip to the undersurface. These stops clamp tight against the edge of the sliding table to line the guides up with the blade. One of the bolts which clamp the fence flange engages a slot at the right side of each guide to lock it in position.

Sand all surfaces and edges, then cover with several applications of wood sealer or wash coats of shellac. As each coat dries, smooth with fine steel wool. Finally, apply paste wax and rub to a hard polish. To further minimize friction, wax the surface of the saw table, as well.

The V-guide is useful for jobs such as bisecting a disc, too. This is a tough cut to make on a table saw without some special jig. The disc can also be quartered or cut into many pie-shaped segments

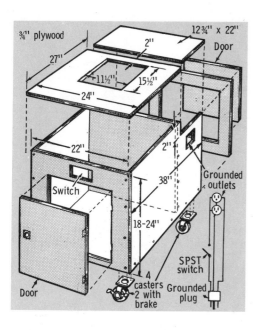

# Rolling saw stand

## BY RALPH TREVES

■ RIPPING AND CROSSCUTTING long lumber in a narrow basement shop becomes a lot simpler when you have your bench saw mounted on a caster-fitted stand which can be swung around easily to let you saw "with the room." Here's a handy stand that fills the bill.

18 and 24 in. Use 2½-in. plate-type casters, the two for the front equipped with locking levers. The step-down in the top permits the motor to rest securely in its belt. The entire base is made of ¾-in. fir plywood, cut from a 4 x 10-ft. sheet, joined with glue and screws.

The base is fitted with grounded ganged outlets near the rear that are controlled from a front switch box. Use a dustproof switch box. Plugging in the motor, instead of wiring it permanently, permits it to be moved easily to another power tool.

A sawdust bin at the front of the base keeps the shop clean. Weatherstrip the door all around to seal it

Saw accessories and blades find a home in the rear compartment. Cabinet catches hold the doors shut

The overall height should be between 34 and 40 in., depending on your own height. Allow 3 in. for casters and 13 in. for the 10-in. saw shown. The height of the base, then, is between

---

**bench-top holder:** see holder, bench-top
**bench vise:** see knurling; punch

---

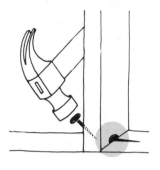

To toenail a stud, drive
the head of a horizontal
nail into the sill.

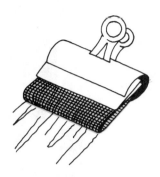

Make a glue brush from a
paper clamp and a scrap
of window screen.

Wrap an ax handle at the
top with plastic tape
to strengthen it.

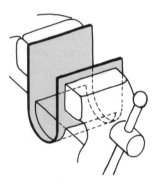

A thick leather strip
with a cut-out makes a
fine vise-jaw pad.

This sawhorse jig sup-
ports long boards being
cut on a table saw.

A C-clamp can be used as
a handle on the end of a
file for heavy work.

Scraps fastened to the
ends of shelves let you
paint both sides.

Three finger holes drilled
through a T-square
allow better control.

Straighten bent wire by
snaking it between spaced
nails held in a vise.

# Metal benders
# for the shop

BY MANLY BANISTER

Here are three different benders
to give your home shop
real metalworking versatility

"GIVE ME A PLACE to stand and I will move the Earth," said Archimedes, to dramatize the potential of the lever. In the centuries since, the lever has indeed moved the world through a long history of technological development. There's never been a mechanical contrivance that didn't make use of the lever principle.

The bending jig shown above is no exception. By putting that principle to work around a circle, it lets you bend ½-in. steel rod (or ³⁄₁₆-in. strap iron up to 1 in. wide) as easily as a circus strong man would—and a lot more accurately.

To use this bender, you select pins (or collars) of suitable size, position them in holes just far enough apart to accept the material to be bent, then bring the point of the peen against the work and secure it by tightening the retaining bolts. That done, you swing the handle around—clockwise, as shown in the inset sketch, or counter-clockwise if the work is reversed, as for lefthanded use. A full turn produces an eye;

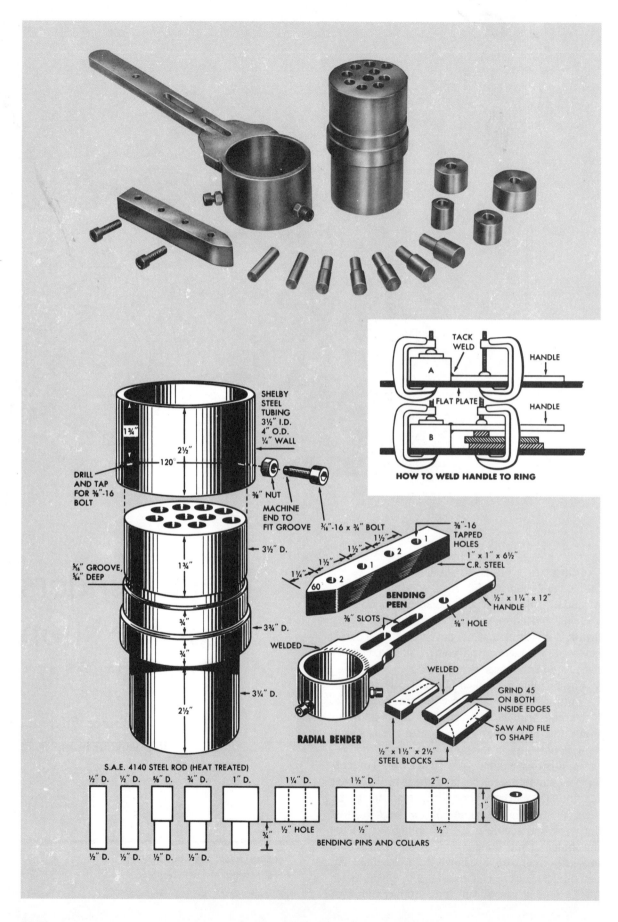

SHELBY STEEL TUBING 3½" I.D. 4" O.D. ¼" WALL

1¾"

2½"

120°

DRILL AND TAP FOR ⅜"-16 BOLT

⅜" NUT

MACHINE END TO FIT GROOVE

3/16"-16 x ¾" BOLT

3½" D.

3/16" GROOVE, 5/64" DEEP

1¾"

¾"

¾"

3¾" D.

3¼" D.

2½"

S.A.E. 4140 STEEL ROD (HEAT TREATED)

½" D.   ½" D.   ⅝" D.   ¾" D.   1" D.   1¼" D.   1½" D.   2" D.

½" D.   ½" D.   ½" D.   ½" D.

¾"

½" HOLE   ½"   ½"   1"

BENDING PINS AND COLLARS

TACK WELD

A   HANDLE

FLAT PLATE

B   HANDLE

**HOW TO WELD HANDLE TO RING**

⅜"-16 TAPPED HOLES

1½"   1

1½"   2

1½"   1

1¼"   2

60

1" x 1" x 6½" C.R. STEEL

**BENDING PEEN**

⅜" SLOTS

WELDED

½" x 1¼" x 12" HANDLE

⅝" HOLE

WELDED

GRIND 45 ON BOTH INSIDE EDGES

SAW AND FILE TO SHAPE

**RADIAL BENDER**

½" x 1½" x 2½" STEEL BLOCKS

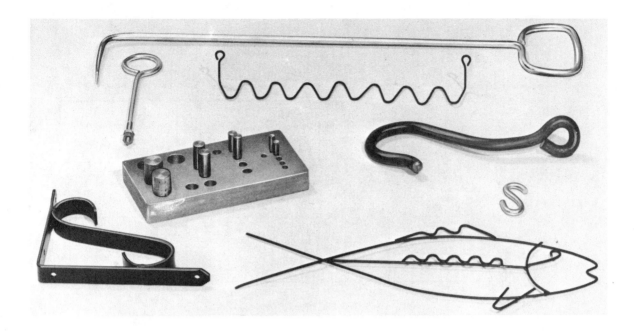

a half-turn makes a U-bend; a quarter-turn forms a right-angle. Excess length is not needed, as it is when the work must supply its own leverage by extending well beyond the bend.

A second, simpler jig—and a sampling of the work it will do—is shown in the photo on this page. Its capacity is strip metal up to ¼ in. thick by ¾ in. wide, but using the smallest set of pins, it's ideal for bending wire. With this jig, the material to be bent becomes its own lever as you pull it against the pins.

It has no moving parts and is actually only a

socket plate for clamping in a heavy-duty vise. Though simpler in construction, it is even more versatile, since it's four jigs in one, utilizing pins of ¼, ⅜, ½ and ¾ in. diameter, which handle a range of material from coat-hanger wire up through the heaviest material you can bend by hand—either cold or hot. If you want to make wire jewelry, add a series of ³⁄₁₆ and ⅛-in. holes, and cut matching pins. These will be just right for copper and silver wire.

Any bending jig must provide a variety of pin sockets since the best spacing between the anchor pin and the radius pin is just enough to pass the thickness or diameter of the work. In the radial jig, ½-in. sockets spiral outward at increasing distances from the center hole. A layout for drilling these holes is given on this page. Make a full-size pattern on tracing paper, tape this to the face of the bending table and transfer hole-centers to the steel with a prick punch. Retap these with a centerpunch before you go to the drill press. Then start with ⅛-in. pilot holes and work up to the final diameter through several drill sizes to keep drill-whip from enlarging or oblating the holes.

The steel used for the body of the jig is a chrome-molybdenum alloy made for maximum resistance to abrasion, impact, and stress. Its industrial designation is A.I.S.I. A-4142 (SAE 4140) Moly-Krome. It's available both annealed and heat-treated. The latter requires no further treatment for home shop usage. If the annealed type is used, you should have your local machine shop heat-treat it to prevent the pin sockets from

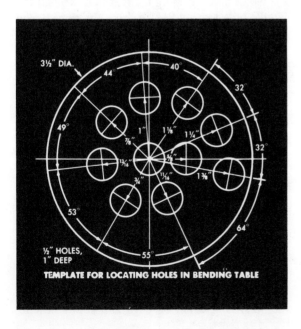

TEMPLATE FOR LOCATING HOLES IN BENDING TABLE

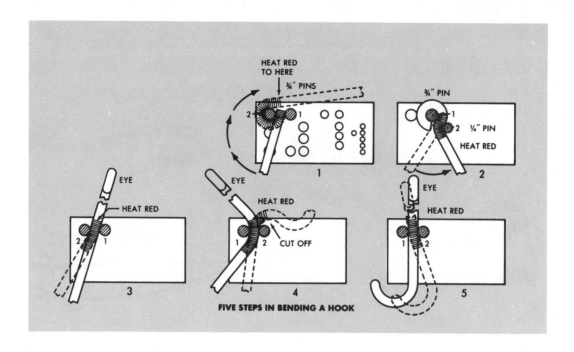

HEAT RED
TO HERE
¾" PINS
¾" PIN
¼" PIN
HEAT RED

EYE
HEAT RED
EYE
HEAT RED
CUT OFF
EYE
HEAT RED

**FIVE STEPS IN BENDING A HOOK**

*metal benders, continued*

"egging." I turned the body on a 6-in. lathe (with a milling attachment for cutting the slots and the peen point). But, be warned—heat-treated Moly-Krome is murder on cutting and drill bits. The groove around the body seats the three collar bolts that prevent the collar from working upward in use.

The top photo on page 258 shows a convenient spread of bending pins and collars. If you make pin sockets from drill rod, you can use them without hardening; but if you choose to harden them, be sure to temper them at not less than 800 deg. Otherwise the steel will be brittle and will snap off under pressure. Pins of low-carbon steel can be case-hardened. The plans call for pins of different diameters for bending arcs of radii. For larger sizes, "doughnut" collars slipped over the center pin are recommended, to save machining.

If you lack facilities to harden and temper the pins and other pieces, your local machine shop can do the job for two or three dollars. If you have a forge or blast furnace, bring the metal to a bright, cherry red, then quench in clean, cold water, stirring vigorously with the tongs to cool as rapidly as possible. To draw some of the hardness and take away the brittleness, temper the metal in a 300 deg. kitchen oven for an hour. Quench again in cold water and polish off the scale in the lathe with fine emery cloth. You'll

know the pieces are properly hardened when they sound like those ball bearings Capt. Queeg always rattled in his hand.

The bending peen has four tapped holes to permit adjustment to various distances from the center pin. Turn retaining bolts into the No. 1 pair for light work. But when you're bending heavy material, you can gain extra leverage by moving the peen back to engage the work an inch or so from the bending point. In such cases, use the No. 2 holes, passing the rear bolt through the handle hole located 8¼ in. from the ring. If you need more leverage than the handle can provide, slip a length of pipe over it.

The peen must be hardened, since the bending is all done with the anvil tip, and this would quickly score to the point of uselessness. This large a piece of tool steel is rather expensive, but cold-rolled steel will serve as well if the point is case hardened. This can be done quite easily with a commercial product called Kasenit, from directions on the can. Or use a hard-surfacing electrode in an arc welder to lay a bead across the point and a couple on each side. Then grind the hard-surfacing deposit to a rounded point.

The handle can be cut from solid ½-in. sheet, or built up as sketched, page 258. After shaping, cut 2¼-in. slots as shown. The ⅜-in. bridge between the slots is merely to avoid weakening the handle. A detail on page 258 shows how to join handle and ring without distortion. First clamp both parts upside down to a piece of flat steel, and tack weld at each side, where the handle joins the ring. When these welds cool, reclamp the unit as shown at B and run a full weld across the top, using a ⅛-in. E6011 electrode at 115 amps. The ring and weld area should be immediately swathed in rags (or covered with sand or ashes) to slow cooling. When the metal is at room temperature, unclamp and grind the weld bead flat with the handle surface. Then clamp the unit upside-down again and run a full weld across the joint, again insulating it for slow cooling.

The flat bender is a simple socket plate. The spacing of the holes is given in o.c. dimensions that create between-pin spaces to take a variety of thicknesses. For easy passage between pins, increase each space a hairline when transferring the pattern centers to the block with a prick punch. Though the pin holes are only ¾-in. deep, drill the ⅛-in. center holes *through* to prevent suction and ease removal of stuck pins.

You'll want a pair of ¼, ⅜, ½ and ¾ in. pins. For occasional use, pins made of hard steel rod (the bright-plated kind, available in 3-ft. lengths at hardware stores) are tough enough. But if you plan to use the jig fairly often, cut the pins from drill rod.

The photo at the top of this page shows the use of the jig for putting a radius bend at the end of a strip of ³⁄₁₆ x ¾-in. hot rolled steel to be used as a handrail. The bend is made a bit at a time by

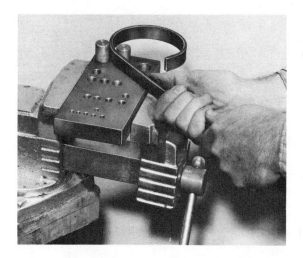

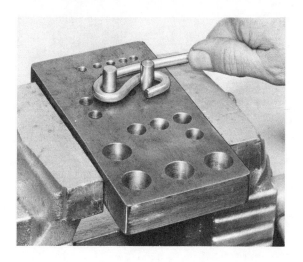

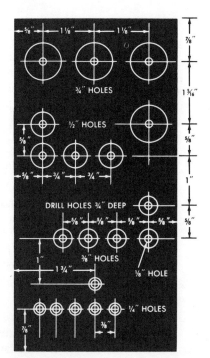

pulling on the work. You can bend ¼-in.-thick strips the same way if the vise is strong enough to withstand the tension. If you're not certain, heat the metal red, first. This is a good idea, too, when you're making tight radius bends in thinner stock.

The second photo above shows steps in bending a big S-hook around ⅜-in. pins. The material is ¼-in. hard steel rod; the pins are spaced ¼ in. for the first bend, then moved as shown for the second. The excess stock is then trimmed off.

Bends with this jig may not always be as well shaped as you need—that is, they may not be snug to a given radius, due to the "spring" inherent in the metal, and to the fact that the material must provide its own leverage. And if a quantity of identical items must be made, you lose some time cutting off each one as it is formed. So, for production or precision work you're better off cutting the stock to straight, finished lengths first, then forming these on a bender.

**See also:** sheet metal; shrink plate; smelting furnace, stake plate.

# Bicycle built for two

BY MANLY BANISTER

Here's a tandem for a few dollars by
using the front half of
a boy's bike and the back
half of a girl's bike

■ EVEN IF THE LADY in your life *isn't* named Daisy, she'll look sweet upon the seat of this custom rig which is as slick as most expensive models you can buy. When kids lose interest in conventional bike-riding, here's a way to get extra mileage and status out of a couple of stored bikes that are only taking up room and serving as a nuisance in the garage or basement. Instead of continuing to step around them, why not put them to good use? And unless the teen-agers appropriate the tandem the minute you snug up the last nut, you'll discover that this type of biking is great sport for adults as well. The cooperative propulsion takes the huff-and-puff out of cross country pedaling—gets you out in the open air for exercise.

Starting with two standard 26-in. bikes in good condition, you can convert them into a tandem for only a few dollars—including the

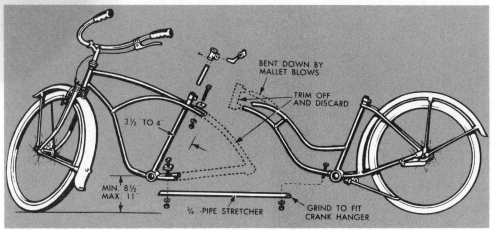

All you add to the two frames is a bottom stretcher. You may have to reshape the cross bars of the girl's bike (right) to join it to the front frame for a good-looking design

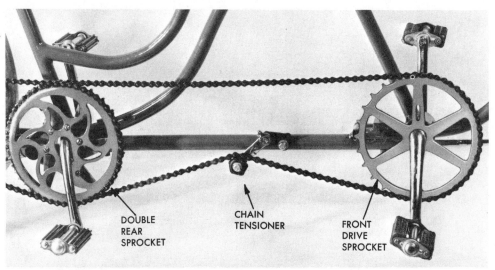

Drive linkage consists of one chain around front sprocket and same-size sprocket on inside of rear assembly—plus second chain from outer sprocket to rear wheel, and tensioner

extra sprocket, all other materials, a can of spray paint—and the cost of having necessary welding done at a local shop.

A boy's bike provides the front wheel and steering column, a girl's bike the rear wheel and seat. The first step is to measure the height of both crankshafts from the ground—which should be between 10 and 11 in. The crank hangers should be kept at this height to provide clearance for the pedals on corner-banking. Actually, in the model shown the frames were dropped somewhat to flow the lines together, so the 6½-in. cranks were replaced with 5½-in. cranks made for 24-in. bikes. But you can avoid this to keep costs at a minimum.

Stand the bikes with the front wheel of the girl's beside the rear wheel of the boy's. Study them. Decide where the frames can be joined for best design and strength. The diagram is only

Outside sprocket of rear drive must have hub hole enlarged to fit over pedal crank. Saw with metal-cutting blade passed through sprocket does job fast; small file in chuck does final shaping

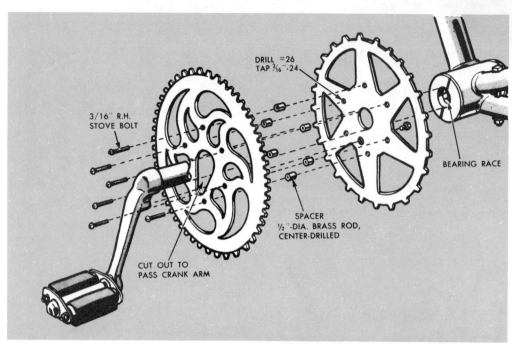

DRILL =26
TAP 3/16"-24

3/16" R.H.
STOVE BOLT

BEARING RACE

SPACER
1/2"-DIA. BRASS ROD,
CENTER-DRILLED

CUT OUT TO
PASS CRANK ARM

Rear crank assembly's sprockets bolt together. Spacers enable the chains to run side-by-side without touching. Shoulder on the crank arm passes through the outer sprocket to seat against the inner one

*bicycle for two, continued*

Worm's-eye view of rear axle shows 3/16-in. thick aluminum washer on far side of hub. This aligns reversed wheel sprocket to outer drive sprocket

Rear handlebar is for gripping—it doesn't steer, so it's anchored by means of a 1/2-in. pipe tee bored out to fit the front saddle stem. Standard handlebar stem is trimmed

To install dual sprocket (foreground) on one-piece crank, you'll probably have to remove pedal, nut, and bearing race (all left-hand threaded) from opposite side and twist crank through hanger

a suggestion, as bike models differ just as automobiles do.

Next, strip both bikes down to their frames. Remove the handlebar and stem from the girl's bike and save them. Discard the front fork.

Crank assemblies differ, but most American bikes have a one-piece crankshaft that must be drawn through the hanger from the sprocket side. For this you must remove the pedal, nut and bearing race on the left side. These have lefthand threads, so turn them in the direction opposite to the way you normally loosen a bolt or nut. The bearing race on the sprocket side has a righthand thread. You'll have to remove this one, too, from the rear crank.

Using a hacksaw, cut through the frame of the girl's bike just behind the steering column. When you saw off the rear frame of the boy's bike, leave several inches of each bar you cut through; you'll need every part of these stubs to attach the bars of the girl's bike, and the extra stretcher which actually helps couple the two bikes together. Now, select the best pair of wheels and fasten them in their respective forks.

To do this properly you should lay the frames on their sides on the floor with both wheels bearing against a wall. The wall represents ground line and lets you adjust the frames to each other while retaining the proper ground-to-center-of-crank-hanger distance. The 8½-in. minimum shown in the exploded diagram on page 263 is for the shorter 24-in. bike cranks substituted in this particular model. To retain the present cranks (assuming you are joining 26-in. bikes), avoid dropping the frames very much. The exploded view in the diagram gives you a very good idea of how all this will fit together.

Once the frame positions are determined, measure between the crank hangers and cut a length of ¾-in. pipe to span this distance. File each end concave for a good fit, and drill for bolts that will secure the stretcher to the frames for welding. A third bolt joins the upper bars of the two frames. The three welds on the model shown were made by a commercial shop for $3. It cost an extra 50¢ later on, to have the rear handlebar unit welded to both the seat stem and the handlebar stem. It was secured with bolts at first, so it could be adjusted during trial runs.

One of the bikes shown had ½-in.-pitch chain, the other 1-in.-pitch. It makes no difference as long as the extra sprocket you buy has the same diameter and pitch as the sprocket on the front frame. This extra sprocket replaces the original rear sprocket if the latter differs in pitch. The original sprocket is then attached to the replacement sprocket and chained to the sprocket on the rear wheel. These last two sprockets must have the same pitch.

### how to adjust chains

The sprockets mounted on the rear crank must be separated sufficiently to let the chains pass. Wrap a length of chain around each sprocket and lay them together, back to face, separating the edges of the chains with bits of ⅛-in. cardboard. Measure the distance between the inside faces of the sprockets and cut pieces of brass rod that length—preferably on a lathe, for uniformity. To determine how many you'll need, check the sprockets to see how many places a bolt may be driven through both. Drill through the center of each spacer to pass a ³⁄₁₆-in. stove bolt. Also drill pass-holes in the outside sprocket at the points selected. Then drill and tap matching holes in the inside sprocket. Make a trial assembly with two bolts and spacers to see how the paired sprockets fit on the crank, filing out the center opening of the outside

The two halves blend into an harmonious whole, losing their original identities. Note pedals are always in same relative positions for smooth rider leg action

sprocket until the assembly seats squarely. Add remaining bolts, turning them tight; trim off and peen the projecting ends.

A chain tensioner is needed to take the slack out of the front chain. The one shown was made from the spring, arm and one sprocket from a broken Simplex tensioner for multi-speed bikes, picked up for $1.50 in a bike shop. But such a shop should be able to supply you a regular tensioner for tandem bikes. Commercial tensioners are for ½-in.-pitch chain. If your chain has a 1-in. pitch, convert the sprocket by cutting out every other tooth. You can do this with a pocket knife.

Before the tandem is ready for a trial spin, move the rear-wheel sprocket out to align with the outside crank sprocket. The girl's bike shown had an English coaster brake; the sprocket nut had a lefthand thread, with an ⅛-in. hub on the inner side. By turning the sprocket over and screwing it back on with a washer between sprocket and brake hub (see the photo), the teeth were moved out enough to be in line with the drive teeth of the dual-sprocket assembly.

Should the sprocket have no hub, you might

obtain a second sprocket (for its threads), turn it down to a washer, and weld it to the original sprocket, from which the threads have been machined.

You'll find that the tandem bicycle is no patchwork job, but that the two halves will blend into a harmonious whole, losing their original identities. A can of spray paint will help to give your new vehicle its finishing touch before you take her out for a trial spin.

An added filip, one which will lend a certain foreign sparkle to the tandem cycle, and one which will provide you with an extra safety margin is the addition of a hand brake. This is especially good for emergency stops and for downhill coasting. It should be installed on the front wheel. This will add only a few dollars to total costs. When you consider that a commercial tandem would set you back nearly $100, you're still way ahead. About as far ahead as you'll be on that first hill when you show the lonely pumpers your dust. That should *really* put you out in front with sweet-sittin' Daisy!

**See also:** bicycle boat; concrete; exercise equipment; paddleboat; parade floats; unicycle.

# Hi-cycle

BY MORRIS G. HULTS

■ THIS UPSIDE-DOWN BICYCLE is guaranteed to keep the kids off the street—high off, that is. Because no welding is involved, it's easy to convert this conversion back to a lowly "earth" bike. Be sure to check your local ordinances to see if this bike is legal before you begin.

First remove the handle bar, seat, wheels, pedal crank and chain; then wash all parts and bearings in solvent and pack with grease. In reassembly, both the rear wheel and pedal crank must be on the opposite side of the frame.

The fork is removed, then reinstalled after the bike is inverted. A 5-ft. pipe forced into the fork serves as a "joy stick." The seat post is also a 5-ft. pipe bolted to the frame.

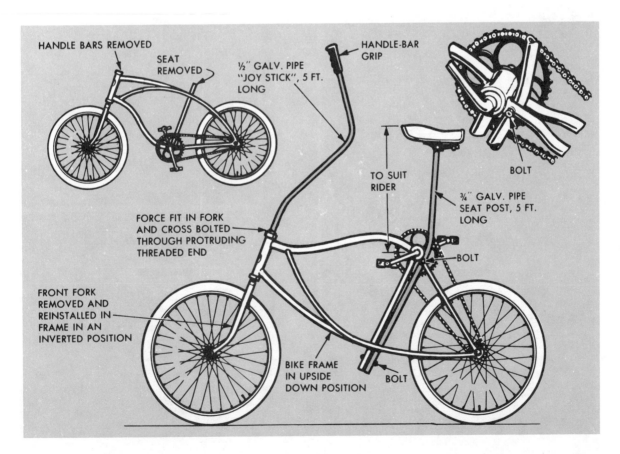

HANDLE BARS REMOVED

SEAT REMOVED

½" GALV. PIPE "JOY STICK", 5 FT. LONG

HANDLE-BAR GRIP

TO SUIT RIDER

BOLT

¾" GALV. PIPE SEAT POST, 5 FT. LONG

FORCE FIT IN FORK AND CROSS BOLTED THROUGH PROTRUDING THREADED END

BOLT

FRONT FORK REMOVED AND REINSTALLED IN FRAME IN AN INVERTED POSITION

BIKE FRAME IN UPSIDE DOWN POSITION

BOLT

# Power or pedal this water bike

BY HANK CLARK

For your next trip to the lake you can build a versatile craft that
offers leg exercise as well as lazy cruises

TAKE YOUR CHOICE: putt-putt-putt or puff-puff-puff. Whether you decide to build up those leg muscles by pedaling or relax and let the motor do the work, you'll have a ball with this either-or bike boat. It's a two-weekend project that offers season after season of low-cost fun on the water.

When you feel energetic, just tilt the motor clear of the water and drop the paddle wheels in by lowering the "liftlock" arm from its hook. This same arm anchors the paddle wheels in the down position. Use the handlebars for steering —they're linked to two rudders astern—and back pedaling when you want to stop or back the boat.

To switch to power, haul the paddles up clear of the water with the lift-lock arm and hook it in

**bicycle exerciser:** see exercise equipment
**bicycle parking block:** see concrete
**bifold sliding doors:** see sliding doors

MOTOR POWER

PEDAL POWER

Fair the top and bottom edges of the sidepieces so they will fit tightly against the plywood planking

the stowed position. Then lower the motor into the water, give a yank on the starter and you're off to the races at a breathtaking 8 mph.

Normally, you'll steer with the handlebars, since the motor is set in a straight-line position with an adjusting nut to keep it from swiveling. To be on the safe side, however, leave that adjusting nut loose enough so you can reach around and override it if a sudden change of direction is necessary.

If you can build a box, you can probably complete the two floats in a couple of evenings. First cut and assemble the sides on the transom, bow block and bulkhead. Note that the width of each sidepiece is 8½ in. at its widest point. Next, install the top piece, by gluing and nailing every 1½ in. The hole for the spreader support may be cut before nailing the top down or when mounting the diagonal braces for these supports.

### secure with glue, nails

Once you've installed all the necessary supports, backing blocks and braces, the bottom can be added. Note that the photo shows a 1 x 4 cross brace between the sidepieces at the end of the bow curve. While not absolutely necessary (it's not shown on the plans), this simplifies the job of planking the bottom since it holds the sides in place during nailing. The bottom, like the top, is secured with glue and boat nails spaced 1½-in. apart. To complete the pontoon, mount the keel and transom filler block, both cut from 1-in. stock.

After sanding all edges slightly round, seal the seams (including those around the spreader support) with fiberglass tape.

The next step is to join the two floats. Set them flat on the ground the proper distance apart and mark the top of each spreader support for cutting, so that it will fit flush against the bottom of the spreader. When you've made these cuts

The front spreader supports are glued and screwed to the sides. A 1 x 3 cross brace is also required

and shaped the spreader, mount the front spreader on the supports by gluing and toenailing through the curved end. The joint is then covered with ¼-in. plywood gussets glued and nailed to both faces to form a rigid arch.

The rear spreader may now be cut to shape. However, its exact location will depend on the bike used, so don't mount it as yet.

The bicycle must be taken apart and modified for mounting on the floats. Begin by removing

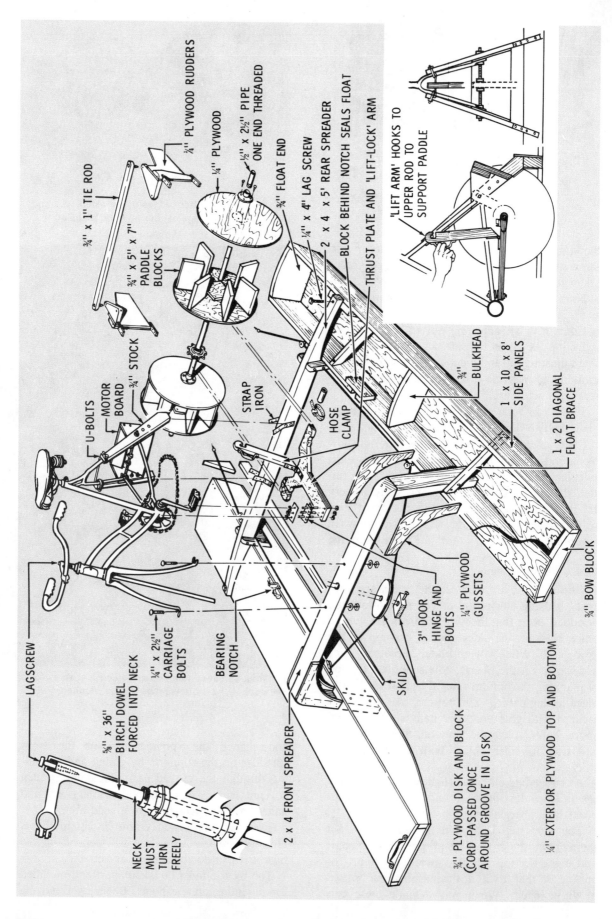

¼" PLYWOOD RUDDERS

¼" PLYWOOD

½" x 2½" PIPE ONE END THREADED

¾" x 1" TIE ROD

¾" FLOAT END

¼" x 4" LAG SCREW

2 x 4 x 5' REAR SPREADER

BLOCK BEHIND NOTCH SEALS FLOAT

THRUST PLATE AND 'LIFT-LOCK' ARM

"LIFT ARM" HOOKS TO UPPER ROD TO SUPPORT PADDLE

¾" x 5" x 7" PADDLE BLOCKS

¾" STOCK

U-BOLTS

MOTOR BOARD

STRAP IRON

HOSE CLAMP

BULKHEAD

¾"

1 x 10 x 8' SIDE PANELS

1 x 2 DIAGONAL FLOAT BRACE

LAGSCREW

⅝" x 36" BIRCH DOWEL FORCED INTO NECK

¼" x 2½" CARRIAGE BOLTS

BEARING NOTCH

2 x 4 FRONT SPREADER

3" DOOR HINGE AND BOLTS

¼" PLYWOOD GUSSETS

SKID

¾" BOW BLOCK

NECK MUST TURN FREELY

¾" PLYWOOD DISK AND BLOCK (CORD PASSED ONCE AROUND GROOVE IN DISK)

¼" EXTERIOR PLYWOOD TOP AND BOTTOM

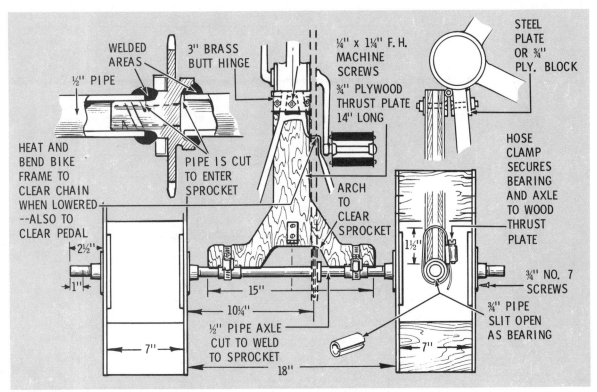

The paddle-wheel drive assembly makes use of an old sprocket welded into the pipe axle. If it's obtainable, a one-to-one ratio between the paddle-wheel drive and the pedal sprocket is best. It makes pedaling your water bike a good deal less strenuous

*water bike, continued*

the wheels and spreading both front and rear forks approximately 1 ft. to provide a more stable support. Then, while propping the rear fork so the bike is level, bend the ends of the front spreader. Drill holes for bolts in the spreader and bolt the front fork to it.

Before the rear fork can be mounted, the paddle wheels must be constructed. After removing the sprocket from the rear wheel, clean it and take it to a welding shop to have it welded to the ½-in. pipe axle. Once the axle is made up, slip the two slitted pipe bearings over it and turn flanges on the ends. The inner axle should be 18 in. long when these are in place. After turning the two short nipples into the other pair of flanges, lay these aside while you assemble the paddle wheels.

Cut out the four 18-in. plywood discs and 14 paddle blades. To locate the blades on the discs, pencil off seven equally spaced radial lines on two discs, and drive three nails along each line so they barely protrude on the opposite side of the plywood. Then apply a generous coat of waterproof glue to one end grain of each blade, allow enough time for it to be absorbed and give it another coat. One at a time, place the blades

## WATER BIKE MATERIALS LIST

| PLYWOOD | AMT. |
|---|---|
| ¼" x 4' x 8' Exterior (AB) | 2 |
| ¼" x 4' x 4' Exterior (AA or AB) | 1 |
| ¾" x 2' x 2' Exterior (AA or AB) | 1 |

| LUMBER | AMT. |
|---|---|
| 1 x 10 x 8' Pine or fir | 4 |
| 1 x 8 x 6' Pine or fir | 1 |
| 1 x 5 x 10' Pine or fir | 1 |
| 1 x 3 x 6' Pine or fir | 2 |
| 2 x 4 x 7' Fir | 2 |
| ⅝" x 36" Birch dowel | 1 |

| MISC. | AMT. |
|---|---|
| ½" x 18" Galv. pipe (ends threaded) | 1 |
| ½" x 2½" Galv. pipe (one end threaded) | 2 |
| ½" Galv. pipe flanges | 4 |
| ¼" x 2½" Carriage bolts with nuts | 2 |
| ⅝" No. 8 f.h. woodscrews | 16 |
| ⅜" x 1' Threaded rod with six nuts | 1 |
| ⅜" x 1' Rod | 1 |
| ⅛" x ¾" x 5" Strap iron | 4 |
| ¾" x 1½" Galv. pipe (slit) | 2 |
| 2" Hose clamps, screw type | 2 |
| 3" Brass butt hinge | 1 |
| 3/16" x 1¼" Machine screws (for hinge) | 6 |
| ¼" x 4" Log screws | 2 |
| 1" Eye pulleys | 4 |
| 20' Steering cable | 1 |
| 1" boat nails, waterproof glue, primer and exterior finish | |

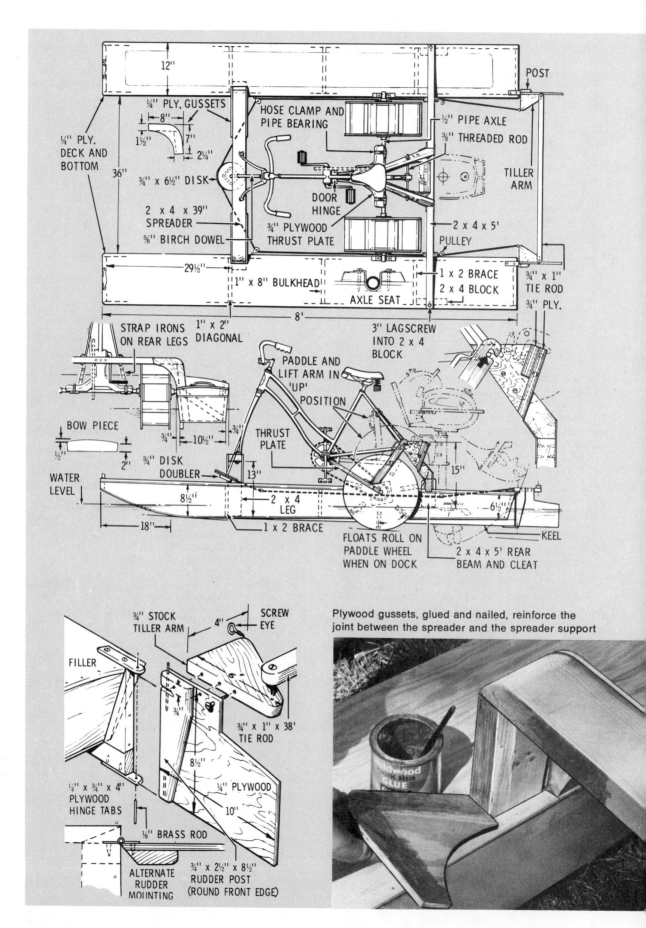

¼" PLY. GUSSETS

12"

8"

1½"

7"

2¼"

POST

HOSE CLAMP AND
PIPE BEARING

½" PIPE AXLE

⅜" THREADED ROD

TILLER
ARM

¼" PLY.
DECK AND
BOTTOM

36"

¾" x 6½" DISK

2 x 4 x 39"
SPREADER

⅝" BIRCH DOWEL

DOOR
HINGE

¾" PLYWOOD
THRUST PLATE

2 x 4 x 5'

PULLEY

¾" x 1"
TIE ROD

¾" PLY.

29½"

1" x 8" BULKHEAD

AXLE SEAT

1 x 2 BRACE
2 x 4 BLOCK

8'

STRAP IRONS
ON REAR LEGS

1" x 2"
DIAGONAL

3" LAGSCREW
INTO 2 x 4
BLOCK

PADDLE AND
LIFT ARM IN
'UP'
POSITION

BOW PIECE

½"

2"

¾"

¾"

¾" DISK
DOUBLER

10½"

13"

THRUST
PLATE

WATER
LEVEL

8½"

2 x 4
LEG

15"

18"

1 x 2 BRACE

FLOATS ROLL ON
PADDLE WHEEL
WHEN ON DOCK

6½"

KEEL

2 x 4 x 5' REAR
BEAM AND CLEAT

¾" STOCK
TILLER ARM

4"

SCREW
EYE

FILLER

¾"

¾" x 1" x 38'
TIE ROD

¼" x ¾" x 4"
PLYWOOD
HINGE TABS

8½"

¼" PLYWOOD

10"

⅛" BRASS ROD

ALTERNATE
RUDDER
MOUNTING

¾" x 2½" x 8½"
RUDDER POST
(ROUND FRONT EDGE)

Plywood gussets, glued and nailed, reinforce the
joint between the spreader and the spreader support

on the nail points, flip the disc over and drive the nails home into the end grain.

To complete each wheel, treat the opposite end of the paddle blades with glue, place a second disc over the blades and nail it in place. However, remember to nail plywood doublers to the inner face of each disc before you secure this second disc. These are needed to provide a grip for the flange screws.

With the two paddle wheels completed, you can now mount the four flanges on them. The completed assembly should measure 37½ in., with about 1 in. on each end for bearing into float notches yet to be cut.

The length of the chain will govern the axle location. With the bike propped level, run the chain onto both sprockets and pull the paddle wheel assembly back until the chain is taut.

Then mark the exact location of the pipe axles on the floats, for this is where the axle seats should be.

You will probably find that the chain rubs on the fork since the axle has been lowered. To provide sufficient clearance for both chain and pedal throw with the axle in this new location, you'll have to heat the frame and twist it with a hammer and wrench. After modifying the frame, make a final check of paddle-wheel rotation to make sure that everything is square and then, with the chain still taut, swing the paddle wheel assembly up so that it will clear the water. The rear spreader should be mounted just aft of this unit, so that it won't hinder paddle-wheel movement when lifting or dropping.

When you're assembling the paddle wheels, glue blocks inside for screws used in mounting flanges

Now cut the tapered 1 x 3 stilts and fasten them to the rear spreader with strap irons. The upper ends are clamped to the fork with U-bolts. To provide support, the rear fork rests on a threaded rod running through holes drilled in the stilts. Nuts inside the fork and outside the stilts hold this in place.

The thrust plate, the final drive item, is designed to take strain off the axle assembly. After cutting this to fit, secure it to the crank housing with a heavy door hinge and machine screws, as shown in the drawing, left. The lift-lock arm is hinged to this plate near the rear axle and notched at its upper end to fit over the unthreaded ⅜-in. rod running between the U-bolt clamps. This same arm serves as a "down lock" when hooked over the threaded rod.

The motor-board assembly is cut to fit between the stilts and bolted rigidly in place. Note that the board itself is doubled at the top to fit the motor clamp.

Follow the detail shown at the left when you are constructing and mounting the rudders. These are controlled from the handlebars by means of steering cables running through pulleys mounted on the floats. First, however, the handlebar unit must be modified.

### ready for a test run

After removing the handlebars and discarding the old taper nut and bolt, drive a heavy dowel up into the neck and secure it in place with a lagscrew plus epoxy. Then drill a hole through the crotch of the fork to allow the dowel to slip through the front fork. Oil the neck so it will swivel freely before you replace the handlebars in the fork assembly. Once these are in place, mount the grooved disc on the end of the dowel, install the steering cable and the boat's ready for a test run.

Take it easy on your first few trial runs with the motor, leaning inside all turns to make sure that the outer float doesn't dig in. Speed is controlled by a lever on the motor, but if you find it inconvenient to reach behind you every time you want to change speed, it's a simple matter to run a cable from this lever to a remote gas control up on the handlebars. An old bicycle handbrake or auto choke control makes a fine remote throttle. Also, oil the chain lightly to prevent rust. Happy cycling!

**See also:** bicycle; canoes; games, boating; kayaks; paddleboat; pontoon boat; sailboard, sailboat.

# Six trick billiard shots

BY ROBERT A. KELLY

These tricky shots
   can make you look
like a pro

■ ONCE YOU'VE LEARNED to hold that billiard cue just right, address the ball with confidence, and sink those shots on a regular basis, *maybe* you'll be ready for the challenging trick shots outlined here by the best cueman of them all, Willie Mosconi, world's billiard champion.

The trick shot by itself, while it draws "oohs and ahs" from onlookers, is like eating dessert minus the meal—it doesn't do much good without the main course. And in billiards, that means learning the basics plus practice, practice, and more practice. Mosconi, perhaps the greatest billiard player of all time, points out that his many championships were won as a result of just plain hard work, the deepest kind of concentration, continuously sharpened skills and a certain amount of luck.

But, for Mosconi, there have nevertheless been moments of truth. For example, asked what he remembers as his most difficult tournament shot, he replied, "Against Andrew Ponzi in the 1948 World Billiards Tournament at Navy Pier in Chicago, I needed one ball and Ponzi needed three to win a crucial game and move into the next round. Ponzi left me a blocked shot situation and I could not risk another scratch (miss). My two

SIX BALLS IN SIX POCKETS . . . Place the 3 and 13 balls in the center of the table, halfway between the side pockets and the diamond. Allow space for the cue ball to pass through. The end balls should be aimed at the corners of the end pockets. Hit the cue ball low center using a hard stroke and balls will go into the pockets traveling the white lines illustrated in the photo at the top of the opposite page

previous shots had been scratches and a third in succession means a 15-point penalty. My only alternative was to attempt to score so I planned out a five-cushion shot and made it to win the match and, ultimately, the world title."

As to the new crop of billiards champions now circling the colorful tables, Mosconi adds, "The trend among the champs today is to be less cautious in attempting shots, and for this reason: Common table size now is 4½ by 9 feet as compared to 5 by 10 championship size in former years. The smaller table permits a player to make a variety of shots easier and he plays a more exciting game.

"Not only that, defensive play is noticeably

**binding, book:** see bookbinding

Mosconi: "Aiming the corner balls to the inside edges of the corner pockets is the critical factor in this shot. Tap each ball on top with the cue ball to set the cluster in a 'frozen' position"

less important in their approach to the game. On the 5 x 10 tables, defensive play was more vital. Don't misunderstand, I am in favor of the smaller size official table. It permits a beginner to learn the game easier and still is an exacting challenge to all players."

While trick shots add spice and color to the game of billiards, Willie is cautious in their use during a championship match. "The only trick shot I use in tournament is an occasional massé shot in which the cue is raised perpendicular to the table to produce drastic English on the cue ball."

But, for those with a burning desire to excel at billiards and to taste the appreciation of the gallery, outlined on these pages are: 1) Three Balls in Rotation; 2) The Spectacular Shot; 3) The Three Ball Shot; 4) Line-Up Shot; 5) Six Balls in Six Pockets; and 6) The Criss-Cross Shot.

Before you step up to address the ball, however, be sure that you have chosen the right cue. Actually, they range in weight from 15 to 21 ounces and average 55 inches in length. In selecting a cue, however, advises Mosconi, always stay within your own physical limitations. Probably the best guide is to choose a cue that has that right "feel" to it. Give special attention to selecting a cue with the right taper. For some players,

a thick shaft will have that feel to it; for others, a slender shaft.

As to the weight of your cue, never select one that is too heavy. This will tend to adversely affect the estimate of force needed for the stroke. On the other hand, a too light cue will cause you to overestimate the force needed for the stroke.

The right *stance* is as important to good pocket billiards performance as to an outstanding golf score. The goal, very simply, is balance and comfort.

Your feet should be slightly apart. With your body weight well-balanced, bend forward at the hips with your head directly over and in line with the cue. Your left hand should be as far forward and as straight as possible. The right hand should be as vertical as possible.

To check your stance, swing your right arm free, forward and back. If it's in line with the shot, your stance is correct.

How you form and use your *"bridge"*—the finger structure which guides the cue—often affects the outcome of the game. It's the firm guidance of the bridge that gives accuracy to a billiard shot.

In forming a bridge, first make a fist with your left hand and rest it on the table, palm side down. Form a circle with the index finger and thumb, resting it against the middle knuckle of the middle finger, holding the cue firmly but not so tightly that you can't move it easily.

To form the base of your bridge, rest the heel of the hand on the table, then extend the last three fingers outward.

### the rail bridge

In billiards, occasions will arise where the cue ball will come to rest against the rail. In these cases, it's easier to use the rail of the table as part of your bridge (hence, the term *"rail bridge"*) rather than attempt the shot with a conventional free-standing bridge.

With the rail bridge, the index and middle finger are used to guide the cue along the thumb. The ring and little finger render firm support to the middle finger. In a shot of this nature you will also have to raise your cue slightly for positive stroke and contact with the cue ball.

For the sake of safety, always chalk your cue before attempting a rail-bridge shot.

Even fundamentals have their share of variations. In addition to the regular bridge and the rail bridge, you occasionally must use the *mechanical bridge*.

Too many times, a billiard player will overex-

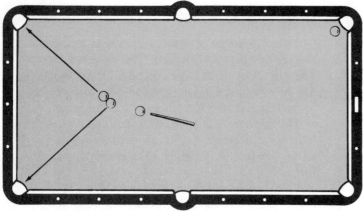

CRISS-CROSS SHOT . . . Place the 10 ball at the second diamond about 1 in. below and to the left of the head spot, making sure it is aimed for the inside corner of the pocket. Place the 3 ball in direct line with and behind the 10 while the 8 is spotted on the center of the lower left pocket. Stroke the cue ball high left, striking the 3 ball ¼ right and sinking the 10 and 3 balls while getting the 8 on the rebound

Mosconi: "Make sure the balls are 'frozen,' or touching, and aimed at the inside edge rather than the center of the pocket"

*trick billiard shots, continued*

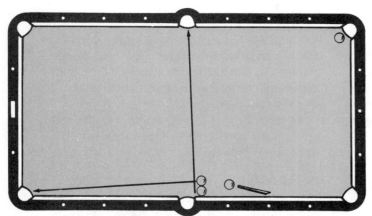

THREE BALL SHOT . . . Place the 8 ball against the cushion and about 1 in. below the side pocket. The 13 ball is placed against the 8 ball while the 15 ball is centered on the lower-left corner pocket. Use a strong high left stroke on the cue ball to strike the 13 ball ¼ right, which propels the 13 to the upper corner, the 8 to the side, and the 15 to the corner

Mosconi: "A sharp stroke is required here to force the 8-ball across the table and bring the cue ball off three cushions to make the 15-ball"

tend himself in reaching for a shot. The result is often a miscued ball.

For the "stretch" shot, the player wisely employs the mechanical or stick bridge. He maintains a firm grip on the butt end of the bridge. His cue rides the middle slot of the bridge and he keeps the distance as short as possible between his cue and the cue ball.

Finally, as he grasps the cue with his thumb

and forefinger, the player is in complete control and can now place a well-directed stroke at the cue ball.

No game is complete without an object, and pocket billiards is no exception. The *object ball* —the ball you wish to "sink"—spotlights the simple formula used to determine exactly where the cue ball must strike the object ball to send it into the pocket. The player draws an imaginary

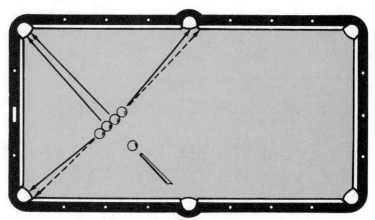

Mosconi: "Because 8-ball and 10-ball travel to same pocket, 8-ball must be hit first, on left side, which sends the cue ball into 10-ball, sending both into corner pocket in that sequence"

LINE-UP SHOT . . . Center the 8 ball at the 2nd diamond, and place the 10 next to it. Make sure the 8 is aimed for the center of the upper left pocket while the 10 is aimed at the inside corner. The 3 and 13 should then fall into line for the upper right and side pockets. Stroke the cue ball low right using a moderate stroke. Cue ball strikes the 8 ball ⅓ left, sending all four balls to the pockets

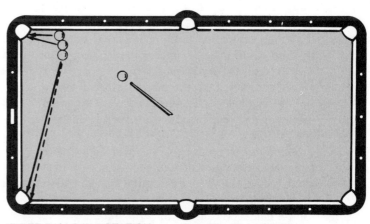

Mosconi: "Again, all three balls must be 'frozen.' The high left stroke is necessary to make the 15-ball hug the cushion on the way to the pocket"

THREE BALLS IN ROTATION . . . Place the 15 against the cushion at the first diamond. The 3 ball should be against the 15 but ½ ball behind and at a light angle from the 15. Line-up the 10 so it is aimed for the outside corner of the right corner pocket. Hit the cue ball with high left stroke using moderate force. Strike the 15 ball on the cushion for the corner pocket; the 3 will follow while the 10 goes into the other corner

line from the center of the pocket to the object ball. Where this line bisects the object ball is his point-of-aim, or where the cue ball must strike it. *Always* keep your eyes on the object ball target.

Just how accurately you hit the cue ball is determined by your *cue stroke*.

Next time you watch a good billiard player, note the smooth rhythm of his arm swinging back and forth in a pendulum arc as he addresses the cue ball.

Keep your cue as level as possible and your bridge firm. Your shoulder, elbow and wrist joints should move in a free and easy action. And when you stroke the cue ball, always follow through. Make sure you're not rigidly poking the ball, but stroking it with a light, springy action.

*Cueing the ball* properly gives it accurate di-

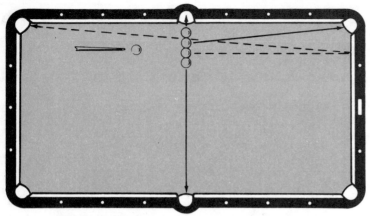

SPECTACULAR SHOT . . . Starting with the 3 ball about ½ in. from and in direct line with the side pocket, line-up all 4 balls. Using a hard stroke, hit the cue ball low center. The cue ball should strike the 8 ball ⅓ left, then carom into the 10. Action will see the 3 drop into the left side pocket, the 13 into the right side pocket, the 10 into the upper left pocket while the 8 will carom into the lower left pocket

Mosconi: "A draw stroke on the cue ball, hitting it below center, is vital to keep the cue ball out of the path followed by the 8 ball"

rection and correct speed. As your game develops, the importance of these two elements will become apparent.

Most professional players avoid "english" as much as possible. Their play emphasizes stroking the cue ball dead center, and applying the follow (or draw) shot for position. Since a standard billiard ball is only 2⅜ inches in diameter, your best target is the dead center.

As you play, take the time to practice stroking the cue ball dead center, and concentrate on accuracy and speed required for scoring and position.

As your game develops and you apply more emphasis on position of your cue ball for the next shot, certain situations will require the cue ball to come back toward you rather than follow the object ball. This calls for the *draw shot*.

To perform this shot, rather than cueing the ball dead center, your point of aim is lowered and "reverse english" is applied. As the cue ball strikes the object ball, the reverse spin applied by the low cueing of the ball forces it to return to you after impact with the object ball.

Occasionally, situations will arise where you will want the cue ball to follow the object ball so that it will stop in good position for your next shot. This is called the *follow shot*. Where you cue the ball about ½-in. below center for the draw shot, the cue ball will do the exact opposite and "get legs" if you cue it about ½-in. above center.

Be careful when you apply this cue-ball action. Should you give too much speed to the cue ball in a straight-in shot, you might miss the ball.

In billiards it pays to look ahead. Therefore, when the words *playing position* are used, it merely means that the billiard player is looking ahead to his next shot.

The player tries to place his first object ball into the corner pocket, but looks ahead to the best position for his cue ball when the time arrives to "bank" (or ricochet) the next object ball against the rail.

His playing strategy tells him that if he hits the first object ball lightly on the right side, he will sink it, at the same time benefiting from the correct speed on the cue ball which places him in excellent position to bank his next object ball.

Remember that a billiard ball is round—it has no flat surfaces. Therefore, it becomes vital to increase the friction between cue-tip and the ball's surface. *Chalking the cue* provides this friction. Be careful not to apply too much by absentmindedly rubbing the chalk against the cue while considering the next shot. A thin film is sufficient for solid contact.

"Practice and concentration on details like bridging, grip, stroke and stance," says World Champion Willie Mosconi, "offer the only chance for improving your billiards game. Coupled with a solid knowledge of the fundamentals discussed here, you can realistically aspire to championship in the highly competitive, colorful and exciting game of pocket billiards."

As we said before, "First the fundamentals, then the crowd-pleasers." *Now* you're ready to try the trick shots just outlined.

**See also:** bowling; games, adult; pool tables.

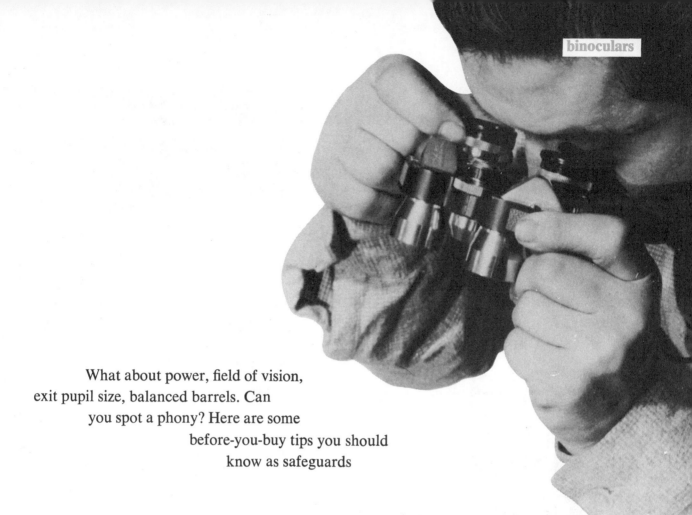

What about power, field of vision,
exit pupil size, balanced barrels. Can
you spot a phony? Here are some
before-you-buy tips you should
know as safeguards

# What to look for
# in buying binoculars

BY KEN WARNER

THE IMPORTANT DATA about any binocular appears in one line in a catalog:

7x35 C.F. (425 ft.) 22 Oz. $87.00

Literally translated, this binocular magnifies seven times, its objective lenses (the ones in front) are 35 mm. in diameter, it has central focusing, gives a 425-ft. field of view at 1000 yards, weighs 22 oz. and lists at $87. What do these specifications mean in terms of performance? Let's take them one by one:

*Magnification:* This expresses the "power" of a binocular to enlarge an object. A 7X glass brings an object 700 ft. away to only 100 feet away.

*Objective diameter:* This determines the size of the exit pupil and the brightness of the scene. The pupil is a round, lighted spot on each rear (ocular) lens when the binocular is held away from the eyes and pointed at a bright surface.

The entrance pupil of the average human eye varies from 2.5 mm. on a bright day to a wide-open 7 mm. at night. At dusk, it's around 5 mm. So, for most binocular viewing, a 5-mm. exit pupil is a good average. To find the size of the exit pupil, divide the diameter of the objective lens by the power of magnification. Thus, 7x35 binoculars have 5-mm. exit pupils.

*Focus:* There are two kinds of focusing arrangements on modern binoculars. *Central* focus (C.F.) types have a wheel on the center hinge to focus both oculars. Turning the right eyepiece adjusts for differences between the user's eyes. On less convenient *individual* focus (I.F.) models, you focus eyepieces separately.

**bins, toy:** see children's furniture

279

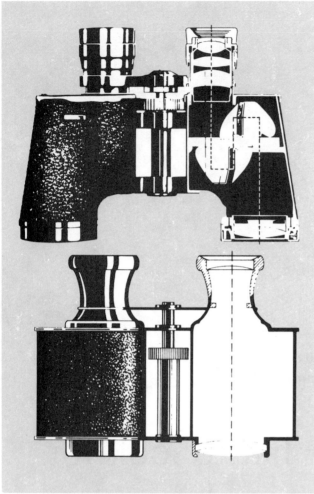

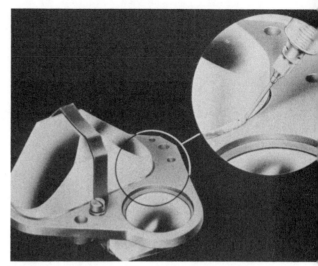

In best method for mounting prisms, small metal strap over prism holds it in a recessed shelf. Injection of plastic fills the gap between the prism and recess

Inadequate prisms in binocular below, show as gray shadows in the exit pupil. Exit pupil of the good glass at right shows as a clear, well defined circle

How to spot a phony is seen in this drawing. At top, objective lenses of most prism binoculars are offset to accommodate prisms. Low-priced Galilean fakes (bottom) resemble binoculars, but have no prisms

*binoculars, continued*

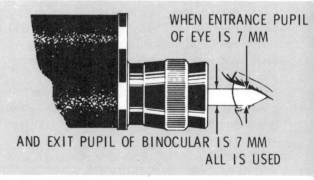

In night glasses, large 7-mm. exit pupils correspond to diameter of the eye's entrance pupil in the dark (drawing, right). However, constriction of eye pupil due to age of viewer or bright light (left) limits that advantage

Look downward through objective lens to determine quality of body castings, method used to mount prisms. Here, screws of prism mount are clearly visible

Interior of shoddy glass shows prism held down by a single levered-in strap, roughness in casting (arrows), lack of antireflecting paint near prism

*Field of view:* This is the diameter of the scene viewed. Most often, it is expressed in feet or yards at 1000 yards. A wide field of view is desirable and, in "normal" glasses, marks a superior optical system. But this doesn't apply to wide-angle binoculars. When a normal 7x35 glass might have a field of about 400 ft., wide-angle types will show over 550 ft.

In practical use, a field approaching 400 feet is quite usable. Wide views are especially useful at close range, such as in watching a play or indoor sports.

*Weight:* Binocular buyers often ignore this factor, to their later regret. An instrument weighing 24 oz. may seem light in the store, but add the case plus ten or more pounds of hunting or camping gear and it becomes a heavyweight. On the other hand, binoculars bought to use from a boat or car, or for spectator sports, may be as heavy as they need to be.

*Price:* Binoculars of approximately the same description may range in price from under $25 to over $200. Unfortunately, though, price is not a good standard for evaluation. True, a $200 instrument from one of the old-line optical firms will be a fine glass likely to outlast the buyer. But low to medium priced binoculars are quite serviceable for average use, provided they pass the inspection detailed later. The exception to this is where failure of performance might result in damages or hardship more costly than the price of a top quality binocular.

Almost all binoculars are discounted somewhere. However, if you must resort to mail order for a discount, be wary. Many binoculars examined for this article arrived defective, damaged or out of alignment. So, deal only with firms giving a no-questions-asked, money-back guarantee.

The reason most binoculars are 6x30, 7x35 and 8x30 or 40 is that these numbers represent the most practical combinations of portability, magnification, field of view and light-gathering ability. The 6x30 is light and portable. The 8x30 or 40 types, with higher magnification, give a smaller field of view but are better at picking out long-distance detail. The 7x35 splits the difference. The average buyer can't go too far wrong in choosing a quality glass in any of these categories.

A hunter using his glass to find game doesn't need a lot of power unless he's in the Western mountains. A bird watcher, on the other hand, can use and appreciate every extra bit of magnification to help identify tiny birds.

In the big-eyed night glasses—the 7x50s and 8x56s—the 7-mm. exit pupils let you keep on seeing through dusk. Also, they are easily aligned with your eyes, even in dim light.

A buyer on a tight budget should note price differences in binocular patterns. The German or Zeiss style has two-piece barrels. In each barrel, a prism is mounted in one casting and an objective lens in the other (which is screwed into the

In glasses suffering from curvature of field, focusing on the center of the image throws edges out of focus (left, above). When you try to focus edges (right), center will become fuzzy. While a slight curvature is easily tolerated by most users, a severe case is grounds for ruling out the glass

Excessive distortion is evident in this glass. Note how image blurs and vertical and horizontal lines are twisted out of shape, making instrument useless

*binoculars, continued*

first casting). The American or Bausch & Lomb style uses one-piece barrels, streamlined and fitted to the shape of the inside parts.

The German pattern is lighter and less expensive to build. The American type is stronger, provides a better seal against dirt and weather, and usually permits a wider field of view.

In the middle price range, German patterns are about $10 cheaper than equivalent American models. When you consider that I.F. models run about $3 to $10 lower than C.F. models, it's easy to see that a $50 German-pattern binocular with individual focus can be a better buy than a $50 American style with central focus. More money is going into the optics.

It's also worth noting that *prismatic* binoculars are the only kind to buy. There are opera glasses and field glasses with magnification up to about

5X. These instruments are adequate for theater use. However, they are sometimes made with phony, binocular-like bulges and illegally represented as binoculars (see sketches). While they may be described as 7x35 or 7x50, their fake bulges do nothing for performance.

How do you spot these phonies? Look for eyepieces and objective lenses to be in line with each other where the price tag runs $20 or less.

In true binoculars, objective lenses are offset from the ocular except in Leitz Trinovid and Zeiss Hensoldt Dialyt models which are specially designed to permit straight tubes.

When the salesman hands you a binocular, don't pitch it up to your eyes and look *through* it. Look *at* it first. Check the markings on the eyepiece end to see that they jibe with the catalog description and with what the salesman says about power, objective lens diameter and field of view. Examine all sides of the instrument for nicks, dents, loose leather or other damage.

### check mechanical function

Next, check mechanical function. Serious flaws can be found this way: Flex the lens barrels slowly back and forth on the center hinge; they may be somewhat stiff, but they should move smoothly. On center-focus models, spin the center wheel slowly through its entire range of movement, feeling for mushiness or hitches and drag. On individual-focus types, run both eyepieces back and forth; do the same for the right eyepiece on center-focus models.

All these adjustments should come to a positive stop at each end of their movement. There should be no crackling noise—an indication that a heavy pack of grease has been used, perhaps to conceal poor fit. It should take definite force to move each adjustment. Any that moves easily when new will be sloppy after use.

If there is anything wrong at this point, ask for another binocular. The next pair, even of the same brand, can be all right.

Now, return all adjustments to zero and tilt up the objectives to look down into the barrels. Hold them so they reflect an overhead fluorescent light and count the reflections. Every white reflection is an uncoated lens surface; dim amber or blue reflections are coated surfaces. Some uncoated surfaces are present in all instruments, but the presence of just one or two coated surfaces with the rest showing white means you may get a dull image with little contrast.

Then, either in sunlight or right under a strong light, look down into the barrels diago-

nally. In some brands, all that is visible is an inner non-reflecting tube and further examination is impossible. Most brands, however, including the best makes, do not use this tube and some of the interior construction is visible. If so, look for three things:

First judge the quality of the body casting by the smoothness of its interior. A sloppy wall with dabs of thick paint indicates a poor casting.

Second, check the prism positioning. You see one side of a prism as you look diagonally toward the center of the binocular. It is vaguely house-shaped and sits on a shelf. Around its edge on the shelf is the positioning device. In a really cheap binocular, this can be just wax or plaster poured around the prism. Most common in low and medium-priced binoculars is peening —a steel punch is used to hump up parts of the prism seat to secure the prism. These peened spots are easily seen. Good binoculars should show one of three prism-positioning methods: A tight-fitting collar held down with screws; a triangular wire tight-fitted inside adjusting screws; a clean job of spotting plastic around the prism.

Third, check the prism retaining strap. There is a metal "roof" over the prism itself, and a metal strap runs over this, held down by a hefty screw into the prism shelf. The "roof" should fit neatly; the strap should be quite sturdy.

### why this is important

These things are important for very practical reasons. A clean body casting doesn't require any filler material which can break loose and float around inside the binocular. Sound prism-mounting is vital since a shift of a thousandth of an inch or so can give trouble. Peening, though it is used in most binoculars now on the market, can put a strain on the prism, making it more subject to damage from later shocks.

Now point the binocular at a large, bright object and examine each exit pupil, which appears as a bright circle on the ocular lens. It should be clean and bright to its edge. Most medium and low-priced binoculars, however, show an exit pupil that appears to be a bright square in a gray circle. If the squares are the same shape, size and position in both exit pupils, this is not so bad. It indicates a skimpy prism, either in design and size, or in the use of inexpensive flint-type glass replacing the barium glass of better prisms.

If the squares are not alike, the prisms are out of line and the binocular needs complete

Slim design reminiscent of old-fashioned field glasses has been achieved by some German makers. Special prisms permit straight optical arrangement

*binoculars, continued*

refitting. You'll be wasting money if you buy it.

Prisms in wide-angle binoculars, incidentally, by their basic design, eliminate this test. Surrounding the exit pupil in these models you'll see a series of dim squares. They are normal.

If the binocular has passed so far, it's time to look *through* it.

Since a dropped pair of binoculars is embarrassing, put the strap around your neck. Then, get permission to go outdoors, if possible, as most of the following tests involve using the glasses at full range.

Adjust the binocular to your eyes in this way: flex the barrels on their hinge until you can see one clean sharp circle— not two like in the movies. Now, cover the right objective lens with your right hand, and focus the left lens by rotating the center wheel in C.F. models or twisting the left eyepiece in I.F. models. Sight on a far-distant object—at least a city block away— and adjust back and forth until it appears very sharp. Then reverse the procedure, covering the left lens while you turn the right eyepiece. In C.F. models, this will require a slight adjustment, unless your eyes are very different; in I.F. models, it will take as much twisting as the left lens.

At this point, if the eye relief (the distance from your eyes to the eyepiece) suits you, adjust the eyecups (if any, and if they are adjustable) until you get a full field without having to shift the glasses. You should have the sensation of looking through a large, clean plate-glass window on a clear day. There should be no strain in your eyes.

In other words, you want more than mere magnification. Distant detail should be as plain as if the object were close by. Shadows should "open up" so you can see detail. If these things are not observed, here is what may be the matter:

*Faulty collimation:* Properly assembled and adjusted binoculars should have both barrels looking at precisely the same field of view. If not, the viewer feels a twisting sensation in the eyes and sees the vague impression of two images.

For a quick check, set the binoculars on a flat surface with the barrels level. With one eye closed, align the field of view with the other so there is an object at the top of the field. Then shift that eye to the other barrel without moving the instrument. If the object is now to one side, half out of sight or well down into the field, the alignment or collimation is faulty. Repeat this test, placing an object at the sides and bottom of the field.

*Distortion:* Straight lines should be straight. If the edge of a building or other long line appears to curve at the edge of the field, the instrument is distorting. No binocular can be absolutely perfect in this respect, but distortions should not be too obvious or they will prove much too bothersome.

### sharp and fuzzy zones

*Curvature of field:* If, when focused sharply in the center, the edges of the field are slightly fuzzy, and when refocused to get the edges sharp, the center is fuzzy, the instrument has a curved field. That is, instead of a flat plane of focus, there is a bowl-shaped sharp zone. Many low-priced instruments have this fault. If not exaggerated, it can be tolerated.

*Chromatic aberration:* If trees, poles or buildings against the bright sky show bright fringes of color, the lens-and-prism system is not bringing light of different colors to the same focus. Definition suffers greatly as a result.

The only one of these faults a dealer can correct—and that only to a limited extent—is collimation. Modern binoculars have front elements set in an eccentric ring. A man who knows something about it can adjust alignment enough to get by, but a professional technician is needed if you want a really precise job.

**See also:** camping; mountain climbing; navigation; pheasant hunting.

It's easier to tote a
stack of heavy asphalt tile
if they are put in a
child's wagon.

Protect your birdfood from squirrels
by tying a plastic bleach bottle
to the feeder pole.

Apron strings are easier to tie if exten-
sions are sewn to them so that they
can be tied in front.

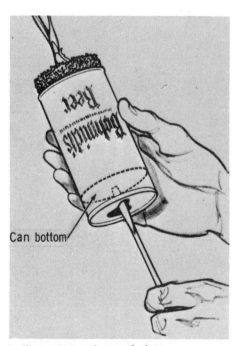

Pull-top cans make good plant
starters. Use the cut-out bottom to
cover the "drain" hole in the top.
Remove the plant with a screwdriver.

# Easy-to-cast birdbath

BY  HI  SIBLEY

■ BIRDS WILL flock to this oasis in hot weather. The simple form consists of two templates, used individually, pivoted on a carriage bolt. The smaller template shapes the convex clay form. It is then removed and the larger one is attached to the bolt. The template is rotated to form the outer bowl shape and give a uniform thickness.

The conical base is poured first, using a sheet metal form. Nipples and a pipe tee anchor the length of pipe that reinforces the column, which is poured after the base has set. The stovepipe, used as a column form, is unfastened at its edges and held together with wire. A suitable concrete mix is 1 part cement to 2 parts each of sand and gravel. The concrete must be kept moist for several days.

**See also:** bird feeders; birdhouses; bird photography; game-bird feeders.

The form for the base is a piece of sheet metal. A stovepipe with its edges unfastened except for a temporary wire binding serves to form the column. The templates, made of pine, are pivoted on a bolt and are used separately. The smaller one shapes the clay and the other forms the concrete

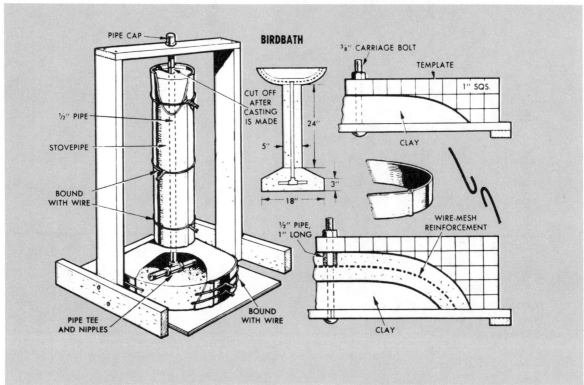

# Bird cafeteria

■ WHETHER YOU hang it from a bracket outside a window or from a pole in the yard, this economy bird feeder will give bird watchers hours of winter pleasure. The key to the whole design is the use of a low-cost muffin tin.

Dimensions listed in the drawing below are designed to accommodate a six-cup muffin tin. However, the cutout of the hardboard platform must fit the cup area of the tin, so check this carefully before cutting. If you wish to use a larger tin, enlarge the platform accordingly, leaving the upright lengths the same.

Fasten the platform to the framing strips with countersunk flathead wood screws. Then fasten the uprights to the frame. The screw eyes do double duty as anchors for the 12-inch lengths of chain used to hang the feeder. Give the muffin tin a coat of paint and sprinkle sand over the wet paint. This will prevent the bird's feet from sticking to the metal in extremely cold weather.

**See also:** birdbath; birdhouses; bird photography; game-bird feeders.

A screw eye on each corner secures the roof to uprights and anchors the hanging chains

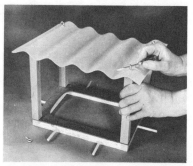

A split ring slipped through the center link of each chain can be slipped over a hook

Diagram labels:
- Screw eyes
- 11" x 14" corrugated fiberglass
- ¾ x ¾ x 7"
- ¾ x ¾ x 8"
- Muffin pan
- ⅛" tempered hardboard
- 5¾ x 9" cutout
- 8 x 11" frame, ¾ x ¾" stock
- ¼" dowels, 2½" long

# Bird automat

BY P. T. HENNIG

Simply by lighting on a perch, birds
serve themselves at this convenient
little automat

YOUR FEATHERED friends need no nickels to serve themselves at this ingenious bird automat. They have only to discover that by lighting on the feeder perch, seed will be dispensed from a hopper onto a feeding plaform.

The complete structure consists of two main compartments; one, the hopper, is located above the feeding platform and stores seed until it is released by a perching bird. The hopper has a removable roof which keeps the seed dry and prevents it from blowing all over the yard. Twin-glass walls make it possible to determine at a glance whether the hopper needs to be refilled. Nine 4-in. dowels, additionally, are located to one side of the hopper, like ladder rungs, and provide a catch for suet and other treats.

The lower feeding platform is open on both sides but has raised edges to keep the seed from blowing.

Paint the entire structure, if you wish, or give it a coat of varnish. Then, set it in a favorite spot in your yard where all the action is observable. In watching the birds, you'll be surprised how quickly they learn the technique of getting extra helpings.

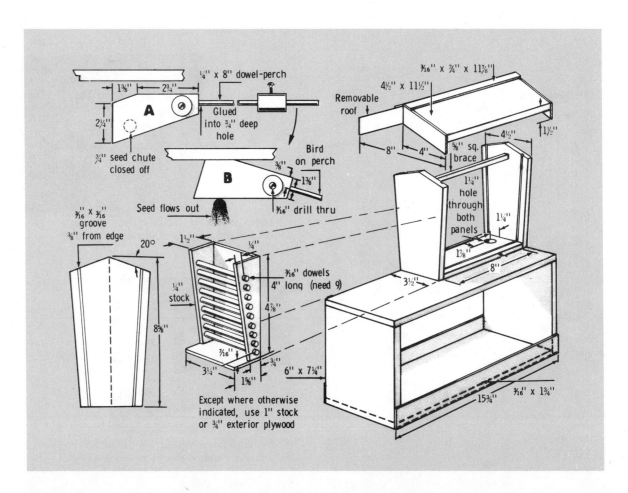

#12 x 2⅛" FH screws
through roof of feeding platform

1⅛" hole
2¼" deep

1½" block,
3¼" sq.

1½" x 3"
x 4⅛"

½" x 3"
dowel-pivot

2½"        1 9/16"

25°

¾"

¾"

¾"

3/4"

1"

½"

9/16" hole through
both blocks

#7 RH screws

1" x ¼" dowel-washer

1" x 1⅝"
counter-weight

# A barrel full of birds

BY  MANLY  BANISTER

These eighteen apartments built in a
barrel should say "welcome" to every
purple martin that flies past in search of a nesting site

■ YOU WON'T BE LONG hanging out a "no vacancy" sign when you get this martin apartment house set on the peak of your garage or atop a pole in a sunny, open area.

You can locate the barrel near your house (but not closer than fifty feet) so that you can enjoy the melodious chatter and flashing wings of a house-nesting colony all spring and summer. But remember that the house must be located in the open, never under or near large trees. Purple martins are graceful, acrobatic flyers and they like lots of wing room. Once they're home, though, they don't mind crowding.

The barrel used for the original pictured above was a paraffin-lined oak keg intended for vinegar or wine. A plain fir barrel would do as well. It might not look as handsome to you, but martins don't choose by appearance. It'll be less trouble,

because the oak keg's thick paraffin lining had to be scraped out. Don't use an old whiskey barrel: martins probably won't like the smell— or the charred inside. The dimensions of the barrel you get should be checked very closely before you cut any stock; the partition assembly detailed may not fit. It was designed for a typical 15-gallon cask. Your barrel should have both heads, but if it doesn't, you can cut additional plywood disks.

First step is to make a barrel buck like that in drawing on pg.292 to support the barrel while you sand it smooth between the hoops, bore the holes and then cut it in half with your saber saw. Locate the holes so they're 1 in. above the floor levels. For the perches, drill ⅜-in. holes 1 in. below each entrance port. On the barrel shown, the top and bottom rows of the perches

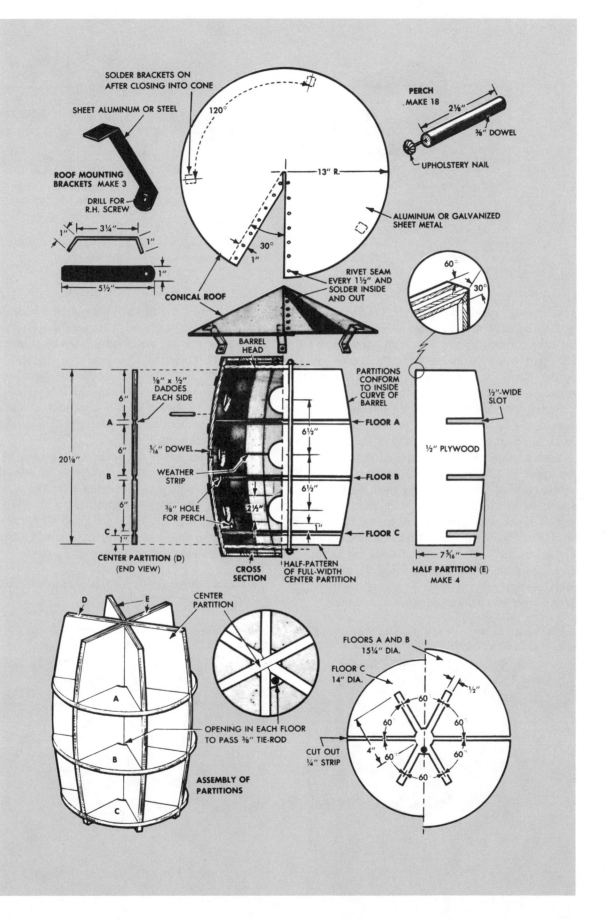

SOLDER BRACKETS ON AFTER CLOSING INTO CONE

SHEET ALUMINUM OR STEEL

ROOF MOUNTING BRACKETS MAKE 3

DRILL FOR R.H. SCREW

120°

13" R.

PERCH MAKE 18

2⅛"

⅜" DOWEL

UPHOLSTERY NAIL

1"

3¼"

1"

5½"

1"

30°

1"

CONICAL ROOF

ALUMINUM OR GALVANIZED SHEET METAL

RIVET SEAM EVERY 1½" AND SOLDER INSIDE AND OUT

60°

30°

BARREL HEAD

⅛" x ½" DADOES EACH SIDE

6"

A

6"

B

6"

C

1"

20⅛"

⅝₁₆" DOWEL

WEATHER STRIP

⅜" HOLE FOR PERCH

2½"

PARTITIONS CONFORM TO INSIDE CURVE OF BARREL

FLOOR A

6½"

FLOOR B

6½"

FLOOR C

1"

½"-WIDE SLOT

½" PLYWOOD

7⁵⁄₁₆"

HALF PARTITION (E) MAKE 4

CENTER PARTITION (D) (END VIEW)

CROSS SECTION

HALF-PATTERN OF FULL-WIDTH CENTER PARTITION

D

E

CENTER PARTITION

A

OPENING IN EACH FLOOR TO PASS ⅜" TIE-ROD

B

C

ASSEMBLY OF PARTITIONS

CUT OUT ¼" STRIP

FLOORS A AND B 15¼" DIA.

FLOOR C 14" DIA.

½"

60

60

60

60

60

60

60

4"

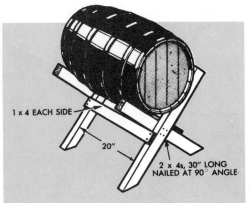

Sand the keg with an orbital sander or by hand. Use a rasp between the end bands

You'll need a buck this size to support a 15-gallon barrel during construction

were offset to avoid drilling through the bands.

The center barrel bands are nailed or screwed to each stave to make sure the barrel won't fall apart when it's cut in two. The lower half of the barrel is weather-stripped with an adhesive-backed felt strip. Finally, drill two 5/16-in. holes, 180 degrees apart and centered on the edge of the lower half of the barrel. Drill to a depth of about 3/4-in. Then, using dowel centers, locate and drill registering holes in the edge of the upper half of the barrel. Glue dowels in the bottom pair of holes, trimming them to project about 5/8 in. and rounding the ends. These dowels serve as aligners. Then, in the final assembly of the partition-and-floor structure the half floors are glued into the dadoes cut in the center partition, D. Before fastening any of these parts permanently together, do a trial assembly. Some work may be necessary for a good fit.

Cut perches and drive in place with a spot of glue on the end of each. Let each dowel project about 1½ in. After attaching the roof to the barrel (bending the brackets slightly if necessary to level the top), finish the barrel all over with two coats of spar varnish. If aluminum is used for the top, it need not be finished. Galvanized sheet metal can be sprayed with a couple of coats of aluminum paint.

If you want to set the barrel on top of a garage or shed, you'll have to design a platform to fit over the roof ridge. Whatever mounting you use, check the purple-martin return date for your locality (usually late April) and don't raise the house before, as sparrows, starlings and other undesirables may take over.

**See also:** birdbath; bird feeders; birdhouses; bird photography; game-bird feeders.

Cut 18 entrances with hole saw, spacing them evenly around circumference. Nail bands to each stave

Insert saber-saw blade in one of center holes; cut barrel in half on larger circumference line

Weatherstrip lower half of keg with adhesive-backed felt strip. Notch felt for easy fit

Cut floors with saber saw. Lay out circles, cut out center strip, stack halves, trim

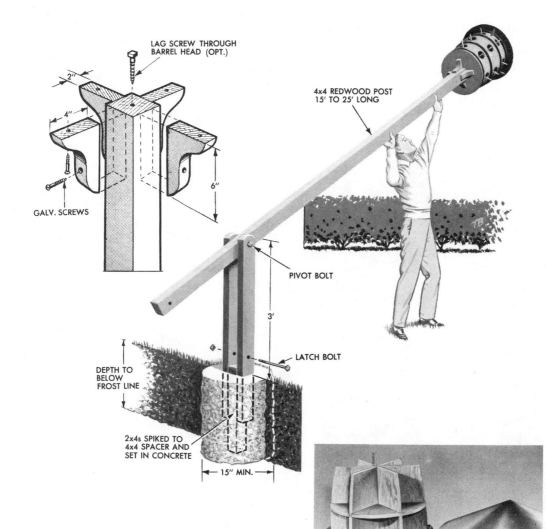

LAG SCREW THROUGH BARREL HEAD (OPT.)

2"

4"

6"

GALV. SCREWS

4x4 REDWOOD POST 15' TO 25' LONG

PIVOT BOLT

3'

LATCH BOLT

DEPTH TO BELOW FROST LINE

2x4s SPIKED TO 4x4 SPACER AND SET IN CONCRETE

15" MIN.

Pivoting post makes maintenance a snap. At end of nesting season, just lower the barrel and detach the tie rod so you can lift off top half. Then partition assembly pulls out for cleaning. By storing barrel indoors till next martin return-date, unwanted squatters are foiled

# Insulated birdhouse beats the heat

BY GORDON HANCOCK

With this inviting house to welcome them, your feathered friends are sure to "keep their cool" even on the hottest days of summer

■ EVEN ON the sunniest summer day, residents of this compact birdhouse will maintain their "cool," thanks to an insulating air space built into the double roof. As dimensioned, the house is suitable for wrens and similar birds. Scrap stock can be used to make it; in fact, a couple of wooden crates will provide adequate material. Don't forget to paint the inner surfaces of the double roof before assembly. All parts are assembled with nails and waterproof glue, except for the bottom, which is fastened with wood screws so it can be removed for cleaning.

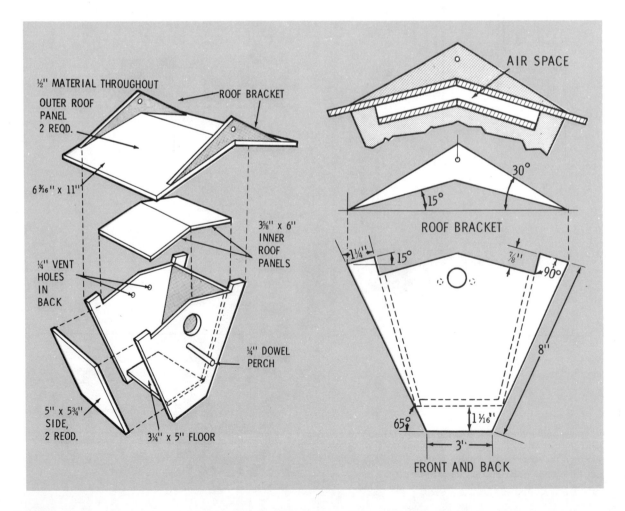

# Dish-pan apartment house

### BY KENNETH W. NIGHTENHELSER

THE SKY is the limit when building this high-rise martin house—you can add as many dish-pan units as you want since each one simply slides down over the pole. Each aluminum pan is divided into four apartments by inner walls which are nailed together to provide a central well for the supporting pole. The removable pans make for easy cleaning of the apartments.

Except for the penthouse apartment, a pipe hole is cut in the bottom of each pan, in addition to four entrance holes in the side. These can be cut neatly with duckbill tinsnips. Sharp edges are covered with squares of hardwood having smaller holes. Each pan is attached to its plywood base with sheet-metal screws through the rim. An extra hole through both the rim and the plywood will serve as a drainhole. A 1½-in. TV mast makes a fine pole, with the house resting on the guy-wire collar. A weather-vane tops off this attractive home for birds.

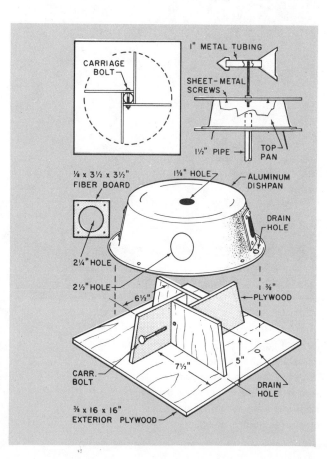

You can finish the job neatly by painting pans and plywood platforms before assembling. Hardboard entrance covers are applied last

# How to capture birds on film

BY FRANK TINKER

All birds, from the beautiful to the comical, can be captured on film . . . even with a simple box camera

ANYONE WHO likes birds or photography will sooner or later try to combine the two.

If the results are less than satisfactory, it's usually because the average snapshooter has overlooked some basic facts.

A bird (1) is usually quite small, (2) is unbelievably fast and (3) doesn't trust people. The basic problem is to get close enough to this tiny creature for the resultant image to be more than a pinpoint on a negative. To do this, you must know your equipment well enough so that when the fleeting opportunity arrives for that one good picture you will make the most of it.

Let's start with the simplest methods. The window feeding station, which many thoughtful people have incorporated as part of their homes, provides an ideal setup for the amateur. The birds become accustomed to their surroundings, a window only a few feet away affords screening for the photographer and the birds can often be caught at rest. In this situation, you can either hold your camera, or put it on a tripod, pre-focus it on the station and trip the shutter with a long cable or bulb release.

As a general rule, it is always wise to use a tripod to avoid the possibility of blurred pictures. But when prowling for good bird shots, tripods are frequently not practical. For hand-held shots, if you hold your breath while snapping the shutter, there is less chance for camera motion.

The cameras need not be expensive. Most cheaper box cameras have a fixed focus which requires that the subject be at least six feet away. Those using 35-mm. film will focus to three feet or less, and auxiliary lenses can be added to allow focusing within a few inches.

To show the range of equipment which can be built around this setup, one family has a cheap camera permanently arranged in this fashion and any time a member notices an interesting bird at the station he simply pulls the cord. Another hobbyist with a much larger pocketbook has a

Soaring birds (left) can be caught with the camera by following their flight and snapping the shutter when they fill the frame. Don't snap them flying past

The baby pelican in the inset at the left, like most fledglings, is too young to fly. The trick is to find the nesting area, then move in close to shoot

The water ouzel was photographed with the arrangement shown in the diagram. Wires attached to the flash units were strung along the bridge to the camera position.

*capture birds on film, continued*

Even a box camera can be used in bird photography if you give some thought to proper arrangements first. Here a string is used to trip the shutter from a remote position

A flash unit was set up near the ouzel's nest. A study of the bird's habits was made before setting up the equipment. Another flash unit was put near a rock that birds always landed on

layout which includes an electric eye to trigger the shutter whenever a bird lands at the station, a supplementary electronic flash to light the subject and stop its motion, and a spring-loaded film-winding attachment which readies the camera for the next shot automatically.

To approach birds that do not choose to mingle with people, blinds can easily be set up in the field. They can be located near a nest or any place the quarry is known to congregate.

The blind, like your other equipment, can range from the elaborate permanent type, complete with flash reflectors angling on the bird from every angle, to a simple piece of canvas thrown over the person's head. All these blinds have a single objective—to erase the human form.

The standard blind, however, is a small tent which allows sufficient elevation for the camera and the person sitting behind it as well as apertures for the lens. Again, as long as the bird does not see the person, the slow movement of this lens poked out the slit in the canvas does not ordinarily frighten him. Since overhead cover is not usually essential, the simplest form of blind consists of several poles driven into the ground with a large tarp wrapped around them. Vertical slits can serve as lens windows or U-shaped flaps can be sewn over larger holes.

The last method for approaching these most elusive creatures is by optical means—binoculars, field glasses or telephoto lens.

The bird photographer is particularly fortunate

Mother swallow (left) feeding its
young required fast shutter. The
shore bird above needed a telephoto

today, since the recent advances such as the sin-
gle-lens reflex camera, auxiliary lenses, binocular attachments and cheap telephoto lenses seem
to have been designed almost specifically for him.
Undoubtedly the best of these substitutes for distance are the telephoto lenses. Usually designed
for 35-mm. use, a good 300-mm. or 400-mm.
lens can now be purchased for well under $100.

Using these long lenses requires a little extra
care, however. The focus becomes quite critical,
and the slightest movement of the camera will
tend to blur the picture. The use of a tripod or
other brace is recommended whenever possible.
For the same reason, a high shutter speed is
usually mandatory. The rule of thumb is to use a
speed to correspond with the focal length of the
lens—that is, for a 400-mm. lens use $\frac{1}{400}$ of a
second, for a 200-mm. lens use $\frac{1}{200}$, etc.

This water walker, a coot, was caught from a shore blind using both fast speed and telephoto

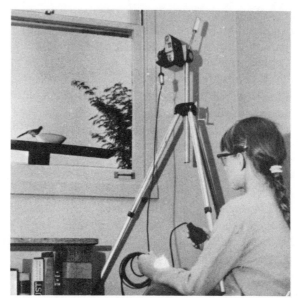

A complete outfit can cost under $200, but for a window-station rig, the cost can be less

With all this talk of speed, the question immediately arises as to whether or not an adequate exposure can be given the film. In many cases, it cannot without supplementary flash. Birds seek the shade because insect food is more abundant here, because it affords protective obscuration and because most species would be unable to endure the glare of the sun indefinitely. The telephoto lens, though, has a tendency to give a soft monotone to pictures that are taken in shadow.

Flash lighting is the next answer to some situations found in the field. The type of flash will depend entirely on the circumstances and the type of camera. If this light source can be fixed—at a nest, for instance—an electronic unit will eliminate the need for changing bulbs with every shot. The contact wires can be spliced and trailed from the photographer's blind to the unit if he intends

Field photography is possible with a simple canvas blind. This grouse was shot from 10 ft.

to hold the camera, or the whole unit can be operated by remote control. A simple solenoid arrangement can be rigged to trip the shutter at distances too great for regular release cords, and even radio-controlled units are now available.

If the unit is to be carried, however, bulbs will probably be most serviceable. Most reflex cameras using the telephoto lenses have a focal-plane shutter which can be synchronized with the electronic units only at very slow speeds. Exposure at these speeds will leave "ghost" images or worse on the negative when used in natural light. The No. 6 or No. 26 bulbs, made for focal-plane shutters, can be used at any speed and seem to reach out farther than the electronic units.

If the camera being used is equipped with a regular leaf shutter, of course, a properly rated electronic unit would be suitable for almost all situations as long as it was not too heavy. Remember that you will frequently be led into rough terrain if you intend to follow the birds very far. Also, remember that with flash you will probably get only one picture at a time. Most birds depart at first when the bulb pops, but become used to it later. The shorter flash of an electronic unit does not disturb them as much.

Let's translate all these do's and don'ts into an actual case. This past winter the author set out to photograph one of the most interesting of western birds—the dipper, or water ouzel. This little sparrow-sized bird, although not a water bird as such, has the unique ability to walk on the bottom of mountain streams, clutching the rocks from which he plucks nymphs and other larvae. Unfortunately, his coat does not match his colorful ways, being completely gray.

### patient stalking needed

Since feeding stations and cameras at the bottom of an icy mountain stream are impractical, the only way to approach the ouzel was by simple stalking through difficult terrain. Also, since he was quite small, very active, and usually frequented the shade, a telephoto lens mounted on a bellows with a flash unit attached seemed to be the answer. Using this rig and much patience, theoretically, would produce good shots.

Making this a reality, however, involved several other things, most important of which was a familiarity with the subject. Few people will try to photograph an auto race, a football game or a movie star without learning first what angles or positions might be best and what might be risky. So it is here, and for really good bird pictures

the photographer is advised to obtain a copy of one of the excellent natural history books available in any library. The Audubon Society, at 1130 Fifth Ave., N.Y., is an inexhaustible and cheap source of information about all birds.

Thus armed with much written information on the ouzel, the writer sought out the bird—and soon found that much remained to be written. For one thing, although all the writers had explained that the ouzel was called a dipper because he dipped up and down constantly, none of them had mentioned that this dipping occurred with a surprising regularity, exactly once a second. Until the photographer learned this, and timed his shots to occur between the dips, the results were somewhat blurred. Other birds move with the same regular, quick movements, ranging from twice or three times a second for a wren to long intervals for crows. Predatory species such as the hawk and owl lack these rhythmic movements, as do most water birds.

### nesting photos in spring

With the coming of spring, the ouzel nested, and the approach shifted accordingly. Flash was provided by an electronic unit attached to the forest footbridge under which a nest was situated and the photographer was concealed in a natural blind at the edge of the stream. Another flash was focused a short distance away from a rock, on which every bird stopped as it bore food back to the nest. Having ascertained these things about the ouzel beforehand, including its pattern of flight, its length of stay at the rock and the nest, a good photographic record of its life could be obtained, whereas a person blind to the bird's habits might have obtained one picture but certainly no more.

The total cost of the ouzel effort was many rolls of film, obtained cheaply by buying it in bulk and respooling it at home, a lot of pleasant time afield, plus a certain amount of penicillin needed to get rid of the pneumonia acquired while crawling through snowbanks. The reward: some excellent shots of a fascinating bird which showed not only the bird itself but proved the fact that the photographer was able to obtain them. Pneumonia is not an inevitable part of bird photography, but the pleasure which comes from a really good picture is always a sort of triumph. Now that the expense has been removed from this challenge, the field is wide open.

**See also:** birdbath; bird feeders; birdhouses; cameras, used; darkrooms; game-bird feeders; photography.

When your wife's necklace breaks, pipe cleaners are perfect temporary holders for the loose beads.

When joggling paper to align the edges for cutting or stapling, sandwich them between two pieces of cardboad to protect the ends and corners.

If a whetstone isn't handy, the edge of a clay flowerpot does a good job.

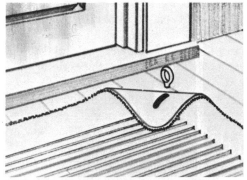

To hold a doormat in place on a wooden porch floor, cut buttonhole slits in the corners near the door and use screw eyes as turnbuttons.

A clothespin clamped to the edge of a pail supports the pail and makes it easier to engage a hoisting hook.

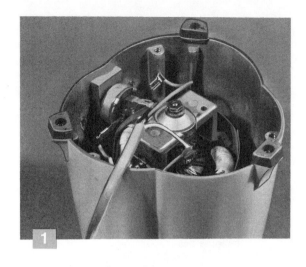

1

2

# How to repair an electric blender

BY JOHN PENNINGTON

It may be the cord, or perhaps the brushes, but chances are it's just a simple operation

■ ONE THING to keep in mind in connection with routine operation of your food blender is to be careful about what you put in it. It will grind and blend almost anything edible to a pulpy, appetizing mass, but a peach or prune pit or a gravel particle that goes in with a few lettuce leaves—well, a blender just isn't built for crushing pits or stones! Other than that, you haven't much to worry about in its operation, unless you drop it, or the parts just plain wear out.

Cords usually go first, but not always. When something goes wrong—the unit doesn't operate properly or won't run at all—the experienced appliance serviceman generally thinks first of the power cord and the motor brushes. That's your cue in fix-it-yourself. If there's reason to suspect the cord, go over it inch by inch, looking for breaks, a cracked plug or a loose wire, either at the plug or other end of the cord at the terminals. If you see anything wrong with the cord, or if it looks like it might go bad, replace it.

With the cord examined and passed, the motor brushes are next. To get at them you have to take the unit apart. When you turn the blender over and remove the bottom plate you'll see something similar to Fig. 1. Likely you'll have to take the motor out to reach the brush retaining screws, Fig. 2. Remember when you turn out screws: easy does it. And don't let the brushes pop out when the retainer is loosened; they're spring-loaded, you know. If the brushes are still good—not badly worn, cracked or chipped—

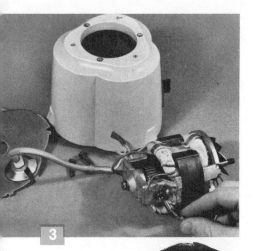

3

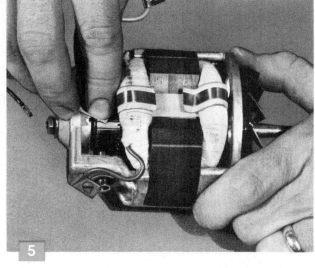

5

4

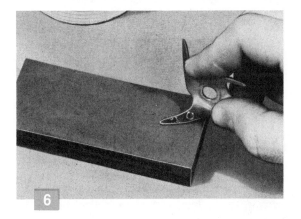

6

clean it with a piece of fine sandpaper, as in Fig. 5. Don't use emery cloth or any similar abrasive as just one grain of these abrasives can cut out an armature bearing in no time.

Often in servicing it may be advisable to test the resistance in the switch. This is done as in Fig. 4, by applying the common lead to the power terminal and the ohm lead to the high and low-speed terminals in turn (most blenders have a two-speed switch). The ohmmeter will register the amount of resistance in the switch. If this seems high, the switch should be replaced.

The three or four-blade cutter in your blender must be quite sharp to do a good job of blending. Touch up the blades on an oilstone as in Fig. 6, being careful to get a uniform bevel.

make sure that you put them back just as they came out. Don't turn them over or interchange them, Fig. 3. This is important, as in use the ends of the brushes have worn to an almost perfect seat on the commutator. If you turn them over or interchange them, you'll get an imperfect contact and a stream of sparks from each brush when the motor is running. This can cause rapid wear of brushes.

Anytime you have the unit apart so that the motor can be seen, examine the commutator. If the brush track appears reasonably clean and a uniform color, just wipe with a dry cloth and let well enough alone. But if it appears blackened and slightly pitted, then it's permissible to

**See also:** appliances; clothes dryers, electric; coffeemakers; electrical wiring; floor polishers; guarantees; irons; mixers, food; testers, electric; toasters.

# Try camping afloat

BY PATRICK PERRETT

Camp overnight in an outboard runabout? It's easy, once you know how—and lots of fun

CAMPING ABOARD a small open boat requires a lot of ingenuity and planning, but once you get used to it, this becomes a real part of the enjoyment of the outing. There are three main considerations: sleeping, cooking, and recreational activities (including fishing, skiing, swimming and cruising).

Sleeping accommodations don't usually present a problem. Those back-to-back seats that convert to sun lounges make excellent bunks for a couple of adults, and in most boats there is room for a youngster or two to bed down on the cockpit floor. Some boat campers rig a tot's bed that fits nicely under the foredeck.

Pipe bunks, popular in travel-camping vehicles, can be fitted into many boats. Four U-shaped brackets support the bunk ends. The bunk itself, which rolls up for daytime storage, is simply canvas supported by two side pipes.

An air mattress or a soft pad is a necessity, not a luxury. Its easy-to-stow size makes it ideal. Foam rubber mattresses designed especially for camping are comfortable but require considerably more storage room.

Even in summer months, occasional rain can

---

**boat convertible top:** see convertible top, boat

**boat cooking:** see cooking, boat

**boat cover:** see cover, boat

**boat decks:** see deck, boat; finishes, non-skid

**boat docks:** see floats and docks

---

be expected in most areas, so it's well to provide some sort of shelter. Boat-tents can range from a simple fly, rigged with a couple of poles, some line and your boat cover, to an elaborate canvas camper top. If your boat has a folding canvas top there are many designs and methods for joining another canvas piece to the rear of the top and spreading it over the boat, tent fashion. You can even design your own boat-tent. Once you've snuggled down in your sleeping bag it's a good feeling to know a sudden shower won't disturb your slumber all through the night.

Cooking probably is the greatest challenge to the boat camper. Meals can range from elaborate menus to simple snacks. We usually stick to a simple meal with only one special dish.

### a big breakfast

Our favorite breakfast fare is eggs and sausage (much easier to handle than bacon) served with hot rolls or freshly baked biscuits prepared in the folding camp oven. The biscuits are refrigerated and come in a cardboard tube, ready for the oven. Six-ounce cans of juice provide easy-to-store individual servings. Instant coffee or tea suits us although many of our camping friends enjoy freshly brewed coffee.

The above is a much bigger breakfast than our family usually consumes at home but, with the swimming and skiing (not to mention the fact that when camping afloat, we usually arise shortly after the sun), it barely tides us over until lunch time. The midday meal is quickly assembled, using standard sandwich makings, fresh fruit, cookies and drinks from the ice chest. To tide appetites over in the middle of the afternoon, members of the crew usually can find some cookies or a hard-boiled egg somewhere in the galley.

If the fish haven't been biting, broil hamburger or steak for dinner. Green salads, premixed at home, will stay cold and crisp in a plastic bag in the ice chest. Simple, bottled dressings are added on board. When the steaks are done, you can use the grill to toast French bread. In the cool of the evening with the grill still giving off warmth and a light breeze stealing across the water . . . that's living!

There are many suitable stoves available. An alcohol stove is universally accepted for marine use. Alcohol fumes, being lighter than air, quickly dissipate themselves. Also, alcohol flames can be extinguished with water.

Still, many boat campers prefer a gasoline stove because of the hotter flame or because they already have one on hand for conventional

Ready for bed when the sun went down, these campers took care of all chores during daylight

Nobody stumbles over shoes and other articles stored out of the way in a hammock net. The nets will stretch to hold all kinds of objects

Odds and ends that every camper needs—such as staples and paper plates—are best stored in a wooden box with a hinged lid that doubles as a bench or table

Let it rain. With the homemade Dacron covering over the rear of the cockpit, the boat's occupants are well protected from rain or dew

Homemade support for a Dacron covering that fits over the rear of the cockpit is made of aluminum tubing and held in place with cord

camping use. Even though small boaters live constantly with gasoline fuel tanks, extra care must be exercised when cooking with such a stove aboard a small boat. Observe all necessary safety precautions.

Stoves should be kept in excellent working order and operated as high in the boat and as far from fuel tanks as practicable. The high placement gives better ventilation and produces increased heat during operation.

Needless to say, you'll have an approved-type fire extinguisher on board, stowed where it can be reached in a split-second when needed.

Although on the heavy side, a favorite charcoal brazier for boat use is the Japanese hibachi, which is inexpensive and comes in many sizes and shapes. It is designed to use a small amount of fuel for the maximum amount of heat produced. Carefully timed, an entire meal can be cooked with a single load of briquets. An even better system for charcoal broiling is to use a brazier which hangs overboard. Marine stores offer several styles or you can fashion your own from a heavy-gauge, industrial-type bucket.

A compact and easy-to-use stove for boat camping is one using LP gas. The fuel comes in disposable cans which are inserted into place. The stove is lighted by turning a handle and using a match. There's no pumping or priming or lighter fuel to fiddle with.

Paper plates and cups are a must (buy plastic-coated plates and hot cups).

An aluminum nesting cook kit is ideal for providing a variety of pans, but you'll probably be happiest if you include a cast-iron or heavy-duty aluminum frying pan along with your cook kit. Square frying pans pack easier, and if you

get one that is divided in the middle you can prepare eggs and sausage at the same time.

When boat camping, it's much more convenient to store your fresh water in several small containers instead of one that is too cumbersome to handle easily. An ideal container is a gallon plastic bottle used for distilled water.

How about food? Few small boats are outfitted with lockers, so to store food, utensils and stove you will need something more durable than cardboard boxes which inevitably get wet and begin to come apart. A couple of medium-sized wooden boxes, rather than one large container, are best for ease in handling and stowing. Wooden boxes will stand abuse and can be stacked one on another; they can also serve as tables or benches. Suitable used wooden boxes are difficult to find, so your best bet is to construct them from lightly framed ¼-inch plywood.

Frankly, our first camp-out aboard a 17-ft. runabout was less than a rousing success.

Once we pulled away from the launching ramp, it didn't take long to realize that we had twice as much gear as we needed. There was barely room to sit, much less stretch our legs, and cooking dinner was a nightmare.

We made out that night, but in the morning we headed right back to the launching ramp and transferred all the useless extras, which we previously had thought were necessities, to the trunk of the car.

So that's how we learned the first two rules of small-boat camping:

1. Keep equipment to an absolute minimum.
2. Have a detailed plan for stowing everything you take along.

You'll soon develop your own short-cuts in shopping and packing for a trip, but keep a note pad and pencil on board so you can make a list of things to bring along (and things to leave at home) the next time you go boat-camping.

**See also:** boat equipment; boat handling; boat repair; boats, buying; boats, used; camping; pick-up camper; sleeping bags; tents; trailers; wild foods.

# Helmsman's step holds tools

### BY HANK CLARK

GOOD SAILORS start young, but often are too short to assume the wheel. This step-and-tool-box combination is the perfect solution to the problem.

Hinged to the deck, the box swings up and locks against the bulkhead when not in use. Pull it down and it becomes a stable platform elevated 8 in. above the deck. Spare parts and tools are stowed away neatly inside.

Construction of the box itself is simple. Butt joints are used throughout, secured with both glue and nails. Narrow strips of foam-rubber (weatherstripping is fine) tacked to the underside of the lid form a gasket to seal the box against spray or rain. To provide a cushioning effect, ten rubber bumpers are required—four on the rear of the box, four on the legs and two on the support arms.

Materials and finish will depend on your pocketbook and personal taste. If your boat has mahogany trim, then that's the logical material for the box. Give it a couple of coats of urethane or spar varnish. Finally, mount a rubber stair tread on top of the box with waterproof glue, and relinquish the wheel to "Shorty."

See also: anchors, boat; boat camping; boat handling; boat repair; boats, buying; boats, used; convertible top, boat; cover, boat; deck, boat; ladder, boat; outboard motors, used.

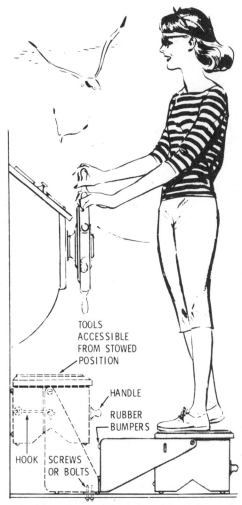

TOOLS ACCESSIBLE FROM STOWED POSITION

HANDLE

RUBBER BUMPERS

HOOK SCREWS OR BOLTS

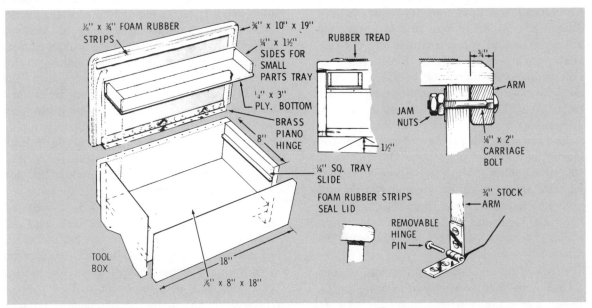

⅛" x ¾" FOAM RUBBER STRIPS

¾" x 10" x 19"

¼" x 1½" SIDES FOR SMALL PARTS TRAY

¼" x 3" PLY. BOTTOM

BRASS PIANO HINGE

8"

¼" SQ. TRAY SLIDE

TOOL BOX

18"

¾" x 8" x 18"

RUBBER TREAD

1½"

FOAM RUBBER STRIPS SEAL LID

¾"

ARM

JAM NUTS

¼" x 2" CARRIAGE BOLT

¾" STOCK ARM

REMOVABLE HINGE PIN

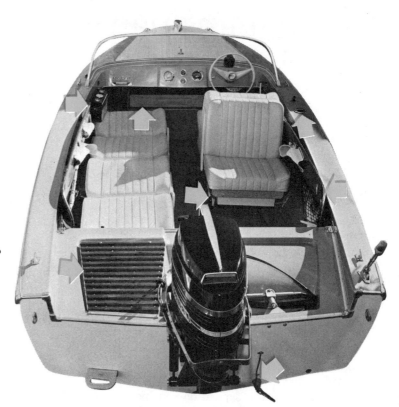

# Personal touches for your boat

BY PATRICK PERRETT

There is no place in the world as small
as the cockpit of a boat
when you are looking for places to stow
gear. Here are tips for finding space

■ WHETHER YOUR INTEREST IN BOATING tends toward skiing, fishing, skin diving or just plain family boat riding, cockpit clutter is bound to be a problem. It is difficult enough to stow the basic equipment that every boat should carry, but when you add the specialized gear for your particular hobby—water skis, or fishing tackle or skin diving gear—the result is likely to be a tangle of loose equipment tumbling freely around the cockpit. This is not only a nuisance, it is also unsafe.

You can solve this problem of stowage by following the example of Tommy Gillean, North Hollywood, Calif., whose wide-ranging boating interests are matched by a commendable passion for neatness. After purchasing a 16-ft. fiberglass runabout, he immediately set about adding a number of simple and functional accessories to meet his needs.

A few of his additions were inexpensive commercial items that he purchased from his marine dealer. The majority were homemade racks and

compartments which could easily be tailored to fit your boat.

For instance, the multi-purpose grill mounted over one side of the motor well provides an excellent place to cut bait and clean fish, because it keeps all of the mess out of the cockpit proper. To clean it is a simple matter of sluicing scales down into the well and out the well drain. This grill also serves as an auxiliary deck when used in conjunction with a combination hand grip and step mounted on the transom, because it provides an easy method of taking swimmers and skiers into the boat. Much of the water they bring into the boat as they come over the side is carried away in the well.

The transom seat-stowage box is upholstered to match the boat's back-to-back seats, and will hold all sorts of odd gear. The box has the added advantage of being stowable itself, since when you want maximum cockpit space for fishing, you can slide it back under the well.

Space on the underside of the seat lid is a

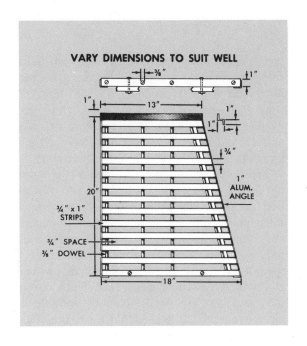

**VARY DIMENSIONS TO SUIT WELL**

3/8"

1"

1"

13"

1"

1"

3/4"

20"

1"
ALUM.
ANGLE

3/4" x 1"
STRIPS

3/4" SPACE

3/8" DOWEL

18"

This multi-purpose grill serves as a boarding platform and as a handy fish-cleaning table. It is made from mahogany strips, and the dimensions will differ from boat to boat. Aluminum angle is used for the frame

The front of the seat-stowage box provides a handy mounting spot for fish knives, rod holders, and lights

Stowage space inside of the box will easily hold bulky gear. You can slide it out of the way when not in use

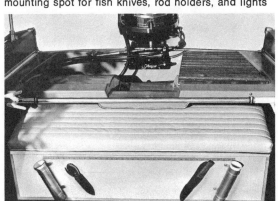

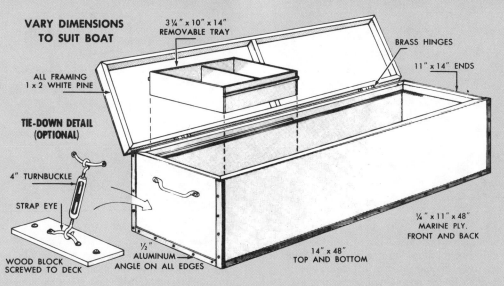

**VARY DIMENSIONS TO SUIT BOAT**

3 1/4" x 10" x 14"
REMOVABLE TRAY

BRASS HINGES

ALL FRAMING
1 x 2 WHITE PINE

11" x 14" ENDS

**TIE-DOWN DETAIL (OPTIONAL)**

4" TURNBUCKLE

STRAP EYE

1/4" x 11" x 48"
MARINE PLY.
FRONT AND BACK

WOOD BLOCK
SCREWED TO DECK

1/2"
ALUMINUM
ANGLE ON ALL EDGES

14" x 48"
TOP AND BOTTOM

311

fine spot for the boat's registration certificate and for mounting a chart of the local boating waters. In the tray inside of the seat you can stow a first-aid kit and other items which you might need in a hurry. If you mount a handle at each end of the seat box, you have a foot-locker that you can carry ashore if necessary.

The bottom frame which supports the back-to-back seats converts easily to handy off-the-deck stowage space by simply adding a bottom. It's a great place for tow lines, dock bumpers, props and bulky items. Water skis and fishing rods fit neatly in rubber-padded recesses of a special rack constructed of aluminum channel and mahogany. The padded strip which covers the rod recess and holds the rods securely in place is hinged and latched. Ski hooks are made from strap aluminum.

Take a look at the other ideas that Tommy developed. You'll find they don't involve expensive gadgetry, and with the exception of instrumentation, cost very little. Best of all, they'll put more fun in your boating.

Every boat is a little different, of course, and you have to adapt some of these ideas to fit your boat. But you'll also find that once you start thinking about storage space and convenience in your boat, you'll develop some new inventiveness of your own.

Mesh hammocks slung under the gunwales hold foul weather gear, jackets, wet suits and towels. Hammocks are available at most marine dealers and are hard to beat for neat, out-of-the-way storage

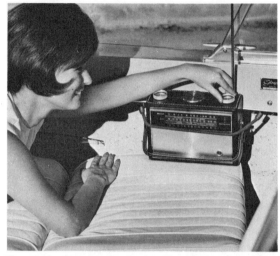

The marine-band radio sits on the padded edge of the seat, protected against the jarring impact of a rough chop. A shock-cord clipped on two eye bolts mounted on the inside of the combing holds it in place

A hand-held spotlight plugs into the cigarette lighter in the dash. Other instrumentation includes a speedometer, an ammeter, an engine hour meter and a tach. The compass is mounted on the dash

A compartment under the dash is a 6 x 7-in. box running the full width of the dash. It has a hinged lid to protect items like binoculars and cameras from spray. For security, install a lock in the lid

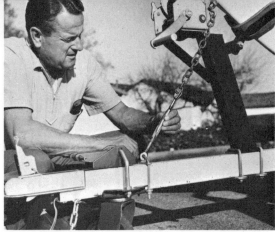

As an extra measure of safety, a chain and turn-buckle are used to tie the boat securely to the trailer. This prevents damage during travel over rough back-country roads by removing strain from the winch

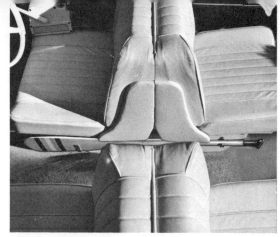

An emergency paddle is held securely in aircraft-type clips mounted on the sides of the wooden seat supports. A similar pair of clips on the port seat holds a fish gaff ready for instant use

This custom-made kit for tools and spare parts fits between the twin fuel tanks under the motor well. The tanks rest on rubber-link door mats to keep them from shifting and to prevent corrosion

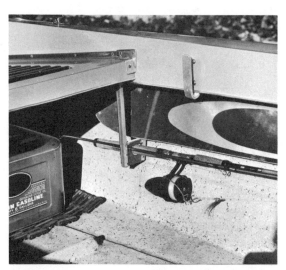

A rack constructed of aluminum channel and mahogany with rubber-padded recesses holds fishing rods neatly in place. The padded strip covering the rod recess is hinged and latched

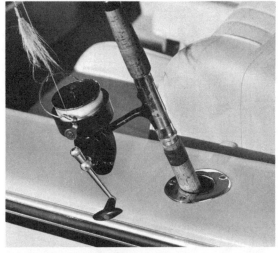

If you want to keep an eye on both the course and the fishing rod at the same time, mount a rod holder in the gunwale at the pilot seat. Two other rods can be placed in holders mounted on the transom seat box

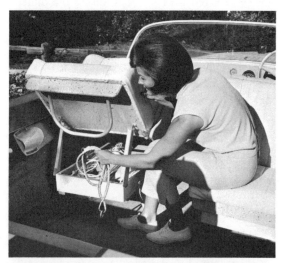

The bottom frame which supports the back-to-back seats converts to a handy off-the-deck stowage space by simply adding a bottom. It makes a convenient storage space for lines, bumpers and spare props

# Six bits of luxury for your boat

BY PATRICK K. SNOOK

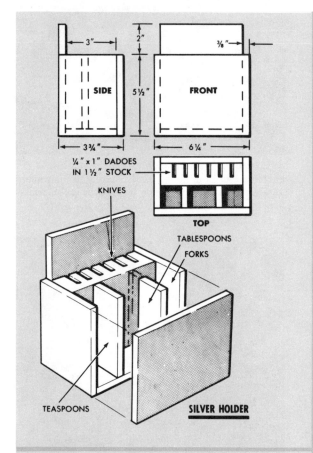

SILVER HOLDER

■ ANY SKIPPER worth his salt knows that there's nothing quite so annoying as loose or sloppily stowed gear, particularly when a chop starts kicking up.

These six simple built-ins will provide tailor-made storage space for some of the more awkward-to-stow articles commonly found aboard a large runabout or small cruiser. All six can be built with hand tools, and they represent a total investment of about $10 for lumber. The pilot models were made from solid Honduras mahogany and finished with a dark mahogany stain followed by several coats of spar varnish. However, other materials and finishes may be substituted if desired.

All units should be constructed to fit your particular needs, so be sure to check the dimensions given in the drawings against those of your equipment. They can easily be altered if necessary. By the same token, you may wish to enlarge the capacity of a unit, making a rack for six charts or eight glasses. Such modifications can easily be made.

All parts should be cut, checked for fit and sanded before final assembly. Use liberal amounts of *waterproof* glue on all joints. When the glue is dry, give the piece a careful final sanding and apply the desired finish.

Line the bottom of the binocular box with a square of ¼-in. foam rubber to protect the glasses. For easy cleaning, use a loose piece of vinyl tile in the bottom of the sandwich shelf of the lunch box. Other liners (for the glass rack, galley box and sunglasses shelf of the binocular box) can be cut from a sheet of automotive gasket cork after making a paper pattern.

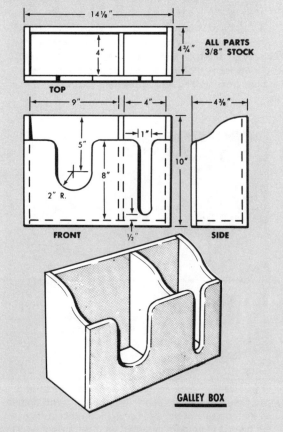

GALLEY BOX

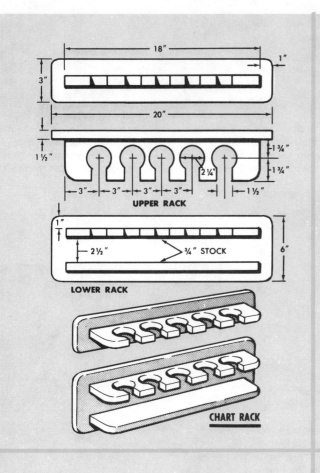

UPPER RACK

LOWER RACK

2½"  ¾" STOCK

CHART RACK

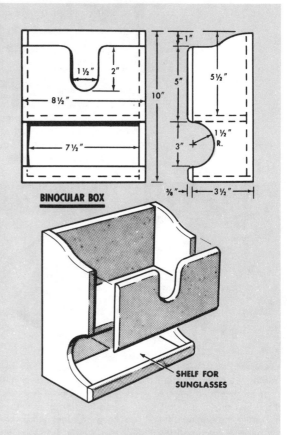

BINOCULAR BOX

SHELF FOR
SUNGLASSES

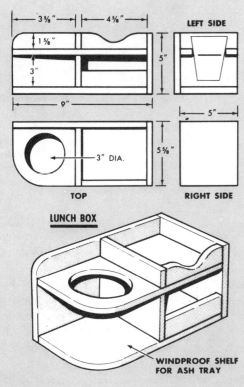

LEFT SIDE

TOP

RIGHT SIDE

3" DIA.

LUNCH BOX

WINDPROOF SHELF
FOR ASH TRAY

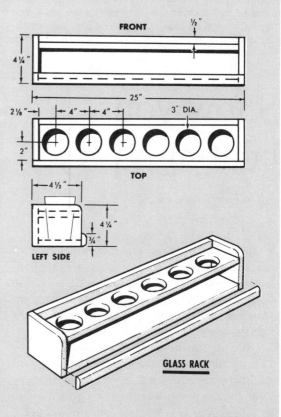

FRONT

TOP

3" DIA.

LEFT SIDE

GLASS RACK

Lead with power when towing another boat in a crowded mooring or narrow channel. Because an outboard responds first at the stern to steering-wheel turns, you'll have a lot more control of your boat and the one you are towing if the boats are attached bow to bow with a short line. Use your reverse gear to get you to open water, where you can tow conventionally

Run your motor dry before putting it in storage for an extended time. At the end of the last day's run, pull the fuel line while the engine still is running. This will use up all the fuel in the carburetor. To further protect the engine, use a cover but don't tie it so tightly that damaging condensation will collect

Always start your engine before un-tying your boat from its mooring. A free-floating boat without power can be a problem. After the engine kicks over, untie the stern lines. Swing the stern free of the pier. Then sit behind the wheel and free the bow lines and, with the engine in gear, slowly ease away from the pier

When you approach a pier or other boats, don't depend upon your reverse gear as a brake. Your engine could fail. If it does don't panic. Put the gears into neutral as quickly as possible and go through standard starting procedures

# Show your boating savvy

BY BARRY BURGOON

■ OUTBOARD OWNERS generally are aware of standard boat-handling techniques. But some of the finer points of outboard boating aren't so widely known. The tips shown here include information that should provide most outboard skippers—even the more skilled ones—with at least one or two new ideas.

Just getting behind the wheel of an outboard and operating it without any serious difficulty is not enough if you want to enjoy your boat to the fullest. You also need to know how to ease it away from dockside without damaging boat,

pier or motor. What's the best way to stow your fuel tank? What's the best way to tow another boat out of shallow water or down a narrow channel? Suppose there are big waves or heavy wakes rolling toward you. What's the best procedure for riding into them? What about the problems you create with your wake? And what's the best way to come in to a pier for docking? Here are some answers.

**See also:** boat camping; boat equipment; boat repair; boats, buying; boats, used; games, boating; navigation; remote controls, outboard.

When you turn the steering wheel of a boat, the part that turns first is the back, not the front. New boaters most often have problems with this kind of steering when they pull away from a pier. They turn the wheel away from the pier and thus turn the rear into the pier. To get away without damage to the boat or your ego, ease away from the pier stern first

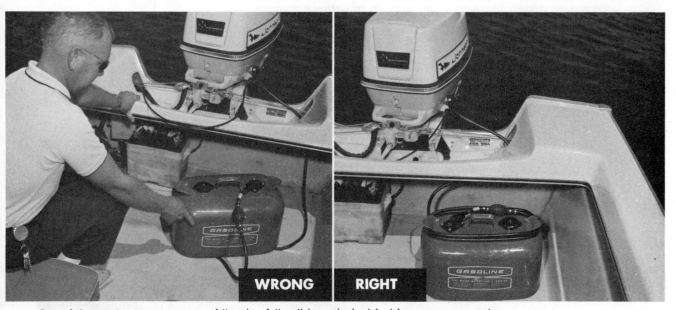

One of the most common causes of "engine failure" is a pinched fuel hose, so never put a fuel tank on the hose. The 36 pounds of fuel in a standard fuel can will choke off the flow of gasoline to the engine. Coil surplus hose on the tank brackets. Also, always make sure the fuel lines are attached tightly to both the engine and the tank after you switch tanks

**RIGHT**

**WRONG**

Watch out for heavy wakes and waves. They'll cause your boat to bounce and yaw. When you see one coming, steer into it at an angle of about 20 degrees. Ease off on your throttle just before your bow hits the crest. Then accelerate when you're through

*boating savvy, continued*

**RIGHT**

**WRONG**

Watch your wake. Power-boat operators always are responsible for their wake and should be moving at a "wakeless" speed well before they get close to other boats

Suddenly throttling back your boat will not as suddenly stop its wake. Boats mushing into the water after slowing from high speed displace a lot of water and cause a wake to go out. Such a wave can damage anchored boats

If it looks like you're in for a rough ride, batten down. Close tackle boxes and brace or tie down loose equipment, including oars. Loose items can get lost in a bad blow. Put everything you can at the lowest point in the boat. If you have a wearable life preserver put it on. If you have a floating cushion, tie it to your belt. Untie your shoes and loosen heavy clothes so you can get rid of them in case you get tossed into the water and must swim

# How to survive rough water

## What to do before and during a storm

■ THERE YOU ARE, out on the water and minding your own business when the wind comes up suddenly or a rough rain squall blows up. Suddenly you realize that the once-friendly water has become an enemy. You have the problem of getting your boat to a haven fast, where wind and water cannot toss you about helplessly.

The first decision you must make is whether to head for home or a strange but safe shore. Head for home if the wind will be in your face as you do and the waves aren't so big you can't get through them. The old rule of heading into a

**boat ladder:** see ladder, boat

319

Keep the boat trimmed to meet the waves. By shifting the position of the gear and passengers, you can keep the bow high for running into the wind or the stern high to keep a following wave from swamping the boat and giving you serious problems. Hit waves at a slight angle and keep as much weight as possible on the downwind side to present the maximum amount of freeboard to oncoming waves. That will keep the inside of your boat as free of excess water as possible. But don't tip the boat so far to the downwind side that a wave could capsize you. A floating cushion tied to your belt (below, left) will stay with you if you get tossed overboard, and a line tied to an oarlock (below, right) gives you a firm handhold

*surviving rough water, continued*

blow applies here. Almost any boat will ride over waves if you take them almost head on and cut back on your throttle just as you reach the crest. Pour on the gas as you come down the other side.

If the wind is too strong and you can't make headway against it, you'll have to turn and run before the wind. Manage your speed so you don't overrun a crest ahead or allow a wave to come in over the stern.

Waves usually are biggest in shallow water, so stay in deep water until ready to run for shore.

If things get really bad, turn and run with the storm until you can work your way to safety. You can tell when you're in serious trouble if your boat starts to dig in at the bow when you come off a wave crest, if you pitch violently as you go up and over, or your engine roars loudly as the lower unit comes out of the water. A short, rough chop can be troublesome, and an irregular wave pattern can cause the worst problems. Long, smooth waves with a lot of time between crests usually will give you time to maneuver between them safely.

Sometimes you can beat a diagonal course through waves too high to take any way but on your bow. Watch the interval between crests until you've learned the timing, then make progress to the side between crests. Then turn back into the wind to take each wave dead ahead

*turn page*

If you find yourself in a heavy blow, quickly get ready for the possibility of losing your power. Rig a sea anchor, which has one purpose—to keep the bow of your boat directly into the wind, so your boat won't get swamped by waves hitting broadside or stern first

Turning around or changing course in a heavy sea is a trick that requires careful timing. As you pass through a crest, put the tiller hard over and turn in the relatively calm waters of the trough. Warn your crew before you do this. Speed before the next wave hits

WIND

If things get really rough, get ashore any place you can. Ideally, run downwind to a sand beach, timing your speed to the speed of the waves so you come in riding a crest. As you hit bottom, tilt up the motor, get out fast and pull the boat as far ashore as possible

Keep your weight as low as possible. Get passengers on the floor of the boat to give the skipper a clear view ahead. Either sit on or brace yourself against the fuel can to keep it from bouncing around and disconnecting the fuel line, killing the engine. Also, try to fix your back against a cushion jammed between you and the seat, to prevent back damage

*surviving rough water, continued*

Don't forget your fuel supply. Before you plan a long run for home, check to determine how much gasoline you have. Remember that, in rough water, you'll burn more fuel than you will on a calm lake, so make sure you have much more than enough fuel to reach safety.

To prepare for the always-possible problem of engine failure in a storm, have your passenger rig a sea anchor. Anything that will float—a bait pail, a floating cushion or even a jacket—tied strongly to a stout line can be thrown overboard should you suddenly lose power. Have the sea-anchor line tied to the bow of the boat, which should be pointed into the wind if you don't have power.

If worst comes to worst and your boat gets flipped or fills with water, stay with the boat. Hang on to it. It should float. An overturned boat has air trapped under it and should stay afloat for a long time if the boat doesn't break up. Knot a line or some of your clothing around hand holds on the boat and hang on for dear life. Work your way to the up-wind side, so waves don't slam it into you.

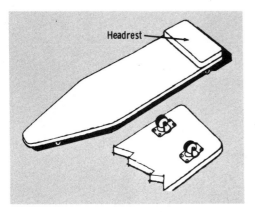

An old ironing board can easily be converted to a wheeled garage creeper. Remove the legs, then attach four swivel coasters.

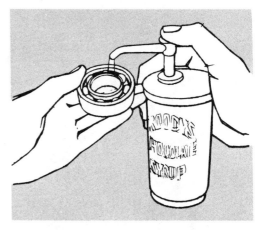

Those chocolate syrup containers that kids use make good grease dispensers. Just rinse them clean and fill them with grease.

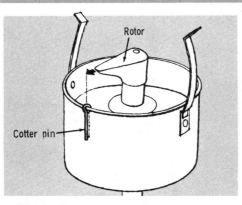

If you mark the rotor position with a cotter pin when you remove the distributor cap, you will eliminate the danger of reassembling the distributor in reverse firing order.

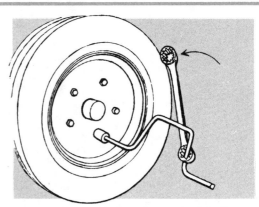

A box-end wrench slipped over the handle of your lug wrench will give you added leverage when removing too-tight lug bolts.

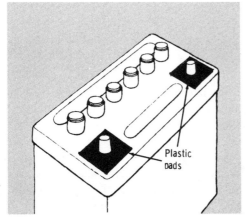

Pads cut from a plastic container prevent acid buildup on the battery connectors in your car.

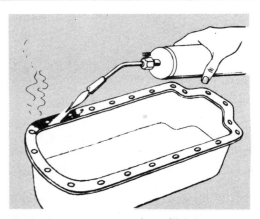

To remove a wornout gasket which has stuck to an oil pan, wash all excess oil from the pan, then use a propane torch to loosen the gasket adhesive.

It's actually just a wooden
waterskier, but it skims over the
surface like a hydrofoil

# Build a water bug

BY ROY L. CLOUGH, JR.

INSPIRED BY those little aquatic insects called "water striders," this unusual model boat flits along the surface of the water on three flipper-shaped planing feet mounted at the ends of long legs.

Although it travels fastest on calm water, *Water Bug* can run through 4 to 5 in. ripples—the scale equivalent of 5-ft.waves—with no trouble. The struts simply slice through the wavelets and keep going. The boat is very stable and can be run with a guide line or turned loose in small ponds where recovery is easy. The original model showed no tendency to trip or tip over, even with the rudder bent sharply for free-running turns.

The hull is a simple box structure of ⅛-in. sheet balsa. It should offer no problems, but re-

---

**boat port:** see cover, boat
**boat propellers:** see propellers, boat

---

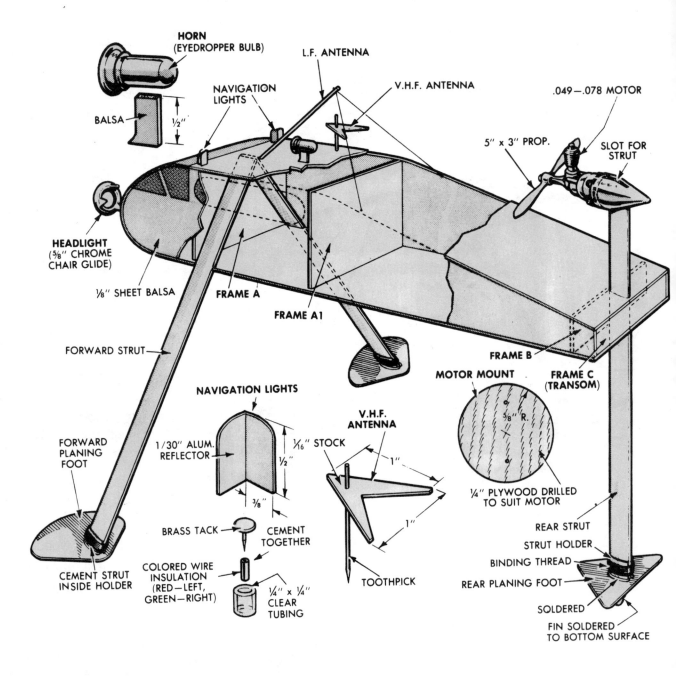

HORN
(EYEDROPPER BULB)

L.F. ANTENNA

V.H.F. ANTENNA

.049 — .078 MOTOR

NAVIGATION
LIGHTS

BALSA

½"

5" x 3" PROP.

SLOT FOR
STRUT

HEADLIGHT
(⅝" CHROME
CHAIR GLIDE)

⅛" SHEET BALSA

FRAME A

FRAME A1

FRAME B

MOTOR MOUNT

FRAME C
(TRANSOM)

FORWARD STRUT

NAVIGATION LIGHTS

V.H.F.
ANTENNA

FORWARD
PLANING
FOOT

1/30" ALUM.
REFLECTOR

1/16" STOCK

½"

⅝" R.

⅜"

1"

1"

¼" PLYWOOD DRILLED
TO SUIT MOTOR

BRASS TACK

CEMENT
TOGETHER

REAR STRUT

STRUT HOLDER

CEMENT STRUT
INSIDE HOLDER

COLORED WIRE
INSULATION
(RED — LEFT,
GREEN — RIGHT)

¼" x ¼"
CLEAR
TUBING

TOOTHPICK

BINDING THREAD

REAR PLANING FOOT

SOLDERED

FIN SOLDERED
TO BOTTOM SURFACE

*build a water bug, continued*

member to soak the sheeting which covers the front section in hot water before bending. Finish the boat with a couple of coats of sanding sealer and one of dope, or cover the bare wood with a layer of lightweight model tissue laid on with heavy dope.

The motor mount is a disc of plywood pinned and cemented to the rear leg. Drill for the engine mounting bolts, set the engine in place and build up the fairing on the rear of the bulkhead with scrap balsa left over from the hull planking.

Don't worry about access to the rear of the bulkhead to tighten up the nuts. If built-in blind this way, they'll stay put. The thrust line of the motor should be almost parallel to the bottom of the boat, but pointed slightly downward.

Cut the planing feet out of .019 sheet metal, then make up the holders and rudder and solder them to the feet at the angles shown. Attach the feet to the struts by lashing and cementing securely.

Finish off the model with scale radio masts,

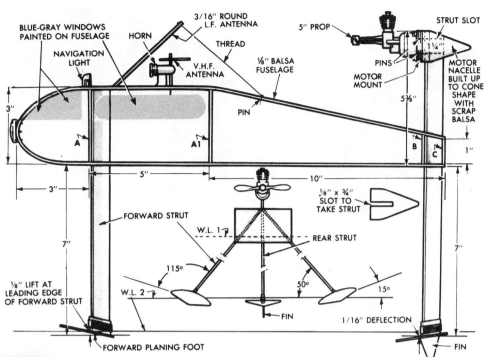

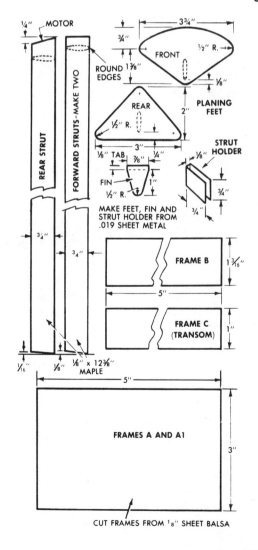

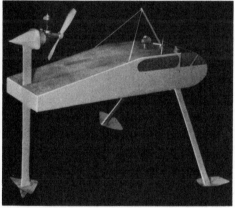

running lights and foghorn. A couple of screw eyes are used for the restraining bridle. If you use a tether, attach it in such a fashion that the boat dangles level when suspended by it.

If you don't have a model boat basin with tether post, you can run *Water Bug* off a spinning rod from a rowboat.

To launch the boat hold it by the motor mount and give a gentle push. It should climb out of the water in about 6 ft. with an immediate increase in speed. If it doesn't, turn up the front edges of the forward planing feet slightly.

**See also:** hydroplane models; rotor ship model; sailboat model; steamboat model; submarine model.

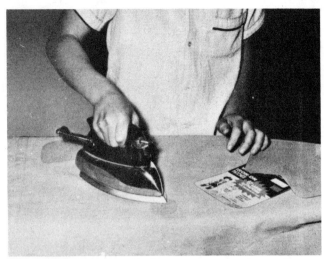

Those irksome holes or tears in your canvas boating equipment—boat covers, convertible tops, duffel bags even sails—can be repaired quickly and easily with iron-on patches. Since these patches are available in a wide variety of colors and sizes, it shouldn't be difficult to find the right one for each job

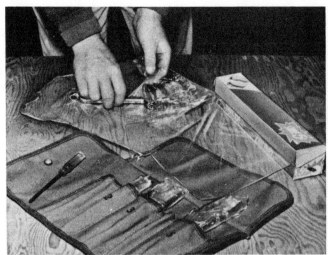

A good mechanic doesn't like to work with rusty tools, yet it's almost inevitable that those carried aboard a boat will start corroding because of the ever-present moisture. To guard your tools against moisture, wrap each one snugly in transparent plastic sandwich wrap before putting it back in the pouch or chest

Bicycle inner tubes, plastic bleach
bottles and transparent sandwich wrap
have surprising uses aboard a boat

# Tips for boaters

Chafing guards for your anchor, bumper and mooring lines will protect both the lines and the surrounding paintwork. Make the guards out of the type of inner tubes that are used on racing bikes. Owners of bicycle repair shops will be glad to give you worn or blown out tubes that you can use for cutting the guards

If you want to put your cruiser in the garage but can't because the windshield is too high, take off the permanent mounting brackets and replace them with quick-change bronze bolts and wing nuts. Apply rubber molding under the edge, then drill a series of holes for the mounting bolts spaced about 10 in. apart

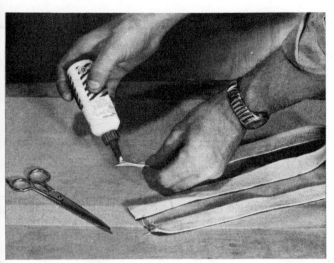

The strap webbing on such boating accessories as canopies and life jackets often becomes frayed at the ends. To correct this condition and prevent it from recurring, cut off the frayed portion of the strap and coat the first inch of material above this cut with white glue to hold the strands of webbing in place

If you need an oversize funnel when you're working around your boat, make one by cutting the bottom from a large plastic bottle or jug, such as those in which bleach is sold. When you put the cap back on, the funnel becomes an emergency bailing bucket that will come in handy in rough weather on the water

Here's another use for those large plastic bleach bottles. Turn them into marker buoys. All you do is attach one end of a length of light line to the handle and the other end to a weight. This type of buoy costs little, but it can be most useful when you want to mark an anchorage or a fishing spot

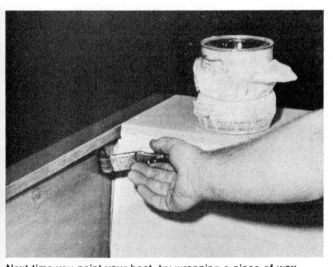

Next time you paint your boat, try wrapping a piece of wax paper or aluminum foil around the bottom of the paint can and securing it with a rubber band or length of string. This not only will stop paint from running down the side of the can and leaving stains, but it will keep the deck from getting scratched

**See also:** boat equipment; boats, buying; boats, used; carburetors, outboard; magnetos, outboard; outboard motors, overhauling; outboard motors, repair; outboard motors, used; spark plugs, marine; tools, boat.

Before you pour a patio in which redwood dividers are set, drive large nails into the sides of the redwood below surface level to anchor the divider strips.

When laying stair treads, measure at only two points—top and bottom steps—and then use a piece of string tacked to these stairs to align the others.

Moth balls can be hung in your closet in a vaporizer made from an old nylon stocking knotted at the end.

This flip-top shelf for your stepladder holds tools or a can of paint. Make it with hinges bolted to the top of your ladder.

■ SHOPPING AROUND for a boat is one of life's real pleasures. You thump hulls, talk boats with the dealers, possibly take a test ride. Maybe you buy, maybe not. Either way, it's been fun.

It's even more fun if you know what you're looking for. The following tips on shopping for five different types of boats are offered by experts. You'll find specific information which will be helpful even if your boat has to be a compromise in its design.

We've omitted the pros and cons of aluminum, fiberglass and wood because this has to be *your* preference. It's important, though, so make up your mind which kind you want.

Remember, somewhere there's a boat that will suit your needs and pocketbook. The trick is to find it, and that's not a problem. It's fun.

A word of caution. Boats, like pets, are easy to love at first sight, so don't be impulsive.

Can you tell a good boat
from a not-so-good boat?
Here's some expert advice
backed up by a total of
100 years' experience

# How to buy
# your first boat

## HOW TO BUY A RUNABOUT

BY JACK SEVILLE

■ ANYONE IN THE MARKET for a runabout today had better forget yesterday's criteria of just what a fun boat should look like.

First of all, your boat may not have a foredeck. Some of today's best runabouts use the space for another cockpit. You'll get more out of it as a seating area than as a rope locker. It also makes a first-rate place to stand when casting a plug.

No matter what the configuration, though, never buy a boat without taking it out for a test run. While you're finding out what kind of a ride it has and how well it handles, you can check out other important features from the cockpit.

The steering, for instance. Be sure the wheel gives positive control without too much play or too much travel. Otherwise, when maneuvering at any speed you'll have to make like a pretzel bender.

A firm seat that holds you erect and gives full visibility is a must. So is a footrest.

Today's runabout may or may not have a windshield. If there is one, it should be sturdy enough to support a passenger who might grab it when he is thrown off balance or who uses it to maneuver himself into or out of the boat.

It is important to note that if the windshield is fitted with glass, rather than Plexiglas, it should be shatterproof. Anything else on a runabout is hazardous.

### get good instruments

A full set of gauges is a good deal, but only as good as the instruments themselves. If there is a tachometer, ask the dealer to check the calibration before you buy. Give the speedometer a two-way scrutiny on a measured mile. On four-cycle engines, you'll also want an oil-pressure gauge and an engine temperature gauge.

If there's a forward deck, make up your mind now that there are going to be occasions when you'll have to get out on it to tie up, or to drop or retrieve an anchor. Don't settle for a deck that isn't going to provide you with sure footing. If it bends underfoot, look out. If it is slippery, turn thumbs down, particularly if it is of a type that can not be refinished with nonskid paint.

Most manufacturers install a label indicating maximum safe load and maximum safe power. Consider the load you are planning to carry and don't skimp on boat size. The larger it is, the more safety and comfort. And don't overpower.

We're discussing a boat that is supposed to get up and go, yet be controllable, so choice of power can be critical. Should it be inboard, stern-drive, or outboard? Should it be jet-powered? Jet power, without a prop or other sharp appendages, eliminates a danger to skin divers and skiers, and lets you run your boat through shallows that turn other boats back.

Prices for a 16-ft. outboard runabout begin at about $1000, as this is written. It will take that much again to bolt on a 75- or 80-hp. outboard motor and another $300 will get you the top end of the horsepower range. To get into a stern-drive runabout, with anything over 100 hp., it will probably cost you $3000 and up.

Does the boat you're considering have plenty of space for stowing sports equipment—skis, fishing tackle and the like?

Finally, you might want to consider a folding canvas top—sometimes it's as much relief to get out of a broiling sun as it is to get shelter from a cold, pelting rain. And, with sun-lounge seats, side curtains and an adventuresome spirit, you can use it as a camping cruiser.

### POINTS TO CHECK
- ☐ **Fuel capacity:** related to fuel consumption of engine used to give desired cruising range.
- ☐ **Deck hardware:** through-bolted.
- ☐ **Engine:** properly matched to hull to give desired running speed at ¾ throttle.
- ☐ **Driver's seat:** should have footrest and permit good visibility in all directions.
- ☐ **Flotation:** sufficient to keep boat afloat when filled with water and maximum load. (Check specs.)
- ☐ **Fuel and engine compartment:** vented according to latest Coast Guard regulation. (Read it before you go out shopping.)
- ☐ **Stowage space:** adequate to hold skis, fishing tackle or anything else you plan to carry.

# HOW TO BUY A SAILBOAT

BY JOHN WESTLAKE

IF YOU'RE THINKING of buying a sailboat, it's probably safe to assume you've been sailing at least once or twice with a friend and know a little something about his boat. This is a good starting point, but when shopping for your own boat, you really ought to familiarize yourself with some of the hundreds of other sailboats available today.

You can divide all these sailboats into two main groups—keelboats and center boarders. I'm leaving out catamarans (twin-hulled) and trimarans (three-hulled), because I wouldn't recommend either of these as a first boat for a

beginner. Their sailing characteristics are unique. Learning to sail on a multihull is a little like learning the glockenspiel as a first musical instrument. To a certain extent, the same objection applies to small sailing "boards"—surfboards equipped with a mast, sail and centerboard.

A keelboat has a fixed fin (ballast keel) projecting down below the hull to grip the water and prevent the boat from sliding sideways. This fin is weighted with lead or cast iron which lowers the center of gravity.

A centerboarder has a movable fin of wood or metal which can be pulled up through a slot in the keel into a "well" or "trunk" inside the boat. The top of this well is above the waterline, so water rises inside but can't enter the boat. As a rule, the fin has no extra weight.

Generally, keelboats are slower and heavier, harder to take out of the water for servicing and harder to trailer. They usually draw more water than center-boarders, so there's more danger of running aground. And once aground, a keelboat is harder to sail free.

On the other hand, they're safer because of the lower center of gravity. Being heavier, keelboats have more momentum and won't stop dead in their tracks when meeting an oncoming wave, as many centerboarders do. They have the feel of a big boat. Finally, there's no centerboard well, which is not only an obstacle but a source of leakage.

The centerboarder's main advantages, then, are "shoal" (shallow) draft and peppier sailing, plus being much easier to trailer and haul out for maintenance.

The choice of a particular boat becomes largely a matter of your more detailed personal preferences and how much you want to pay. Let's look at a representative example of each type.

Take the Bull's Eye, for instance. It's a fiberglass keelboat only 15-ft. long and quite tame because of its ballast and small sail area. The cockpit is large enough to take four adults comfortably on a day's sail. If you live near an exposed, rather rough body of water, this would be an excellent choice. New, a Bull's Eye goes for about $2200. A used one can be under $1000.

The Blue Jay, a 13-ft. wooden centerboarder, gives away security for thrills. It's especially popular as a first boat for training. In spite of its small size, though, it will still take three adults in the cockpit, and can pass a Bull's Eye. In this boat, it's advisable to stay in protected water with breezes under 20 mph. You'd better not be a novice if you exceed these limits, for unlike Bull's Eyes, "Jays" will dump the unskilled into the drink. New, about $1000, used, roughly $400.

A good general rule to keep in mind is that comfort and security generally work against sailing sharpness. As one increases, the other decreases. So the basic question in choosing a sailboat is which of these qualities is more important to you personally. And how much.

## POINTS TO CHECK

- [ ] **Standing rigging:** stainless steel and without kinks.
- [ ] **Turnbuckles:** heavy enough for boat to be heeled over 90 deg. by hauling on the main halyard when boat is afloat.
- [ ] **Running rigging:** Dacron or some other non-stretch synthetic.
- [ ] **Centerboard trunk:** completely rigid.
- [ ] **Keel bolt heads:** bear on large washers.
- [ ] **Cockpit:** large and deep enough for adults to move fast (especially in centerboards).
- [ ] **Dimensions:** must be correct if boat is a "one-design" you intend to race. (The class secretary can supply you with specs.)
- [ ] **Sails:** Dacron, properly fitted (when main is hoisted fully, boom should be horizontal).

# HOW TO BUY
# A FISHING BOAT

BY PAT RICHARDS

■ AS A FISHERMAN, you have a lot going for you when picking out your first boat. Almost any boat will do a fair job for fishing, so you can't go too far wrong. More important, though, you've probably used dozens of boats—rented

or owned by friends—before you set out to buy one for yourself.

If you're like most first-time buyers, you'll already have a pretty good idea of what you want or need before you do any serious shopping. In case you haven't reached that point yet, here are a few suggestions to mull over.

If your fishing is done with finesse—with flies or light tackle on small, quiet waters—you'll want a shallow-draft boat that will slide quietly along a shoreline or drift easily down a stream. Your best bet would be a canoe or a "johnboat-type" cartop boat, the first if you want delicate maneuverability, the latter if you want to stand and cast, as most fly fishermen do.

The canoe will take more skill to operate and will be more expensive. An 8- to 12-ft. aluminum cartopper johnboat is the lightest, most stable and least expensive of fishing craft.

If your fishing runs more to general types on a variety of inland waters, and if you like to take someone along, you'll want more boat than that.

Best bet for general use, then, is a more conventional hull in the 12- to 16-ft. area. They're light enough to carry on a cartop, yet big enough to take a 10-hp. outboard and carry two or three men with their gear. In addition, they're seaworthy enough to be comfortable on a choppy day, or to run home through a squall.

A compromise possibility, with shallow-draft delicacy but enough hull and free-board for most inland waters, is a bigger johnboat hull, anywhere from 12 to 18 ft. Even at that size, they're light enough to be easily handled, and still the least expensive boat for the size.

If your favorite water is a big lake, a rough stream, or shoreline salt water, you'll need still more boat. With heavier gear, a bigger outboard (or possibly two) and bigger fish to handle, you'll need 16 to 20 ft. of hull with a good vee or round

bottom and high freeboard for stability and dry running. Also a deep forefoot and wide bow flare to get you out of trouble in case of a blow. Rigged with twin middle-sized motors, or a big running motor and a small fishing motor, such boats take two to four men in comfort.

For really deluxe accommodations— though at a price—don't overlook the many "utility" runabouts on the market. Running from 14 to 20-ft., they offer very sophisticated and specialized hulls, many good built-in features, lots of deck and seating space, and are often available with stern-drive or inboard power from economical four-cycle engines. And don't forget their big attraction to many fishermen: They do double duty as a family runabout and ski boat.

One great fishing boat often underrated by buyers is the stable, inexpensive, comfortable pontoon boat. It probably offers more square feet of deck for a dollar than anything else afloat.

Pontoon boats are harder to trailer and store than the more conventional hulls, but if you keep your boat in the water, they're great. It's like having your own private fishing dock and floating patio.

Another type of boat most fishermen overlook is the inflatable or folding boat. They're smaller and more expensive than rigid hulls, but offer great stability, easy portability and the easiest storage of all.

One happy thought: No matter what boat you pick, the fishing will be great!

---

### POINTS TO CHECK
☐ **Seating arrangement:** matched to the type of fishing you do most.
☐ **Capacity:** adequate for your normal fishing group. (If three or four, consider going together on a couple of small boats.)
☐ **Motor:** sufficient to power hull properly, yet small enough for trolling. (On large boats, consider using two—one for each.)
☐ **Hull shape and size:** takes roughest kind of water in which you'll be using the boat. (If you have to cross a big lake to reach your spot, buy a hull for lake crossing.)
☐ **Portability:** judged realistically, if it's important in your fishing. (Can you and a friend really get it on and off a car easily, or do you need a trailer?)

# HOW TO BUY
# A SKI BOAT

BY PAT CALLAN

■ WITH MORE THAN nine million water skiers in America today, there are bound to be a number of different opinions on just what characteristics the ideal water-ski boat should have. However, almost every skier agrees that a good towboat is extremely important, especially for beginners. With first-time skiers, it can make the difference

between a fun-packed introduction to the exciting sport and a discouraging failure.

The American Water Ski Association has been working with boat manufacturers on developing suitable tournament rules for quite some time. Some of the most frequently mentioned requirements are:

—Broad, flat planing surface for quick planing, clean wake, and high-speed capability.

—Responsive steering for good performance on turns.

—Low freeboard for maximum visibility and easy boarding.

—Ample storage for skis, belts and line.

—Nonskid cockpit floor.

—Proper equipment (rear-facing observer seat, rear-view mirror, a sturdy tow pylon and a water speedometer).

—Sufficient power to pull the skier.

A good ski towboat answering this general description is a hull in the 16-ft class with a 60-hp. outboard. Such a combination will give you a chance to advance from the beginner stage —riding on two skis inside the wake—to slalom runs and even simple tricks.

It's true that you can pull a skier with a smaller outboard than this, and with children it's even possible to give a good tow if the proper propel-

ler is used. With adults, however, more power is required.

The reasons for the other requirements are obvious. A quick-planing bottom cuts down on the amount of time the skier has to hold against that strong pull of the boat, before he reaches a plane and stands up; if the boat skids or porpoises in a turn instead of responding quickly, there will be a loss of power on the towline and the skier will begin to sink. When the boat takes hold again and the rope snaps tight, it may be snatched from his hands.

Low freeboard not only makes it easier for a fallen skier to climb into the boat, but it also simplifies picking up lost skis. In addition, it cuts wind resistance and gives the driver good visibility.

The tow hook should be installed ahead of the motor near the center of gravity to keep the stern from swaying from side to side when the skier is criss-crossing the wake. The speedometer is actually optional for weekend skiing, but it's a big help when trying to maintain constant speed.

Finally, make sure that your dealer equips the engine with proper propeller for skiing.

---

☐ **Hull:** large enough to take safely an engine with adequate power for skiing.

☐ **Transom:** wide and flat-bottomed for quick takeoff and clean wake.

☐ **Freeboard:** low for easy boarding and maximum visibility.

☐ **Seating arrangement:** include at least one rear-facing seat for an observer.

☐ **Storage compartments:** large enough to hold belts, line and other gear. (If they won't take skis, you can sometimes add racks inside the cockpit if space is there.)

☐ **Cockpit floor:** nonskid textured surface.

☐ **Engine:** powerful enough for full range of skiing activities from beginner stage to slalom or trick runs.

---

# HOW TO BUY
# A CRUISER

BY JACK SEVILLE

■ JUST ABOUT ANY BOAT that provides sleeping space, sanitary facilities, and cooking equipment, all under shelter, can be called a cruiser. When shopping for one of these boats, you'll have to measure your pocketbook against how much cruising capacity you want. To get further and cruise in comfort for longer periods, independent

of shoreside facilities, you're going to want to be able to stand up to your full height, stretch out in full-size beds and enjoy most of the other comforts of home.

Naturally, big boats with all these comforts cost more than smaller cruisers.

One escape from this dilemma is to buy a houseboat and use it as a combination vacation home and a cruising boat. Another is to put up with sitting headroom in the cabin of a small cruiser and do your leg-stretching in the open cockpit, letting that area serve double duty by adding a canvas cover and side curtains.

Before you make your decision, however, go over all the manufacturers' literature you can lay your hands on. Hit the boat shows and check your local dealers.

Note the equipment listed as standard. How many necessities are listed as optional extras? For example, does the base price include all the safety equipment required by the Coast Guard? If not, you're going to have to buy it separately.

Then, try before you buy. Go over the boat with a fine-tooth comb, noting the provisions for creature comfort, but also being supercritical about safety features.

Your cruising range is going to be dependent upon fuel capacity and fuel consumption. Your aim should be sufficient power to obtain comfortable speed at ¾ throttle. Does the boat of your choice carry enough fuel to cover your local cruising conditions? How about the fresh-water capacity? And is there storage space for normal needs of "housekeeping," plus a little extra?

Look for good access to the forward deck. The hatch should be large enough to allow you to get through, and it should be constructed so that it can be dogged down tight—watertight. A chain pipe leading to the forepeak rope locker will avoid slopping mud on the V-berths.

Look for a sturdy bow rail and a strong safety-glass windshield. All decks should have nonskid

surfaces free of toe stubbers. To make side decks safe, there should be handrails along the cabin top.

For cruising comfort, you'll want to be sure the boat doesn't act as a sounding board for excessive engine noise and vibration. As a matter of fact, too much engine noise or vibration probably means something has come unstuck, because today's engines are about 100 percent quieter than they were just a few years ago.

Also in the comfort department, look for adequate provisions for privacy (two-way doors and draw curtains) and proper cabin ventilation.

For safety as well as comfort, take particular note of the boat's attitude underway. There should be good visibility from the helm in all directions and at all speeds. Watch out for a bow-high angle which can cut off forward visibility.

Choose a hull with enough beam to be stable. Perhaps a cathedral hull or another version of a multi-hull will provide the level ride and steady platform you want. If you choose a conventional hull, then look for a full high bow with plenty of flare forward to give you a dry ride.

You'll find a tremendous choice of power units available. Within trailering size, inboard outdrives rack up a lot of advantages. Somewhere around 26 ft. and over, the inboard engine with fixed shaft—possibly in pairs—might be your best choice.

Hopefully, you are going to spend a lot of time on your new cruiser. If you have to skimp on some features, you can afford to give up a little to comfort, but you shouldn't skimp on safety.

## POINTS TO CHECK

☐ **Power:** sufficient to give comfortable speed at ¾ throttle.

☐ **Engine compartment:** well-vented and large enough to give access for service.

☐ **Fuel tanks:** located in a well-vented area, equipped with shutoff valves.

☐ **Foredeck:** easily accessible and free of unnecessary obstructions; nonskid surface.

☐ **Fuel capacity:** to provide the desired cruising range. (Divide it by mpg.)

☐ **Electrical fuses:** should be accessible; system should be wired for shore current.

☐ **Hull configuration:** suited to water conditions in which you'll be using boat. (Get some ideas by wandering around your local yards and marinas.)

**See also:** boat equipment; boats, used; outboard motors, used; propellers, boat.

Shopping the lots can be a pleasant experience if you know exactly what you are looking for and how much you should pay for it

# You can buy a good used boat

BY FRED CLARK JR.

"Pre-owned" boats can be bargains
or headaches, depending upon your
skill as a shopper

IT'S STILL POSSIBLE to get stung when buying a used boat, but you have to make a real effort. Here's how: Hurry into a deal before someone beats you to that "steal," don't ask for advice, choose off-brand gear that's no longer being made. Follow these guides and you'll stand an excellent chance of ending up with a big, juicy lemon.

The smart buyer does his homework before he starts touring the lots and checking the classified ads. If he's not sure of the type of boat he wants, he bums rides with friends, tries out rental boats, takes every chance he can to familiarize himself with boats he *might* want to buy.

He also checks out the price picture of new boats. A few visits to dealers' showrooms and a few evenings studying manufacturers' price sheets will equip you to exercise some judgment when it comes to pricing a used boat. Don't be surprised if you find a price variation of as much as 50 percent between stripped and deluxe versions of the same basic boat.

The big depreciation bite comes in the first year—up to 25 or even 33 percent of list price. After this it drops back to between 7 and 10 percent of list until the halfway mark is reached. From then on it's condition that sets the tab.

Once you have a line on the market and know

# FIBERGLASS BOATS

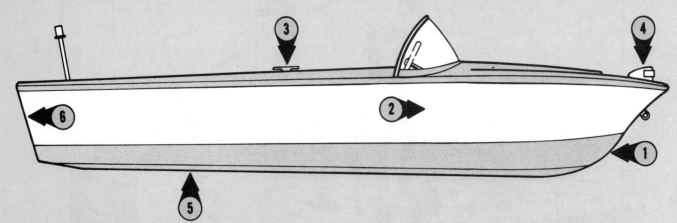

1. Examine the hull for gouges or deep scratches that will require filling. If any are particularly bad, check to make sure structural damage isn't there
2. Go over the gel coat for crazing or fading that indicates that an expensive job is going to be necessary soon after you become the boat's owner
3. Carefully inspect all fittings to make sure that they are tight and well braced. Loose fittings can rip out large sections of fiberglass boats

4. Running lights and equipment should conform to local regulations. If anything is missing, you're going to have to replace it before using the boat
5. Stand off and examine the lines. If the boat is on a trailer, make sure that the rollers support the hull and, especially, the transom correctly
6. Look for cracks at the joints and at connections, such as the chines, keel, transom and stem. Such cracks can mean water seepage and serious problems

# WOODEN BOATS

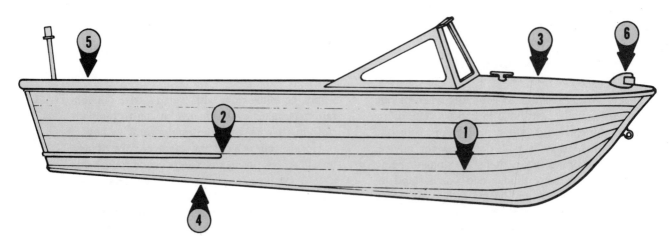

1. If you're considering the purchase of a plywood boat, take the time to look for delamination, especially on the edges of the strakes
2. Are all joints and seams tight? If you find a leak anywhere, it could mean anything from a simple re-calking job to new fastenings, planks or even ribs
3. How's the finish? Repainting a wooden boat isn't a particularly difficult job, but remember that few people look upon it as enjoyable recreation

4. Stand back from the boat you are considering and check the hull lines to see that they haven't been deformed by improper storage
5. Check poorly ventilated areas for dry rot. Don't use a knife or ice pick. Tap suspicious areas. If it's rotted, it will sound dead when hit
6. Find a set of local regulations. The local Coast Guard Auxiliary unit will provide them. Take them along as you check equipment, lights and fittings

# ALUMINUM BOATS

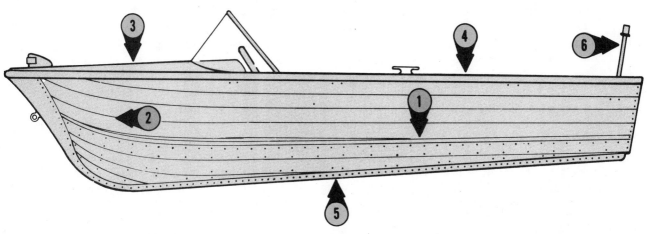

1. Go over all seams carefully for loose or missing rivets, and pay particular attention to spots below the waterline where it looks like a rivet should be
2. Dents should be examined carefully, although, with a nonhardening seam filler, even a dented seam might be only a cosmetic problem that can be corrected
3. If it's painted, must it be repainted? Don't worry about white powder deposits on unpainted aluminum boats. These can be brushed off easily

4. Make doubly sure that the lines of the hull are fair and true, and be certain that they are free of abrupt hooks or rockers
5. Check the flotation. Air-tank flotation should be sound and tight, and foam flotation should be in good condition and securely in place
6. As you would with any boat, use a check list of equipment that is required by local regulations. If it isn't on the boat, you'll have to buy it

*uy a used boat, continued*

what you want, you're ready to shop the classifieds, private owners and dealers.

Each season, people find good buys in gas stations, used car lots and from private owners. You just have to work a little harder checking title and condition, since guarantees can't be as meaningful here as they would be from a dealer. Most of the tricky ones, the boats that would hardly be worth fixing up, change hands on direct deals. That's not to say that all dealers' boats are in perfect shape, but the professional will generally shun a clunker, or junk it for parts.

A dealer usually offers a fair value, good protection and some sort of guarantee. Occasionally, if pressed for space, he'll really wheel and deal.

You've probably already made up your mind about materials—fiberglass, wood or aluminum —so instead of wasting time on the old pros and cons, let's look at the different types of boats.

When you are checking one of these boats, always stand off and take a good look from both

sides and both ends. If the lines aren't fair and smooth flowing, look further to find out why.

Lightweight aluminum canoes and cartoppers may show dents due to handling. If the price is attractive, however, try the boat on the water to see whether performance is affected or whether there are any leaks.

A neglected canvas-covered boat can often be put back in shape, if you're willing to spend time on repairs. Be sure the price is right, however, and if there are quite a few cracked ribs, look elsewhere. Cracks in the cover may be superficial, the result of too many coats of paint.

The most popular boats made today are the 14 to 18-foot planing hulls, so you should have a large selection to choose from. As with a smaller boat, check the hull fore and aft, all around, for fair, continuous lines. It's the most important feature to check, because the condition of the hull bottom determines performance.

Go over the transom closely. This structural

member takes a lot of punishment because it has to transmit the power of the engine to the hull. Get a friend to pull and tug on the engine while you keep an eye on the corners, where the transom mates with the hull. There should be no cracks or movement here.

If the boat is on a trailer, note the location of the rear rollers or bolsters. They should be set to support the transom itself and, thus, the weight of the engine. If they're forward of the transom, the load can cause a concave "hook" in the bottom which does terrible things to performance. The same goes for a hump, or "rocker."

At speed, planing boats ride on the last third of their bottoms, and if this surface isn't straight, the boat will porpoise and buck. Some boats which have perfectly straight planing platforms while sitting in the water will develop a hook when power is applied (a good reason for taking a demonstration ride before buying).

### take a ride

Once you have found a boat that interests you, arrange for an on-the-water demonstration. If you're buying a trailer as part of a package deal, this will give you a chance to check that out, too. Is there a good arch to the springs? Is the axle straight? Flat springs or an axle that could be bent mean trouble.

Observe how the engine starts, idles and runs when opened up. You can't expect perfection in used iron, but on the other hand, you don't want the serious, expensive kind of trouble, either. If an engine starts easily, idles reasonably smoothly, and will take off in high gear, you shouldn't have too much to worry about.

Let the owner or dealer drive the boat at first, while you prowl around looking at the fuel tank and lines, and generally getting a passenger's feel of the boat. Then give her a whirl yourself.

Try normal turns, jumping the wake and tightening the turns gradually. The boat should turn smoothly and steadily. Remember that round-bilge boats will bank more sharply than hard-chine designs. And an unbalanced ride or extreme squatting during acceleration might easily be corrected with inexpensive planing plates.

If the boat looks good, runs smoothly and doesn't take water, you're ready for the final check, which means professional help.

We've bought and sold a lot of boats ourselves, and we've never objected to a buyer's satisfying himself that a boat is in good shape.

But on the other hand, we don't allow anyone who answers an ad to start cutting up our boat or dismantling our engine. If a person is interested enough to hire a service man with the right tools, gaskets and know-how, he's welcome to look at our dome, skirts and rings. The same goes for the hull. The ten, fifteen or even twenty-five bucks you might waste on a rig you turn down could turn out to be the best insurance money you ever spent.

You can't expect a perfect boat from the used-boat market. After all, you're getting from one third to two thirds off the original price, and something has to give. A professional will take this into consideration, while steering you away from boats with serious undercover problems.

Unless you've hung around boats all your life and really know what you're talking about, don't try to outguess the professional or imagine you're smarter than a sharp dealer. Listen to a pro.

### the big boats

Anything over 18 feet should be a survey proposition as soon as you locate a suitable boat within your price range. There's just too much detail and too much expense involved for the average buyer to take a chance on a direct buy in this category, so spend a few bucks and consider it insurance.

Take houseboats, for instance. There are checks for rust on steel hulls or pontoons, fatigue and cracked welds on aluminum. You have to check the exterior and roof for leaks, sags and unfair lines. Black stains on the interior panels almost invariably spell l-e-a-k-y r-o-o-f, which require further inspection by an expert to make sure that the interior framing hasn't rotted.

Then comes the test ride. All houseboats tend to sail around in a wind to some degree, but some are so unstable they're hardly safe, while others show surprisingly good control when the going is tough.

A weekend rental will help you to determine whether a particular layout is functionally suited to your needs, and will also give you a chance to check all the mechanics—water system, head, shower, windows, stove, power plant and generator. But when you come right down to the checkbook, you need the expert knowledge of a surveyor, a professional hired to play on your side.

Savvy, common sense and professional advice will get you an inexpensive, serviceable rig.

**See also:** boat equipment; boat repair; boats, buying outboard motors, used; propellers, boat.

# What you should know about bolts

BY W. CLYDE LAMMEY

Bolts hold things together—make them perform as a unit or as an assembly of functional parts.
Here's how to choose the right one for the job

■ WHEN THE JOB calls for use of a bolt rather than a screw or other type fastener, the homeowner must decide what type and size of bolt is best adapted to the purpose. If the parts to be joined are of metal, then a machine bolt with either a square or hex head usually is best. If the head bears on metal, then no washer will be required under the head in average work. But if the parts are subject to vibration, shear or shake, use a lock washer under the nut.

On the other hand if the parts are of wood, or if the part against which the head must bear is of wood, then it is generally best to use a carriage bolt. The head of the latter is relatively larger in proportion to the body diameter and is crowned in a manner similar to that of an oval-headed screw. The body has square shoulders just below the head. When it is tapped into

a hole, the squared portion of the head prevents the bolt from turning when you tighten or loosen the nut. When the nut is turned down on wood, always use a flat washer under it to prevent crushing or other defacement of the material.

Machine screws differ from machine bolts in that they usually are threaded the full body length and the heads are available in a range of shapes, or types, commonly known as flat, round, oval and fillister, also in the socket (Allen) and Phillips types. The flat and oval heads are much the same as those of ordinary wood-screw heads of the same types, the heads being shaped to seat in countersunk holes in the same manner as flat-head wood screws. But round and fillister-head machine screws are designed to seat directly on a flat surface or onto a lock washer. All machine-screw heads are slotted so that they may

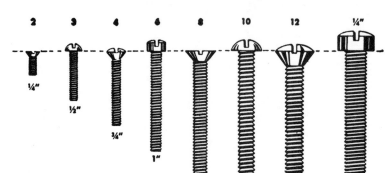

Sizes are designated by length in inches, by diameter in numbers of the American Screw Gauge for diameters less than ¼″, and in fractions of an inch for diameters ¼″ and larger. Designations are for sizes commonly used

| tap size | | drill size no. | drill diameter in inches |
|---|---|---|---|
| diameter | threads per in. | | |
| 2 | 56 | 51 | .0670 |
| 3 | 48 | ⁵⁄₆₄″ | .0781 |
| 4 | 40 | 43 | .0890 |
| 6 | 32 | 36 | .1065 |
| 8 | 32 | 29 | .1360 |
| 10 | 24 | 25 | .1495 |
| 12 | 24 | 17 | .1730 |
| ¼″ | 20 | 8 | .1990 |
| ⁵⁄₁₆″ | 18 | F | .2570 |
| ⅜″ | 16 | ⁵⁄₁₆″ | .3125 |
| ½″ | 13 | ²⁷⁄₆₄″ | .4219 |

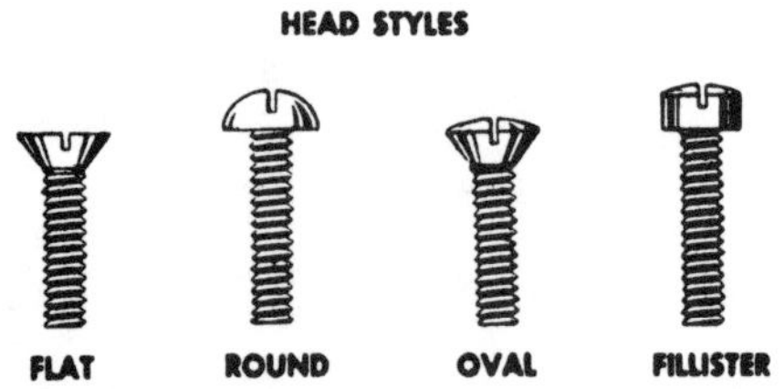

**HEAD STYLES**

FLAT    ROUND    OVAL    FILLISTER

Machine screws—the commercial term for screws to be driven in drilled and tapped holes—are used for assembly of metal parts. Machine screws are regularly made in mild steel and brass, with four types of head—flat, round, oval and fillister. Furnished plain and also with commonly used platings and degrees of finish—nickel, brass, copper, cadmium, electrogalvanized, Parkerized and zinc-plated

be driven with an ordinary screw driver, excepting those with Allen and Phillips heads, the former to be driven with an Allen wrench and the latter with a Phillips driver.

Machine screws are designed mainly for assembly of metal parts, where they usually are driven into tapped holes rather than being drawn tight with nuts. They are widely used in the

assembly of small machines, household appliances, models and experimental apparatus, instruments and in units having parts that must be easily assembled and disassembled in use, or for substitution or replacement. Machine screws come in a wide range of sizes from 0-80 up, are threaded both coarse and fine, and lengths and diameters are held to close dimensions.

| BOLT SIZE diameter of thread and width of square | CARRIAGE-BOLT DIMENSIONS  (in inches) | | | | | |
|---|---|---|---|---|---|---|
| | AMERICAN STANDARD CARRIAGE BOLTS, ROUND HEAD, SQUARE NECK | | | | | |
| | diameter of head | height of head | bolt length and shorter | depth of square | bolt length and longer | depth of square |
| No. 10 (³⁄₁₆″) | ⁷⁄₁₆ | ³⁄₃₂ | 1⅛ | ⅛ | 1¼ | ⁷⁄₃₂ |
| ¼ | ⁹⁄₁₆ | ⅛ | 1¼ | ⁵⁄₃₂ | 1⅜ | ¼ |
| ⁵⁄₁₆ | ¹¹⁄₁₆ | ⁵⁄₃₂ | 1¼ | ³⁄₁₆ | 1⅜ | ⁹⁄₃₂ |
| ⅜ | ¹³⁄₁₆ | ³⁄₁₆ | 1½ | ⁷⁄₃₂ | 1⅝ | ⁵⁄₁₆ |
| ⁷⁄₁₆ | ¹⁵⁄₁₆ | ⁷⁄₃₂ | 1½ | ¼ | 1⅝ | ¹¹⁄₃₂ |
| ½ | 1¹⁄₁₆ | ¼ | 1⅞ | ⁹⁄₃₂ | 2 | ⅜ |
| ⁹⁄₁₆ | 1³⁄₁₆ | ⁹⁄₃₂ | 1⅞ | ⁵⁄₁₆ | 2 | ¹³⁄₃₂ |
| ⅝ | 1⁵⁄₁₆ | ⁵⁄₁₆ | 1⅞ | ¹¹⁄₃₂ | 2 | ⁷⁄₁₆ |
| ¾ | 1⁹⁄₁₆ | ⅜ | 1⅞ | ¹³⁄₃₂ | 2 | ½ |
| ⅞ | 1¹³⁄₁₆ | ⁷⁄₁₆ | 1⅞ | ¹⁵⁄₃₂ | 2 | ⁹⁄₁₆ |
| 1 | 2¹⁄₁₆ | ½ | 1⅞ | ¹⁷⁄₃₂ | 2 | ⅝ |

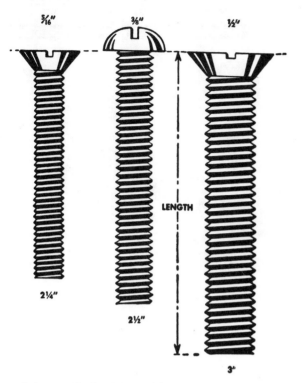

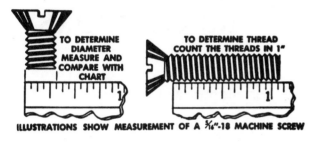

Below, methods of determining diameter of body and number of threads per inch with ordinary rule

TO DETERMINE DIAMETER MEASURE AND COMPARE WITH CHART

TO DETERMINE THREAD COUNT THE THREADS IN 1"

ILLUSTRATIONS SHOW MEASUREMENT OF A 3/16"-18 MACHINE SCREW

American Screw Co.

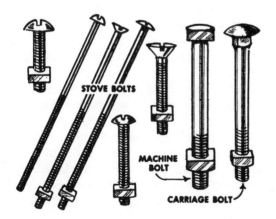

STOVE BOLTS

MACHINE BOLT

CARRIAGE BOLT

Stove bolts usually are carried in stock in standard sizes. Intermediate or extra-length bolts are often available on special order if not stocked. Machine and carriage bolts are ordinarily made with full-diameter shanks. The standard sizes generally are available at any well-stocked hardware store

## stove bolts

"Stove" bolts acquired the name a long time ago and it stuck, even though their use has diversified widely from the purpose for which they were originally designed, that of fasteners in the assembly of stoves. Now they are perhaps among the most widely used fasteners where it is necessary to hold parts together with small bolts. They have slotted heads, like common wood screws, which come either flat or round. They are available in diameters from 5/32 to 1/2 in. and in lengths from 3/8 to 6 in. Stove bolts are not precision-made, being manufactured by upsetting and swaging processes, and the threads generally are rolled rather than die-cut. On the shorter lengths the threads are rolled the full body length. On longer bolts threads may vary from 1 to 2 in. in length. Nuts furnished with stove bolts are ordinarily square, but, any nut tapped with a coarse thread may be used.

## hole size

In wood the diameter of the hole should be the same as that of the bolt. This assures a snug fit and offsets any tendency of the parts to work loose. In metal it is a common practice to drill bolt holes about 1/64 to 1/32 in. oversize so that when the holes are brought into register the bolt will slip easily into place. If holes are drilled the same size as the bolt it may be necessary to tap it rather forcefully. This can swage or upset the threads, making the nut difficult to start.

## length of bolt

Length of the bolt ordinarily should be such that all the threads of the nut engage—with perhaps two or three threads over—when the nut is drawn tight. Of course, you may not always have at hand a bolt, or bolts, that meet this ideal specification. But don't use a bolt of any size that's a thread or two short of full engagement with the nut when the latter is tightened. It might loosen or strip and let you down at some critical time later on. Better to use a bolt that's too long, cutting the excess off the threaded end if clearance is a problem. If you do have occasion to reduce the length of a bolt by cutting off a portion of the threaded end, cut it as nearly square as possible freehand. Then file the end smooth and bevel, or "break" it slightly with a file so that the nut will "take" the threads easily. Avoid use of bolts with damaged threads.

**See also:** building; fasteners; framing; hardware; hinges; nails; screws.

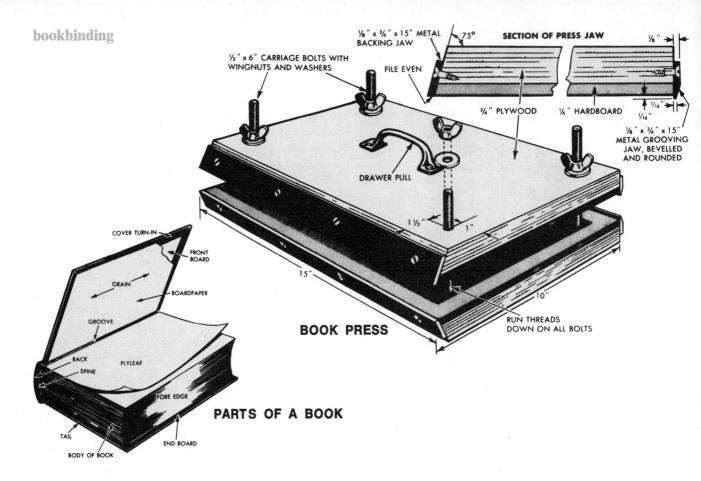

**½" x 6" CARRIAGE BOLTS WITH WINGNUTS AND WASHERS**

**⅛" x ¾" x 15" METAL BACKING JAW**

**FILE EVEN**

**75°**

**SECTION OF PRESS JAW**

**⅛"**

**DRAWER PULL**

**¾" PLYWOOD**

**¼" HARDBOARD**

**1/16"**

**1/16"**

**⅛" x ¾" x 15" METAL GROOVING JAW, BEVELLED AND ROUNDED**

**1½"**

**1"**

**15"**

**10"**

**RUN THREADS DOWN ON ALL BOLTS**

**BOOK PRESS**

**COVER TURN-IN**

**FRONT BOARD**

**GRAIN**

**BOARDPAPER**

**GROOVE**

**BACK**

**FLYLEAF**

**SPINE**

**FORE EDGE**

**TAIL**

**END BOARD**

**BODY OF BOOK**

**PARTS OF A BOOK**

# It's fun to rebind damaged books

BY MANLY BANISTER

Don't let your favorite books fall apart. With a homemade press and
a few common tools you can do a professional rebinding job

NOBODY WANTS to throw out a good book just because the binding is damaged. Chances are it's one of your favorites, for these always receive the most handling. Often, the damage can be repaired in a couple of minutes with a little glue or paste. Sometimes a complete tearing down and rebinding may be required. But in either case the investment in time and materials is negligible when measured by the result.

You don't need a lot of expensive equipment to repair books. The most important piece of equipment is a book press, and the easy-to-build unit detailed above is more than satisfactory for most book-repairing jobs. In addition, you'll need scissors; a ruler; a hammer or mallet; a bone "folder" (or make a wooden one by curv-

ing the ends of a flat stick and rounding the edges); a sharp knife, and a large needle.

Materials used in repairing books are also inexpensive. In addition to the paper, mesh-cloth "super," cover boards and book cloth, you'll have to buy a spool of No. 25 linen thread, a cake of beeswax for waxing the thread, a small can of hide glue and a jar of library paste. All of these may be obtained at a bookbinder's supply house.

One thing to keep in mind when repairing books: Paper, like wood, has a grain running in a given direction, and every piece of paper put into a book must have its grain running vertically, from the head to the tail of the book. Otherwise, it's bound to buckle and cause trouble. One simple way of determining the direction of the grain is to fold a sample sheet and wet the crease. If it dries smooth, the grain runs parallel to the fold.

If the crease buckles, you've folded the paper

To free the body of the book from its covers to start the repair work, use a sharp knife to cut through the "hinges" on both sides

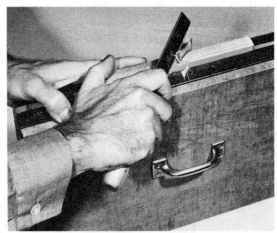

Prepare your book for rebinding by clamping it in the backing jaws of the press and scrape off all paper backing, super and glue

across the grain.

The following steps, numbered to correspond with the illustrations, cover a complete rebinding. This will probably only be necessary if the book is in very bad shape, with the sewing loose and sections coming apart. To repair less severe damage—broken cover boards, torn flyleaves, etc.—simply follow the appropriate steps.

**Step 1.** Cut the body of the book free of its cover by slashing through the hinges on both sides with a *sharp* knife. Tear off the flyleaves and throw them away.

**Step 2.** Clamp the book in the angled backing jaws of the press and dampen the spine. If old glue is really hardened, spread on a layer of library paste and let it stand a while. Scrape off the paper backing, the mesh super and the glue, down to the folds of the sections.

**Step 3.** The body of the book is composed of sections called "signatures" in the trade—a series of sheets folded together, usually forming either 16 or 32 pages. Find the center of the first section, disclosing the sewing thread, and cut each stitch down the "gutter." Do the same to the rest of the sections.

### hammering the groove

**Step 4.** Carefully separate the sections. Note that each is creased close to the fold. This is the "groove," formed in the backing, and it must be hammered out. Protect the face of the section

with a sheet of waste paper and hammer out the groove, one section at a time.

**Step 5.** In separating sections, it often happens that the outside sheet of a section becomes torn. Before resewing the book, it is necessary to repair these sheets. Cut ½-in. strips of 11-lb. bond paper, or similar, as long as the page. Lay out the damaged sheet or sheets with the inside of the fold up. After applying paste to the strip, stick it over the torn fold, being careful not to stretch the paste-dampened strip. Then rub it down and put the sheet aside. When all such sheets have been repaired, gather them together with protective sheets of waxed paper between, squeeze for a few minutes in the press, and lay them aside to dry.

**Step 6.** Reassemble the sections and stack them with the fold to the fore edge in alternating groups of two or three. Place a sheet of waxed paper or aluminum foil on each side and run the press wing-nuts down as tight as you can. Let the sections stand under pressure overnight.

### remove from press

**Step 7.** Take the sections out of the press and assemble them in the proper order. Take care you don't put a section in upside down! Clamp

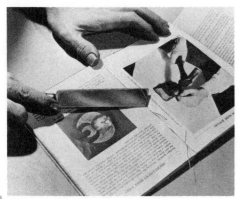

**3** Starting with the first section of the book, find the center and carefully cut each stitch. Then take all other sections and do the same to them

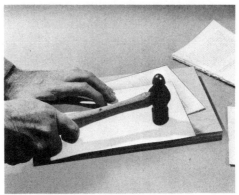

**4** Separate the body of the book into sections and flatten the groove in each of them. Do not tap sections directly with the hammer. Cover them with paper first

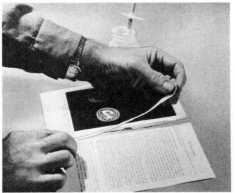

**5** If an outside sheet of a section is torn, repair it by pasting a ½-in. strip of bond paper over the tear. Make sure the bond paper is completely flat

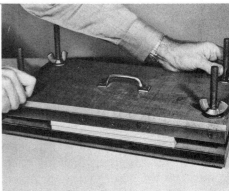

**6** Reassemble the body by stacking sections in the press with their folds to the fore edge in alternating groups. Keep them in the press overnight

*rebinding books, continued*

them in the backing jaws of the press, leaving about ¼ in. projecting. Make four or more unequally spaced marks across the back, and saw each mark with a *dull* saw about ³⁄₃₂ in. deep (deep enough to cut through the innermost fold of each section). The head and tail sawcuts should be placed ¾ in. from the ends of the spine.

**Step 8.** Sewing by the lockstitch method has the advantage that no special equipment is needed. Lay the first section face down on the edge of the worktable.

**thread and sew**

Thread the needle with a couple of feet of thread. Pass the needle into the tail saw cut at the head. Draw loops of thread out through the other sawcuts with a crochet hook or poke them out from inside with the eye end of the needle. Lay on the second section, pass the needle in

through the sawcut at the head and out through the next sawcut down the back. Pass the needle upward through the loop protruding from the section below and back into the same sawcut. Draw the loop firm (but not too tight) to form the lockstitch. Finish sewing section one to section two and tie the two threads together at the tail sawcut with a square knot.

Section three and all following are sewed in the same manner, except that there are no loops protruding. Pass the needle behind the stitch in the next lower section, then back into the section, out at the next sawcut, and so on.

**"kettle stitch"**

At the end of each section, the section is anchored to the one below by means of the "kettle stitch." Pass the needle behind the thread below, then bring it around and up through the

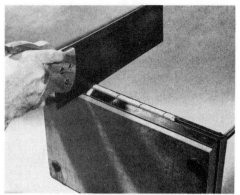

**7** Use a dull saw to make four unequally spaced cuts about ³⁄₃₂-in. deep in the spine of the collected sections. This is necessary before you sew the spines

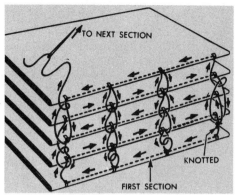

**8** Sew the assembled section together with the lockstitch shown above. This stitch is especially designed for book sewing and is described in the article

**9** Sewing thickens the spine, but pounding with a hammer or mallet will flatten it by embedding threads in the folds. Tap only on a protective paper

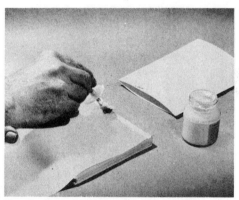

**10** To attach new endpapers, apply a ¼-in. strip of paste down the folded edge of outside sections. Then carefully fix the endpapers in place

*turn page*

loop of thread thus formed and draw it snug. When you come to the end of the thread, tie on another length so that the knot ends up inside a section. When the final section is sewed on, finish off with a couple of kettle stitches down the back and cut off the thread about 1 in. long. This will be glued down to the spine of the book.

**Step 9.** Sewing leaves the spine thicker than the rest because of the bulk of the thread. "Knock down the swell" with a mallet or hammer, embedding the threads in the folds.

#### new endpapers

**Step 10.** New endpapers may be made from regular endpaper stock, obtainable at any bookbinding supply house, or any other strong paper, even Kraft wrapping paper. The fold is made with the grain, and the folded sheet should be exactly the size of the body of the book. Protect-

ing the face of the book with a sheet of paper, apply a ¼-in. strip of paste down the folded edge. Then lay the endpaper over the body and rub it down. Turn the body over and attach the other endpaper in the same way. Let it dry under pressure.

**Step 11.** Normally, the book won't need trimming. However, if the sections are badly uneven, have a printer trim about ⅛ in. from all three open edges with a guillotine. Apply a thin coat of flexible glue or Liquid Cloth to the spine. (You can make flexible glue by adding 1½ teaspoonsful of glycerine to an ounce of liquid hide glue.)

Then, before the adhesive is wholly set, tap the spine into a rounded shape with the hammer. Push in the fore edge with your thumb while drawing the top sections toward you with the fingers.

**11** After applying flexible glue to the spine, tap it gently with a hammer or mallet into a rounded shape before the adhesive has set

**12** With the book clamped in angled backing jaws, turn edges of the sections outward with glancing blows. Tap gently and use paper to protect the sections

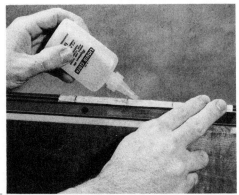

**13** Once shaping of the spine is complete apply a thin coat of flexible glue to it and rub it in well with your fingers. Wipe off excess glue

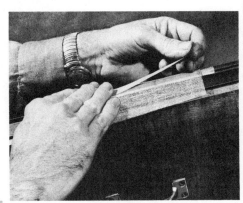

**14** After glue has been rubbed fully into the spine, rub cloth backing, or super, down into the glue. Then cover the backing with a strip of paper

*rebinding books, continued*

### completing the backing

**Step 12.** To complete the backing, place the body in the angled backing jaws of the press, leaving ³⁄₁₆ in. of the endpapers exposed on each side. The idea here is to turn over the sections from the middle toward each side, reforming the groove noted before you tore the book down. Draw the hammer toward you with each stroke, making glancing blows that tend to turn the fold-edges of the sections toward you. Work the full length of each side of the book until a smooth, rounded spine is obtained, with edges bent over against the metal jaws of the press.

**Step 13.** Apply a thin coat of flexible glue to the spine of the book and rub it in well with your fingers.

### preparing the super

**Step 14.** Prepare a piece of super (a mesh cloth) or crinoline, obtainable from a drygoods store. Unbleached muslin can also be used, or canton flannel, stiffened by dipping in a starch solution. Iron the flannel when dry. The super should be long enough to reach from tail kettle stitches to head kettle stitches and wide enough to overhang the book 1¼ in. on each side. Rub the cloth backing down into the glue. Now cut a strip of Kraft paper, or ordinary newspaper, as wide and as long as the book's spine, and glue it over the cloth.

**Step 15.** To cover the book, you will need bookcloth or Fabrikoid, obtainable from a bookbinder's supply house. (For this you can substitute paper, leatherette, or even automobile upholstering plastic in sheet form. If the upholstering plastic has a cloth backing, remove the cloth.) Do not use ordinary cloth or anything else that will let the glue soak through and spoil the appearance of the book.

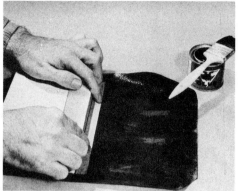

**15** When the bookcloth has been cut, position the body and boards on it and glue spine-size paper in place, fixing it firmly by applying pressure

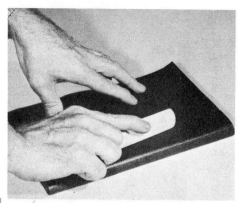

**16** With the body of the book in position, glue the bookcloth to the boards. Work out excess glue and fix the substances together by rubbing with a folder

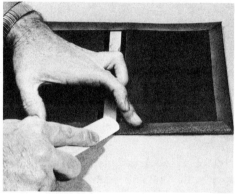

**17** Remove the case and turn excess cloth over the edges all around, making sure everything is taut. Squeeze out excess glue with the folder

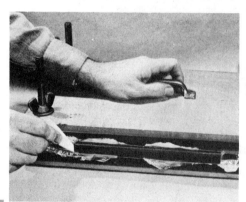

**18** Replace the body in the case and clamp the book in the grooving jaws of the press. Shape all of the corners and then let everything dry overnight

### cutting the boards

You can use the old boards or make new ones from mill board or heavy cardboard. Be sure to cut the boards with grain running from head to tail. Make them the same size as the old boards if the body wasn't trimmed; otherwise, make them as wide as the body and ¼ in. longer. When ⅛ in. is left at the back edge for the groove, the boards will overhang the fore edge ⅛ in. all around.

Cut the bookcloth to wrap completely around the book, plus ¾ in. extra at each end and ¾ in. along each side. Mark a rectangle the exact size that will be covered by the book on the inside face of the cloth, then coat it with thin, runny glue. If the glue is thick, thin it by heating in a pan of water.

Clip off all four corners of the cloth to within ⅛ in. of the corners of the rectangle.

### fixing the body

Lay the end board on the glued cloth in exact position, then position the body of the book on the board. Cut a strip of Kraft paper as wide and as long as the book spine and glue it to the bookcloth, as shown in the photo.

**Step 16.** Don't hurry! Glue sets slowly. Check everything for squareness as you go along. Lay on the front board so that it overhangs evenly all around, leaving a ⅛-in. groove between the back edge of the board and the turn-up on the book. Bring the cloth tightly over the back of the book, lay it down on the front board and rub it down with your folder. Use the rounded edge to rub in the groove. Work the folder from back edge toward fore edge and toward head and tail to work out any excess glue. A sheet of waxed paper placed under the board while you're working will· prevent the glue from running on the edges of

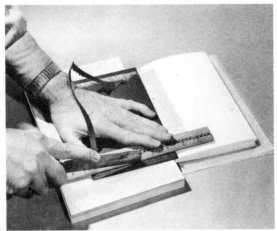

19 Use a straightedge and a sharp cutting tool to trim the excess turn-in on the boards (*not* the spine). Leave about ⅜ in. on all edges

20 Glue the boardpapers to the boards and place the completed book in the grooving jaws for a final 24-hr. pressing

*rebinding books, continued*

the book. Now, turn the book over and rub down the other side.

### removing the case

**Step 17.** Remove the case (as the cover is called) from the body and lay it board-side up on the table. Turn the cloth over the edge all around and rub down the turn-in, squeezing out all excess glue, which can be wiped up with a damp cloth.

**Step 18.** Return the body of the book carefully to the case. Place waxed paper or foil between the boardpapers and the boards and wrap another sheet around the book. Insert in the grooving jaws of the press and tighten the wingnuts. Tear the foil away from the back of the book and pick out and shape the corners of the cloth with a pointed folder or stick. Leave the book in the press overnight.

**Step 19.** Remove the book from the press and separate the case from the body. If the case is stuck along the edges of the back so that the body can't be freed, don't worry about it. The turn-in is trimmed only on the boards. Don't ever try to trim it across the spine, or you'll cut through the cloth and spoil the case. Mark the turn-in ⅜ in. wide around the open edges of each board and trim out with a sharp knife and straightedge. Pull out the excess cloth and discard it.

### glue and pressure

**Step 20.** Place newspaper under the boardpa-

per to protect the book and coat the face of the boardpaper with thin glue. Glue the super tab down to the boardpaper, but keep glue out of the groove. Close the cover on boardpaper, then open and rub the boardpaper down with your fingers.

Withdraw the newspaper, replace it with waxed paper or foil and close the cover, then glue the second boardpaper.

The book is now ready for a final pressing. Be sure to have waxed paper or foil between both boards and the book to prevent moisture from soaking through. Wrap waxed paper around the book and place it in the grooving jaws of press.

The title can be handlettered, typed, or printed if a small handpress is available, on a piece of colored artpaper. Glue the title to the back of the book and leave book in press at least 24 hrs.

To avoid breaking the back when the rebound book is opened, open it this way: Stand book on spine and let covers fall open. Open the book a few sheets at a time, a few at front, and rub them down in the groove; a few at the end, and rub them down.

Continue thus until the middle of the book is reached.

**See also:** book storage; clamps; glues; linoleum-block press; printing press.

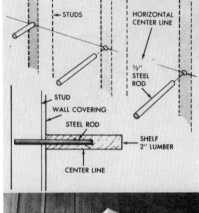

STUDS — HORIZONTAL CENTER LINE — ½" STEEL ROD — STUD — WALL COVERING — STEEL ROD — SHELF 2" LUMBER — CENTER LINE

# Floating bookshelves

BY  R.  J.  DeCRISTOFORO

■ WITH NO VISIBLE means of support, these floating planks are quite "shelf-sufficient" and will hold their weight in books without any danger.

The shelves are simply edge-drilled to slip over ½-in. steel rods projecting from holes drilled through the wall into the studs.

Despite the care needed to bore the holes true so the shelves and rods will register, it's actually a fast way to erect wall shelves and a most attractive one. First, with the aid of a level, draw horizontal lines on the wall at the heights where you want the shelves. Then, after locating the first stud by tapping the wall with a hammer to get the solid sound that indicates a stud, measure across the wall at 16-in. intervals to spot the centers of the other studs. Drill ½-in. holes 3 in. deep in each stud where the lines intersect, drive in the steel rods and mark the shelves for registering holes in the edges by resting them on the rods as shown in the photo.

**See also:** bookbinding; children's furniture; **gifts,** Christmas; remodeling; remodeling ideas; vacation homes; weekend projects.

# Shelves that grow

BY DAVE SWARTWOUT

■ MOST PEOPLE can't keep up with their collection of books. By the time they build a new bookcase, their library has already outgrown it. Paperbacks, especially, proliferate like rabbits. But if you build from the plans on the next page, you've licked the problem. When one two-shelf unit fills up, you just stack another identical unit on top. You might say the sky's the limit, since you can stack to the ceiling—but if you go up too high, it's best to tie the top unit to the wall.

The design is ingenious in several respects: A single unit looks fine by itself, and the protruding end panels serve as built-in bookends for the top shelf. The legs of the next unit slip over these panels to set the new unit's ends flush with

the old—so that no matter how many units you stack, you'll have solid, gapless panels running down each end.

The best thing about this design is the ease of construction. You merely cut 1 x 8 shelving into 3-ft. lengths and bevel each corner to take ¼-in. posts. The backs and ends are pre-finished hardboard; they are glued into the posts' grooves with epoxy cement. In finishing your bookcase, paint all rear faces of the end panels to match the shelves before you assemble them, leaving a narrow strip along the edges for gluing into the posts. As another final step, it's a good idea to roughen the finished edge of the hardboard panels before you glue them.

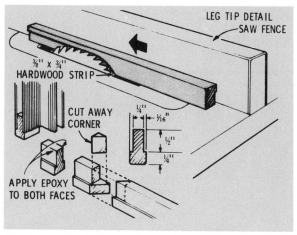

LEG TIP DETAIL
SAW FENCE

⅜" x ¾"
HARDWOOD STRIP

CUT AWAY
CORNER

APPLY EPOXY
TO BOTH FACES

¼"  ¹⁄₁₆"
½"
¼"

The feet for the bottom unit come from T-shaped hardwood strip. Fasten the shelves along the edges of the back panels with epoxy and screws; a notched spacer (below) keeps them parallel

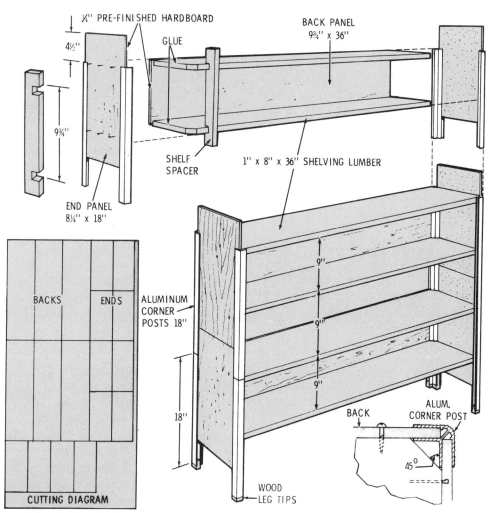

¼" PRE-FINISHED HARDBOARD

4½"

GLUE

BACK PANEL
9¾" x 36"

9¾"

SHELF
SPACER

END PANEL
8¼" x 18"

1" x 8" x 36" SHELVING LUMBER

BACKS     ENDS

ALUMINUM
CORNER
POSTS 18"

9"

9"

9"

18"

CUTTING DIAGRAM

WOOD
LEG TIPS

BACK

ALUM.
CORNER POST

45°

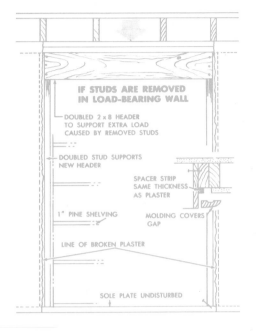

IF STUDS ARE REMOVED
IN LOAD-BEARING WALL

DOUBLED 2 x 8 HEADER
TO SUPPORT EXTRA LOAD
CAUSED BY REMOVED STUDS

DOUBLED STUD SUPPORTS
NEW HEADER

SPACER STRIP
SAME THICKNESS
AS PLASTER

1" PINE SHELVING

MOLDING COVERS
GAP

LINE OF BROKEN PLASTER

SOLE PLATE UNDISTURBED

Two methods are shown here. Above, only wall surface is removed, and shelves are notched to let in studs. For stud-less bookshelf, you cut away studs within the opening, but if wall is load-bearing you must treat opening like a doorway (left) and install extra supports

# In-a-wall bookcase

BY HANK CLARK

◼ FREE-STANDING BOOKSHELVES, shoved against a wall, seldom look as if they belong. Unless the wall is perfectly square with the floor, the bookcase leans away, leaving a gap behind. And there's a limit to how high you can stack such shelves before yelling "Tim-m-m-ber!"

But worst of all, in today's cramped rooms bookcases are space-grabbers, drawing the wall further forward.

All these problems are solved if you sink your shelves *into* the wall, taking advantage of the 4-in. hollow behind the plaster (or wallboard). The diagrams above show how much space you save with standard 8-in. shelves: Recessed, they eat up only *half* as much floor space.

This trick applies to partition walls only, of course. You'd never cut into an *exterior* wall because of insulation and vapor-barrier problems.

354

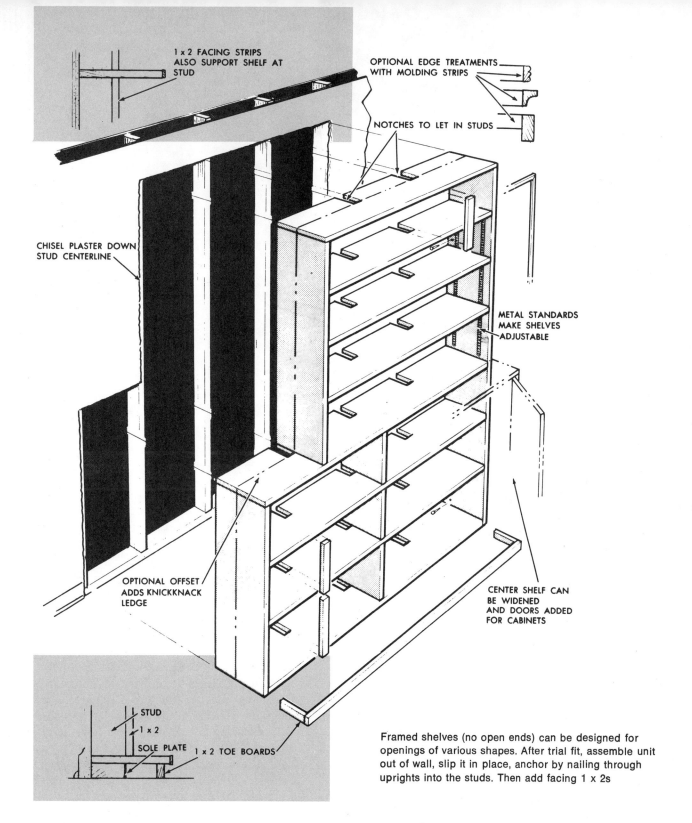

1 x 2 FACING STRIPS ALSO SUPPORT SHELF AT STUD

OPTIONAL EDGE TREATMENTS WITH MOLDING STRIPS

NOTCHES TO LET IN STUDS

CHISEL PLASTER DOWN STUD CENTERLINE

METAL STANDARDS MAKE SHELVES ADJUSTABLE

OPTIONAL OFFSET ADDS KNICKKNACK LEDGE

CENTER SHELF CAN BE WIDENED AND DOORS ADDED FOR CABINETS

STUD
1 x 2
SOLE PLATE
1 x 2 TOE BOARDS

Framed shelves (no open ends) can be designed for openings of various shapes. After trial fit, assemble unit out of wall, slip it in place, anchor by nailing through uprights into the studs. Then add facing 1 x 2s

But most homes have plenty of unused space along partition walls—and some of these walls aren't even load-bearing. In such cases, you can simply trim away the studs within the opening. But where the wall is a structural part of the house—supporting ceiling joists—you'll actually *add* strength by notching your shelves around the studs you bring to light when you cut away the finish wall.

Since these studs are rarely top-grade lumber, you may have to dress them up a bit. When the books are in place, only the front edges of the studs will show, so facing strips, glued on and painted, are an easy solution. If the rear face of the opposite wall is naked lath, you'll want to mask it with panels of ⅛-in. hardboard, fitted between the studs, before you insert the shelf assembly.

355

With a little bit of practice, you can try catching the
returning stick by clapping it between your hands

# Build
# a boomerang

BY DALE RUDOLPH

HOVER, THEN SWOOP BACK TO FEET

FIGURE EIGHT (TOP VIEW)

When you're an expert at regular return tosses, you may
want to try the stunts that an Austrailian aborigine
uses to test his skill as shown above

■ IF THE SPACE AGE began when man first tried
to duplicate the flight of birds, it's not very new.
And it didn't start when Dedalus stuck feathers
to his arms with wax. It goes far back into the
cavern of pre-history, to the heart of the world's
bleakest continent, and starts with a stick.

Perhaps the Space Age dates from that day an
Australian aborigine first whittled the crotch of
an acacia tree into a flat, sickle-shaped blade, for
use as a hunting weapon. (One can imagine his
surprise when he flung his stick at some scamper-
ing animal only to find the thing arcing around
through the air to come spinning *back* at him!)

At any rate, these nomadic people—who
through the centuries have made virtually no

other contribution to civilization—have developed their skills with the flying stick into an art
that makes most of our model flying look pale
and fussy. The primitive Australian can throw
his boomerang in the most erratic, yet precise
patterns. He can make it fly like a runaway saw
blade at a forward speed in excess of 50 m.p.h.
for over 100 yards, then loop around, lift 150 ft.
in the air, circle up to five times and finally knife
into the ground at his feet; or he can make the
stick scribe a broad figure eight in the sky and
then return docilely to his waiting hands; he can
even cause it to dive to the earth and bounce up
again with enough spin to return as if there'd
been no interruption.

This skill comes from a great deal of practice,
and the aborigine boy starts his training as soon
as he learns to walk. Upon reaching manhood,
he graduates from a toy stick to a deadly curved

**booster, FM tuner:** see tuners, FM

356

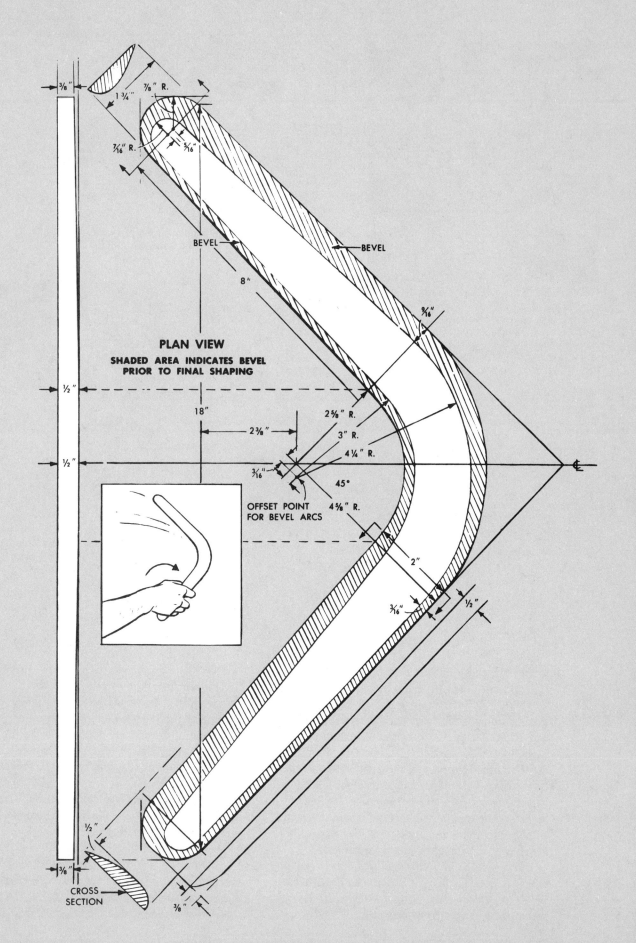

PLAN VIEW

SHADED AREA INDICATES BEVEL
PRIOR TO FINAL SHAPING

BEVEL

BEVEL

8"

⅜"

1¾"

⅞" R.

⁷⁄₁₆" R.

⁵⁄₁₆"

½"

18"

2⅜"

½"

⁹⁄₁₆"

2⅝" R.

3" R.

4¼" R.

45°

4⅝" R.

³⁄₁₆"

OFFSET POINT
FOR BEVEL ARCS

2"

³⁄₁₆"

½"

½"

⅜"

CROSS
SECTION

⅜"

357

Final shaping is done with a wood rasp, to convert the flat bevel into the smoothly rounded half-teardrop cross section sketched on the previous page

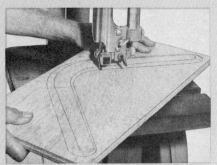

A jigsaw is the fastest way to cut the outline after laying out the pattern on a piece of ½-in. exterior-grade plywood. Sand to the exact pattern after cutting

Rough shaping consists of cutting away corners of upper face to remove the shaded area in the sketch on the preceding page. Use a blockplane or a spokeshave

Brush on a coat of sealer and two coats of a good lacquer. Rub down the entire boomerang with steel wool and apply a coat or two of wax. Rewax as often as necessary

*build a boomerang, continued*

missile which he makes from a tree he must select and cut down for himself.

There are three main types of boomerangs: the returning stick, the hunting stick and the war stick. All three are curved (in shapes from a shallow V to a deep U), but the latter two don't return. Largest and most lethal is the war boomerang. Up to 5 ft. long, this giant is thrown with both hands, wickedly maiming anything in its path. The hunting boomerang is middle-sized, with a maximum range of over 200 yards. It's capable of disabling a full-grown kangaroo.

But the popular returning stick, one type of which is detailed here, is strictly for fun. It can be 18 to 36 in. long, with a 90 to 120-degree spread between its V-shaped arms.

The plans provided are only a suggestion. After experimentation, you can vary the angle and length of the arms. The vital thing is the shaping of the airfoils. Theoretically, the greater the height of the camber, the greater the lift. And remember that the pattern given is for a right-hand boomerang. For left hand, the bevels are reversed.

Leave the bottom face flat, with only a slight rounding of the edges. Then sand and finish all surfaces as smooth as possible.

To throw, hold the stick vertical, the beveled face toward you. Grasp either arm, and throw overhand with a quick snap of the wrists. All it takes is patient experimentation.

**See also:** archery; baseball; marksmanship; targets.

You can wash storm windows without stooping if you build a simple wash rack from scrap lumber.

Stop pump noises from being transmitted into the house by using a good grade of hose instead of a pipe to couple the main supply line to the pump.

Try using paper clips to fasten notes and papers to a file spike. This way you can remove any one paper without disturbing the others.

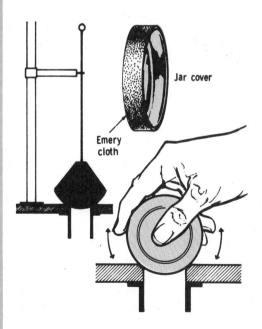

Corrosion on the ball stopper seat can often cause leaky flush tanks. Resurface the seat using a jar cover wrapped with emery cloth. The cover should be the same diameter as the ball.

# Buy the
# right boot

BY  PAT  SNOOK

■ TOP QUALITY LEATHER that is properly tanned, plus superior construction and oil treating, are the things that go into a good boot to insure durability and comfort. These factors can make or break your next outdoor excursion.

Ignore these qualities when buying a boot and you'll pay for it with wet, tired feet, and count your hiking miles in blisters.

The best boot leather is "full grain," which means that when the hide was tanned, only the hair was shaved off the outside. Lower grade hides are "corrected" by removing the thin outer layer of the skin to eliminate blemishes, scars and other imperfections. Unfortunately, when the tough outer surface is ground off, along with the blemishes, the leather loses much of its durability and water resistance. Since corrected leather has an artificial finish, it can often be detected by its unnatural gloss and smoothness. Full grain leather has a dull sheen. Another way to identify full grain leather is to look closely

at the surface. If the hide wasn't corrected, you will be able to see the tiny pore holes. Often, too, full grain will be stamped as such; it's a quality mark.

The leather itself should be soft and supple to the touch. Chrome tanning and oil treating both contribute a great deal to the water resistance and durability of the material. Chrome tanning may be indicated by stamping on the leather or may be pointed out in literature or a sales tag on the boot. If it isn't, check along the exposed cut edges, such as at the eyelet facing. If the leather is chrome-tanned, you will probably be able to see a layer of greenish tinge just under the dye layer.

The best quick check for top quality oil treating is to take the boot and crease the leather sharply. With good oiled leather, this will produce a white streak along the point of the crease. The streak should vanish when you rub it lightly.

Where styling is concerned, the "right" boot depends on how and where you'll use it.

The shoepac, made with watertight rubber bottom and leather upper, is designed for wet snow or shallow marsh. It is ideal for hunting, but for warm weather or long distance walk-

Semi-moccasin style has the quarter extending down to the sole. Triple stitching in this model is a sign of quality. The wedge sole is ideal for mud walking or boating

A rubber bottom and leather top make the shoepac an excellent hunting boot when the hunter hikes through mud and marsh. It is a warm and waterproof boot

The full moccasin has the vamp cut from a single piece of leather. This style has a full back stay, a heel and lug sole, and an 8-in. top. It's ideal on rocks

ing, it is uncomfortable. Unless a completely waterproof bottom is an absolute necessity, the disadvantages far outweigh the advantages.

An engineer boot is almost the opposite. Its loose-fitting upper and absence of laces make it cool and quite comfortable. In some styles, with extra heavy leather in the quarters, it's an ideal solution to the problem of poisonous snakes. Its main disadvantage for general purpose use is that the design is such that it gives little support for negotiating rough terrain.

By far the most popular all-around boot design is the bird shooter. Whether it is beefed up for foot support and called a climbing boot, cut low and called a boat shoe, made in a lightweight model and called a hiking boot, the basic design is all the same.

Almost all bird shooters have what is called "moccasin toe" construction, meaning that the toepiece is a separate piece of leather sewn to the vamp to form a more comfortable boxlike toe shape. On the very high quality boots you will find the toepiece joined to the vamp with an overlap type of construction.

The finest boots you can buy have what is called a true moccasin vamp. This means that the vamp is cut from a single piece of leather and runs from one edge of the toepiece down the side, all the way across the bottom, and back up the other side. The imitation moccasin also has a one-piece vamp, but it only extends down from the toepiece to the mid-sole where it is sewn or "welted" to the sole.

There are also full and semimoccasin types. The full style has a vamp running back to the heel; the semimoccasin extends only a bit behind the front edge of the quarter. In the semi-, the quarter comes all the way down to the sole. The full style has two advantages. It is more watertight and more comfortable, because the seam that joins the quarter to the vamp is up along the side of the boot.

Top-line boots will have stitched reinforcing at the stress points where the toepiece is joined to the vamp and quarter. Good boots have a sturdy rivet here.

Another mark of a good boot is a backstay that runs all the way from the heel to the top of the back of the boot. Double or triple stitching is important here also. A pull loop at the top of the backstay is of no particular value except with a pair of hard-to-get-into boots.

The type of sole on a boot should depend mostly on the use you intend for the boot. The

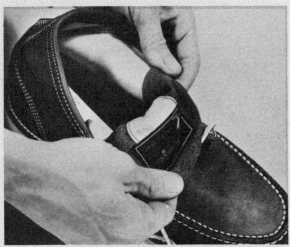

Among the signs of quality in a boot are the bellows-type tongue that extends above the boot top and the added patch of leather on the instep. Superior chrome tanning usually is noted on the manufacturer's label

Although most bootmakers contend that a full glove-leather lining adds nothing to a boot but weight, it's a pretty sure indication that the rest of the workmanship in this boot is of the very best quality

*buy the right boot, continued*

wedge sole is popular for upland game shooting where much of the walking may be in muddy fields. While the completely flat bottom is less likely to collect mud, it is heavier and gives slightly less traction on slippery surfaces. Hikers like a heeled boot because of the increased grip and lighter weight and, to them, mud is rarely a problem. Both of these sole styles are designed for extensive walking, so good models of either should have most of the sole flex between toe and front of the arch. To check, pick the boot up and bend the sole.

A boot that is to be used for climbing or hiking on rock or loose shale should have a lug sole. Metal calks are useless because they skid on the rock. Climbing boots should also have a considerably stiffer and less flexible sole, as should a general-purpose work boot.

Another point of support that is very important to check is the counter. This is the cuplike stiffener in the rear of the boot. It serves as sort of a cradle for your heel. A good counter will feel quite rigid when you squeeze the heel of the boot and it should extend about two inches up the back of the boot.

Heights, measured from the floor to top of the back of the boot, run from 6 to 18 in., although 8 or 9 in. is about standard for a hunting boot. Super-tall models are good for snake country. Climbing boots run 6 to 9 in. and boat shoes are usually 6 in.

A low boot isn't much good in country where there are low weeds, sand, or small loose stones. Anything less than 8 in. in this kind of country means spending half your time dumping out the garbage.

During the past few years, several manufacturers have introduced insulated styles of leather boots. For the most part these are quite effective for use in temperatures down to about the zero mark. Since the construction of an insulated boot is almost identical to that of an uninsulated model, boot quality can be analyzed on the same basis for both. The only drawbacks to insulated boots are that, once you get them wet, they take forever to dry out and they are quite a bit heavier than conventional models.

Weight, incidentally, is quite an important factor if you are going to be covering a lot of ground in your boots. The average pair of lightweight 9-in. bird shooters weighs about 3 lbs. A heavy pair of insulated boots can weigh 4 lbs. or more. If you figure the number of steps involved in ten miles of deer hunting that extra half pound per boot suddenly mounts up to the fact that you have lifted an extra, and possibly unnecessary, five and a half tons during your day of hunting or hiking in the wilds.

**See also:** camping; fishing; mountain climbing; packs, camping; pheasant hunting; shotguns; sleeping bags; tents.

Save those small bags of silica gel which you find packed with photo equipment and instant color film. These crystals are super-efficient in soaking up moisture and can be used in the workshop to protect fine tools from rust. Just place a bag or two in any tool box, preferably not in direct contact with the tools themselves. When the crystals change color, it means they have absorbed all the moisture they can. To reactivate, dry the bags in a low oven.

Always ready when you need it, a simple swing-out bench stop can be made from a large U-bolt. Just drive two large staples into one edge of the bench to support the bolt and bore a hole in the top of the bench to take one of the legs when the bolt is swung into position. Be sure to position the hole so that the bolt will be at right angles to the edge of the bench when it's swung over to act as a stop.

One of the handiest soldering aids for the workshop is a pair of strips cut from an asbestos shingle. When used as pads to hold work to be soldered in a vise, they will prevent the heat from leaking off in the vise jaws.

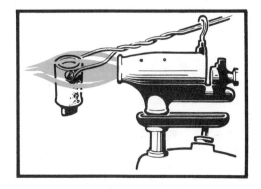

A solder-dipped pigtail joint makes a fine electrical connection, but it's seldom handy to dip a pigtail in a regular ladle, especially if it's in a crowded ceiling box. A miniature pot for such use can be made from a ½-in. pipe coupling with a plug in one end. Tap it for a couple of machine screws to attach a handle bent from No. 9 steel wire.

PIGGY BANK

GIANT FUNNEL

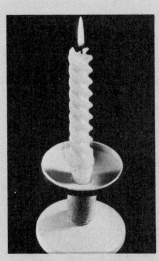

CANDLESTICK

CLOTHESPIN JUG

# Bleach-bottle bonanza

BY WILLARD AND ELMA WALTNER

**bouncer:** see tumbler
**bowhunting:** see archery

THERE'S NO limit to the number of projects that can be made with no-rust, easy-to-cut plastic bleach jugs and detergent bottles. Most of the items shown here are self-explanatory. The candlestick is made by cementing the tops of two detergent bottles together, mouth-to-mouth, and then running a dowel through the necks and wrapping it with cord. To make the clothespin jug, cut an opening in the front and slit the

SAILBOAT

PLANTER

SCOURING-PAD CUP

SUPER SCOOP

TOOL CADDY

handle to hang on the clothesline. Ballast the boat with a little sand, pouring melted paraffin over this to hold it in place. Decorate the items according to personal taste; the picnic set, for example, could be brightened with decals, while the planter might be finished with metallic paint.

**See also:** boat repair; candles; gifts, Christmas; novelties; toys.

PICNIC SET

Only three easily "spotted" angles of delivery will take care of 90 percent of the pin combinations you'll meet.

Learning to use them can add 20 points to your average. Here's how you can do it.

# Play the bowling angles

BY BOB KELLY

▉ ARE YOU A "strike-happy" bowler? Most bowlers are. If their first ball fails to clear the lane, they lose interest in the second delivery, and they miss spares from simple lack of interest—or from lack of knowledge of the easy formula for picking up spares.

How important is the spare to your final score? If you bowled a line, downing nine pins each time and "picking the cherry" with each second delivery, your final score would be a fat 190 without rolling a single strike!

The average more-than-occasional bowler bowls 154, getting two or three strikes and leaving three or four open frames in each line. He picks up four or five spares in the line during the game. But if he'd take the time to learn the facts about picking up spares, Mr. Average Bowler could pick them up around 90 percent of the time—and boost his score by 20 pins.

What's the secret? It's simple. Barring splits or freak hits, one of three basic angles of delivery will pick up every spare in the book. And they're predictable enough that you can learn to spot-bowl them as easily as you can learn to spot-bowl for the strike pocket. No need to change your form or speed. Just learn to position yourself and start the ball over the right target spot on the alley, and the spares come tumblin' down.

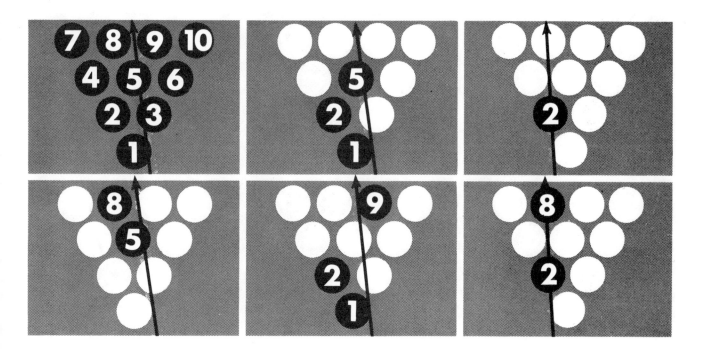

# THE "STRIKE BALL" SPARE

THE FIRST THREE common spares are easy —you can pick them up with exactly the same delivery that you use for the 1-3 strike pocket, since half the balls you roll are aimed at that pocket. Start with your feet in the normal strike position, and deliver the ball over your normal strike target on the alley.

The experts say it's best to forget the urge to aim toward the left on the 1-2-5; your consistent strike delivery will be more likely to connect, and if you overcorrect to the left, you could miss the 5-pin. The 5-8 doesn't offer as much temptation to the would-be sharpshooters.

With the 1-2-9 spare, accuracy becomes very important, since a ball too far right will send the king pin across without taking out the 2, and a ball too far left will miss the 9.

The same delivery picks up the single 2 and the 2-8 spares, but for a sure hit, don't aim from your usual position. Position your feet a pin's width (about 4½ inches) to the left of their usual starting spot, and bowl over a spot the same distance to the left of your usual strike-ball target. The ball follows the same path, adjusted leftward, but otherwise the delivery is the same as for a strike.

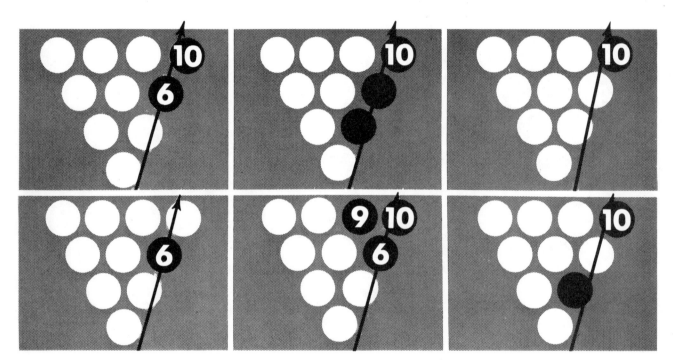

# THE RIGHT-SIDE SPARE

TOUGHEST OF THE common spares for the right-handed bowler are those on the right side of the lane. A standard delivery from the right side gets a narrow sweep of the standing pins, and a natural curve or hook too far to the right can drop into the gutter before it reaches the pins.

To play it smart, move as far as possible to your left, face the pins, and bowl cross-lane. Unless your curve or hook is a natural one, switch to a straight ball. The result is a ball that moves down the 1-10 side of the pin cluster, leaving a maximum margin for error.

For the six common situations shown here,

the delivery path is identical; the ball is aimed to cover the 6-pin. And if it's on target, there's little left to luck and pin action; the ball covers the spots well.

One variation of the right side spare delivery is needed when a light hit leaves the head pin standing, too, as in a 1-3-6-10. With that situation, use the extreme left-side delivery, but aim to hit the 1-3 pocket, heavy on the 3 side.

Again, with a single 6 or 10-pin standing, it's better to stay with the same right-side spot delivery instead of an aimed ball. If your "automatic" delivery is right, it'll go down.

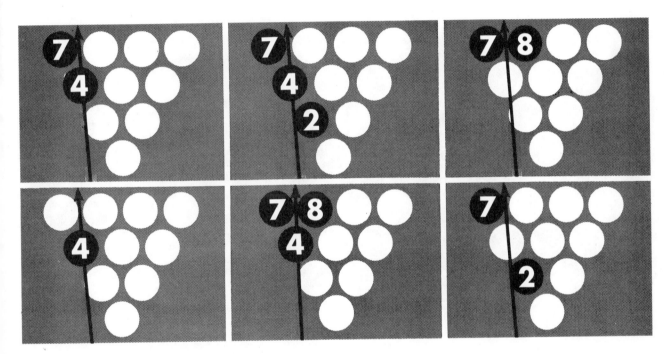

# THE LEFT-SIDE SPARE

EASIER FOR RIGHT-HANDED bowlers, the left-side spares allow a more natural delivery to sweep down the 1-7 side of the cluster, allow a sharper cross-lane delivery angle, and let you use a curve or hook more effectively than on the right-hand spares. But for best results, move as far right as possible, face the pins, and bowl across a target that will put the ball on the 4-pin.

On the 7-8 spare, the ball is only two inches wider than the space between the pins. But if you aim on the 4-pin target, you'll split them right down the middle. It's that advantage that prevents the 7-8 from being classified here as a

split, as are the 4-5 and 5-6 leaves. But in some areas, the 7-8 is still called a "small split."

The pin clusters shown on all these pages are not, of course, all the possible situations you might face, but they're the most common for right-hand bowlers. (If you're a southpaw, your leaves—and everything else—will be reversed; you'll have your easiest time with right-hand spares, and should switch to a straight ball for those on the left side.)

We haven't tried to show the exact foot position and target to bowl over, since lanes may vary somewhat in the position of their markings.

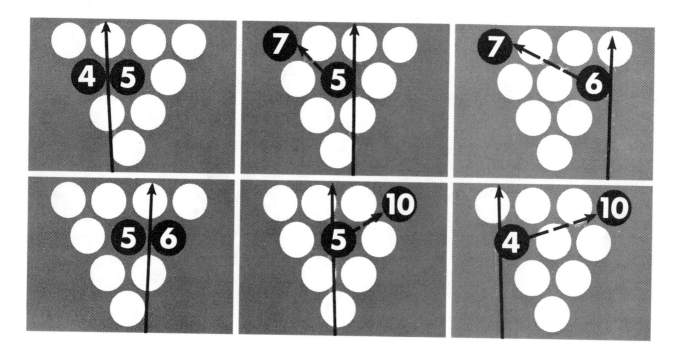

# THE EXCEPTIONS—SPLITS

SPLITS, OR RAILROADS—pins left standing with no other pins between or in front of them—are the toughest shots in bowling and the least amenable to formula treatment. But don't let them worry you; any split can be converted.

Since split conversion requires your steadiest and most accurate delivery, most of the pros recommend that you start from a comfortable spot just to the right of center and aim the ball straight toward the contact point with whatever delivery is easiest for you. Since wide splits are almost as demanding as billiards, your ability to shave the edge of a pin is all-important.

The 4-5 and 5-6 situations are classed as splits even though both pins can be struck by the ball at the same time. With only two inches of hitting area between the pins, a straight-ahead, dead-center shot is considered best.

Three splits aren't shown. The 6-7-10 and 4-7-10 are handled just like the 6-7 and the 4-10; the corner pin is automatic if you hit the front pin properly.

The other one? The 7-10. For this impossible-to-predict, freak or trick shot, go for one single rather than take a chance on missing both. If you can get both pins every time, go on the stage!

**See also:** billiards; games, adult; pool tables.

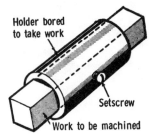

You can chuck a piece of square stock in a three-prong chuck if you bore a hole in round stock of the right size to secure the square stock, and hold it with a set screw.

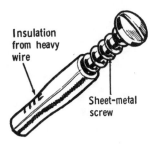

Insulation from No. 6 or 8 wire makes a good improvised screw anchor.

A spiral nail is a quick substitute for a broken ⅛-in. drill bit.

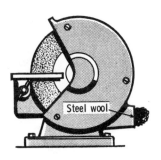

Steel wool makes an efficient throwaway grit catcher for the exhaust chute on your bench grinder.

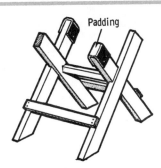

Prevent skinned knuckles when sawing firewood by tacking pieces of inner tubing over the ends of the crossed uprights of the log cradle.

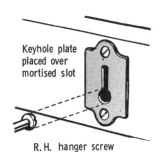

A hidden hanger for a picture frame can be made by cutting a vertical slot in the frame and covering it with an inverted keyhole plate.

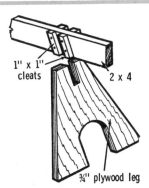

This collapsible sawhorse made from a length of 2 x 4 and ¾-in. plywood is strong, but comes apart easily for storage.

Keep a spare wedge handy when splitting wood. Then if one gets stuck, you can free it by splitting the log the other way.

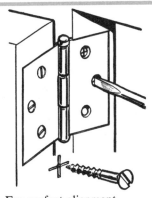

For perfect alignment when mounting a hinge, use a screwdriver with a blade which matches the diameter of the holes. Two taps mark the center.

This is a challenging project for the
advanced woodworker who likes to
sink his chisel into a fine piece
of lathe work

# Four seasons bowl

BY JOHN BURROUGHS

To ORIENTALS, calligraphy—fine brush and ink handwriting—is an esteemed art. The smoothly flowing symbols of the Asiatic languages have beauty in themselves, a decorative value apart from the meaning expressed. Families in Japan, China and Korea hang expertly brushed mottoes or verses on the walls of their homes, just as we hang paintings.

The individual written characters, picturesque even to Westerners, evolved from age-old Chinese picture writing. Unlike the letters of our own alphabet, which indicate sounds, oriental language-characters at one time portrayed ideas, and so were called ideographs. But through the centuries, the primitive picture-symbols have become so stylized that it is no longer easy to recognize what they represent. In a sense they have become abstract designs.

The oriental symbols representing the four seasons of the year can be utilized to create a striking ornamental motif for a woodworking project. They are particularly eye-catching when

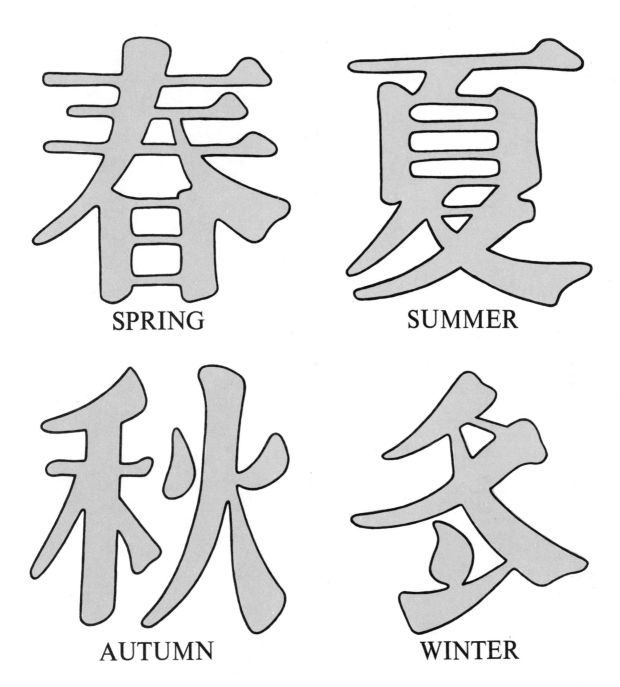

春
SPRING

夏
SUMMER

秋
AUTUMN

冬
WINTER

carved in relief as was done on this stunning lathe-turned fruit bowl.

To make the blank for turning, the edges of eight pieces of 1-in.-thick walnut stock are mitered on a table saw at an exact angle of 22½ deg. This is most important since the fine craftsmanship of the finished bowl depends largely on the fit of the segment joints. The segments are glued to each other and to an octagonal bottom, which likewise must be accurately cut. Because strong joints are essential in this project it is best to use a resorcinol or plastic resin glue. A band clamp makes it easy to hold the pieces snugly while the glue is drying, but if you lack this tool,

some strong twine can serve as a substitute. After the glue has dried thoroughly, attach the blank to a lathe faceplate, being careful that the screws do not poke through the ¾-in. bottom. Operate the lathe at low speed while first working the blank into the round. Then increase the speed for the finishing cuts in turning it into a smooth cylinder, inside and out. A ⅛-in.-high band is left on the outside to provide for the raised designs. The blank's glue lines divide this band into eight segments, just right to accommodate two sets of spring-summer-autumn-winter ideographs. The four seasons symbols are shown actual size and may be traced directly

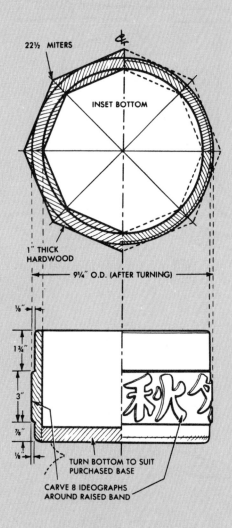

22½ MITERS

INSET BOTTOM

1" THICK
HARDWOOD

9¼" O.D. (AFTER TURNING)

⅛"

1¾"

3"

⅞"

⅛"

TURN BOTTOM TO SUIT
PURCHASED BASE

CARVE 8 IDEOGRAPHS
AROUND RAISED BAND

Sturdy twine effectively holds together the eight segments of the four seasons fruit bowl while the glue dries. Be certain that the alignment of the segments remains correct after the cord is tightened

*four seasons bowl, continued*

from the encyclopedia for transferring to the bowl. The best way to hold the bowl for carving the symbols is to leave it attached to the lathe faceplate. Relief-carving the designs is simply a matter of incising the outlines and gouging the background flush with the bowl's rim-band. The edges of the carving tools should of course be kept as keen as possible so that the cuts will be clean and the symbols will stand out sharply. Though you may never before have tried your

hand at carving you are not likely to encounter any difficulty if you work slowly and make light, shallow cuts. Since the final appearance of the fruit bowl is a direct result of the care used in smoothing the surface, it is important to do a meticulous sanding job. The areas around the symbols are difficult to sand, but your efforts will be well rewarded.

The bowl may be finished in various ways, but rubbed varnish is perhaps the most attractive

The easy way to carve the symbols is to leave the bowl in the lathe after completing the turning. The bowl is held steady, yet may be revolved by hand so the area being carved is in the most comfortable position

choice. The first step is to apply a coat of sealer which is allowed to dry thoroughly and then sanded with a 4/0 or even finer paper. After sanding, a tack rag should be used to wipe the surface of the bowl so that no dust will be imbedded in the rubbing varnish which is next applied. The best results are obtained with spray equipment, but if this is unavailable, a satisfactory job may be done with a high quality varnish brush. At least four coats should be applied,

with a light sanding and thorough use of the tack rag between coats. Allow three days for drying before polishing with pumice and water.

The base shown with the bowl wasn't homemade. It's an imported carved-wood vase stand of a type sold by many stores dealing in oriental novelties.

**See also:** candlestick; carving; cheese board; novelties; routing; tiki god; whittling; woodworking.

# For the boy craftsman

BY FRANK N. STEPHANY

Three practical projects
for youngsters

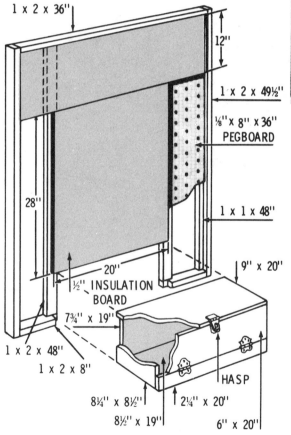

1 x 2 x 36"

12"

1 x 2 x 49½"

⅛" x 8" x 36"
PEGBOARD

28"

1 x 1 x 48"

20"
½" INSULATION
BOARD

9" x 20"

7¾" x 19"

1 x 2 x 48"

1 x 2 x 8"

8¼" x 8½"      2¼" x 20"

HASP

8½" x 19"      6" x 20"

CHEST MADE OF ½" PLYWOOD

---

## TREASURE BOARD STRONGBOX

◾ GIVE YOUR BEDROOM an individual stamp with this combination wall rack for sports equipment, bulletin board, trophy shelf and strongbox. Nailed right into the frame, so nobody can walk off with it, is a lockable chest for cash and treasured items you can't leave around loose.

To make the frame, assemble the 1 x 2s flat on a floor, using glue and finishing nails. Set the five outer pieces on edge, but not the two in the center that back up the meeting edges of the three vertical panels. Form a rabbet to support the outer edges of the pegboard by tacking 1 x 1 strips on the inner faces of the side members.

Cut up a sheet of insulation board (the kind with a prefinished face is best) into two panels and glue these to the backing strips. After nailing the pegboard to the frame, you can provide a finishing touch by butting a molding strip along the exposed edges of the center insulation board panel and on down the sides of the box.

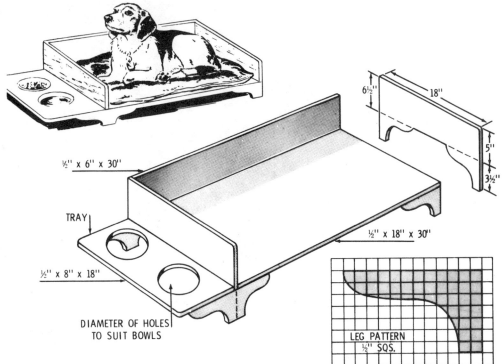

½'' x 6'' x 30''

TRAY

½'' x 8'' x 18''

DIAMETER OF HOLES
TO SUIT BOWLS

6½''  18''

5''

3½''

½'' x 18'' x 30''

LEG PATTERN
½'' SQS.

## DOG BED AND FEEDER

■ EVEN IF YOUR pooch has the run of the house, he'll appreciate a place of his own. This snug bed keeps him up off drafty floors; the attached tray makes his water bowl tip-proof and anchors his food dish so he won't have to chase it as he eats.

Make the unit from ½-in. plywood. If an 18 x 30-in.-size sleeping platform is too cramped for your dog (measure the area he needs when he's lying on the floor), add a few inches to both

dimensions. You can adapt the width of the tray to the size of your dog's bowls. These should be the type with a flanged or turned edge.

Once you've laid out the right end, you can use it as a pattern for the left end, cutting the latter off at the dotted line. Except for the attached legs on the right end, the leg pattern is used to cut separate members (it's doubled at the left) which are glued and screwed flush with the long edges of the bed and tray panels.

## BAMBOO WIND HARP

■ STIRRED BY a breeze, these random-sized pieces of bamboo strike and brush one another to produce a musical sound. Vary the lengths from 6 to 10 in., sawing the ends at 45-deg. angles in a miter box. Clamp each section for cross-drilling a hole ¼ in. from the end. Pass twine through and hang the pieces about ¼ in. apart from a horizontal section, adjusting the relationships of short to long to create the most pleasing sounds.

When you try to feed a cord through the horizontal section, for hanging, you'll doubtless find free passage blocked by a web across each section joint. If you have no facilities for end-drilling this long a piece, you can make yourself a needle by bending a tight eye at one end of a heavy wire. Sharpen and heat the other end so it will burn its way through the webs.

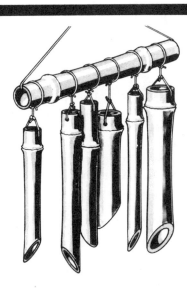

**See also:** bicycles; boomerang; doghouse; games, children's; kites; magic; parade floats; play bouncers; playground equipment; puppet theaters; road racing, model; sleds; stick-model planes; stilts; toboggan; toys; tree houses; unicycle.

To check for leaks in a wheel cylinder, just peel the rubber boot back a bit from each end with a screwdriver. A trickle of fluid tells the sad story: Fluid is getting past the pistons, shown in drawing at the right

# Give your brakes a break

BY MORTON J. SCHULTZ

■ WHEN YOU GO to have a brake job done, you may be faced with two figures as different as male and female. One mechanic may want $10.95; another, $60.

And in scanning the estimates, you may find that on paper both proposed jobs are just about identical—"check linings, check springs, check wheel cylinders, check drums . . ."

In short, one price may seem too low for quality, while the other could hit your pocketbook quite hard.

Can you do the work yourself? To a degree—yes! Some parts of the job involve special equipment and more knowhow than is generally realized. You'd best leave those to a pro. However, other aspects, such as master cylinder and wheel cylinder work, are fairly simple. Why not tackle these yourself?

Result: By saving money on half the job, you can afford the best mechanic in town for the other, more critical half.

First step in a complete brake overhaul is an inspection of the master cylinder. This part is

really an assembly consisting of two sections—a fluid reservoir and a cylinder, in which a piston slides. This piston is operated by a push rod which is connected to the brake pedal (see the drawing at right, p. 379).

Stepping on the brake pedal shoves the piston forward. The piston primary cup closes the compensating port, blocking the flow of fluid to the cylinder. Meanwhile, the piston shoves fluid through a check valve, through the cylinder outlet into the hydraulic lines, and to the wheel cylinders as pictured in the drawing above. The wheel cylinders, in turn, push the brake shoes against the moving drums, creating the friction which stops the wheels.

In other words, the force of the driver's foot is transmitted to the brake shoes by means of the incompressible fluid confined inside the brake system. The same principle is used in hydraulic presses and lifts. In cars equipped with power brakes, the driver's foot is augmented by a mechanical booster.

When you release pressure on the brake pedal, the piston return spring retracts the piston, reopening the compensating port and relieving the pressure on the fluid, which flows back into the master cylinder and reservoir.

The most frequent trouble in the master cylinder is with the primary and secondary cups. To check them out for leaks:

Get in the car, apply *light* pressure to the pedal

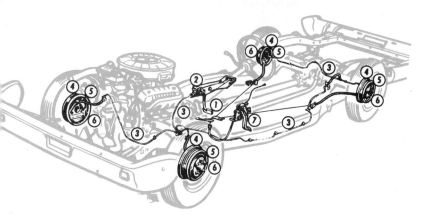

How brakes work: Stepping on the pedal (1) sends fluid from the master cylinder (2) through the lines (3) to wheel cylinders (4), which push brake shoes (5) against drums (6). The parking brake works mechanically via a cable

Leaky secondary cup in the master cylinder lets fluid accumulate to trickle out when you break the boot loose at the pushrod end. This one was taken from the car for the photo

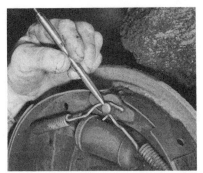

Anchor pins (above) rarely come loose, but check them—just to be safe

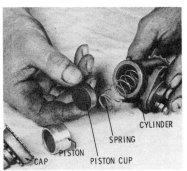

CYLINDER
SPRING
CAP
PISTON
PISTON CUP

The simple components of a wheel cylinder are analogous to those of a master cylinder. The cap pushes on the brake shoe. Other types have pins to pass pressure to the shoes

and maintain it for about a minute. If the pedal fades away slowly, the primary piston cup is probably shot, allowing the brake fluid to leak past it.

Now, check the aft end of the cylinder—the end covered by the rubber boot through which the push rod goes. It is usually located on the left side of the fire wall, where the push rod enters the master cylinder. Break the boot away with a screwdriver. If fluid dribbles out of the boot, the secondary cup is shot (a frequent cause of a low brake pedal).

Often, you can check for a leaking secondary cup by merely examining the engine side of the fire wall for a trickle of fluid running from the master cylinder and down the wall.

If the master cylinder tests indicate internal damage, you can either replace the entire assembly with a new or rebuilt one, or repair it yourself with the aid of a rebuild kit. This job proceeds as follows:

With the cylinder removed from the car, dump any remaining fluid. If there's a threaded cap on the outlet end, start tear-down there. But if your model has that end sealed, start from the rubber-booted end and invert the sequence.

With the threaded outlet removed, check the end-nut rubber washer, which acts as the seat for the check valve. This washer seldom gets damaged, but if it is worn or distorted, replace it. Rebuild kits will generally include replacements for all rubber parts.

Now slide the main spring from its position. In the cylinder pictured, the spring is attached to the check valve.

The main spring has two important functions. First, it holds the check valve against its seat when the brake pedal is applied, to maintain about a 7- to 12-lb. fluid pressure in the hydraulic lines. Then, when the brake is released, the spring forces the piston back, removing the primary cup from the compensating port.

With the spring removed, take out the primary cup and slide the piston from its place. The secondary cup is an integral part of the piston. The whole piston setup, cups and all, will be replaced with new parts from the rebuild kit.

With all parts now removed from the cylinder,

379

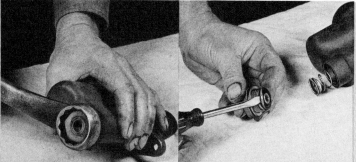

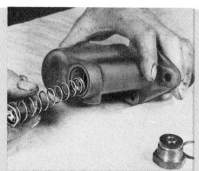

Master cylinder disassembly starts with the cap on the outlet end of the housing (left). The valve seat washer, against which the check valve rests, comes off easily. When rebuilding a master cylinder, replace this and all the rest of the rubber parts; they're included in the rebuild kit

The main spring will slide out of the bore handily after the outlet cap has been removed. It holds the check valve against the valve seat washer and helps the piston return

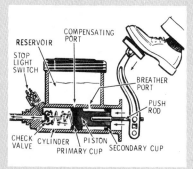

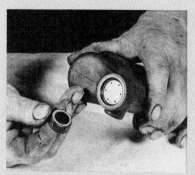

In the master cylinder, brake pedal pressure advances the piston so the primary cup cuts off the compensating port, then passes hydraulic pressure through check valve and lines

The primary cup, at the working end of the piston, is another rubber part that is replaced during rebuilding. The piston face is visible through the opening in the end of the housing

The secondary cup is usually an integral part of the master cylinder piston. It keeps reservoir fluid from leaking past the back end of the piston itself

inspect the bore carefully. Whether rust or pockmarks are apparent or not, the cylinder should always be honed during a rebuild job. Lubricate the bore with denatured alcohol or brake fluid, and grind with a honing stone and electric drill until the cylinder bore is as shiny as a gun barrel. Since it's easy to remove too much metal, check the piston-to-bore clearance with a feeler gauge after honing. If clearance exceeds .005 in., replace the entire master cylinder as it will no longer retain fluid effectively under normal use.

Compensating and breather ports are important, too. The bigger breather port isn't likely to clog, but the compensating port could. It would then be unable to pass fluid back to the reservoir and the brakes might lock. Run a thin wire through it (photo, p. 381), just to be safe.

Next, reassemble the cylinder, by reversing the disassembly procedure already described. Clean out the vent in the reservoir cap hole with a wire,

to prevent a vacuum from forming in the cylinder, which could lead to a dangerous spongy and/ or low pedal. Then put the cylinder back into the car, hook up the push rod and fill the reservoir to within ½ in. of the top with fluid.

This brings us to an easy part of the job—checking the hydraulic lines. In most cases, damage to these lines will consist of either a leak, usually at a wheel cylinder, or a line crimp.

To find leaks, have someone apply firm pressure to the brake pedal as you examine the lines leading into each wheel cylinder. A trace of hydraulic fluid running down the inside of a tire is a sure sign of a leak at the wheel cylinder connection. Obviously, a leak elsewhere in a line will show as drops or traces of fluid on the surface of the line.

To find a line crimp, which causes a wheel to "slide" or keep spinning when the brakes are applied, just inspect each fluid line visually. If you

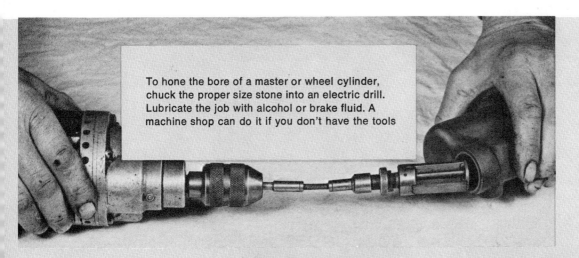

To hone the bore of a master or wheel cylinder, chuck the proper size stone into an electric drill. Lubricate the job with alcohol or brake fluid. A machine shop can do it if you don't have the tools

# WHAT'S INSIDE A MASTER CYLINDER?

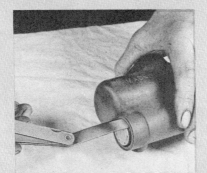

Keep checking the piston-bore clearance to avoid removing too much metal. If clearance is more than .005 in., the cylinder housing will have to be replaced

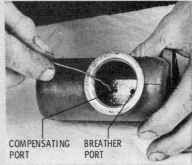

COMPENSATING PORT    BREATHER PORT

To be on the safe side, run a thin wire through the compensating port to remove any possible obstructions. The breather port is bigger, thus rarely does it get clogged up

spot either a fluid leak or a crimp, the line *must* be replaced.

Finally, turn your attention to the last of the "fluid carriers"—the wheel cylinders. Each of these consists of eight parts: one cylinder, one spring, two caps, two pistons and two piston cups.

Usually, each side of the wheel cylinder operates one of the wheel's brake shoes. However, in some cars—including some Chrysler-built products—there are *two* so-called single-action wheel cylinders to a wheel. Each controls only one of the brake shoes. If, when testing, you find one of these cylinders must be replaced or rebuilt, replace or rebuild both, to equalize the pressure on the brake shoes.

As a wheel cylinder receives the force of hydraulic pressure, the pistons are pushed outward, moving in the cylinder bore. In some wheel cylinders (those equipped with rubber caps), the pistons will, in turn, activate the brake shoes by

means of actuating pins. However, in cylinders that have metal caps, the brake shoes are activated by the caps, which are connected directly to the shoes and are pushed outward by the pistons. When the brakes are released, the pressure is taken off the pistons, which then retract to their idle position.

The critical parts of a wheel cylinder, as with a master cylinder, are the piston cups. If these allow fluid to escape, you might experience a low brake pedal or a spongy, springy braking action.

To check a wheel cylinder, "break" each of its boots. If fluid is escaping, it will dribble out immediately.

Incidentally, any time you do a complete brake overhaul, you should either replace or rebuild all wheel cylinders, even if they show no sign of damage. Why renew everything else only to have a cylinder fail shortly afterward?

If you decide to rebuild, the procedure is sim-

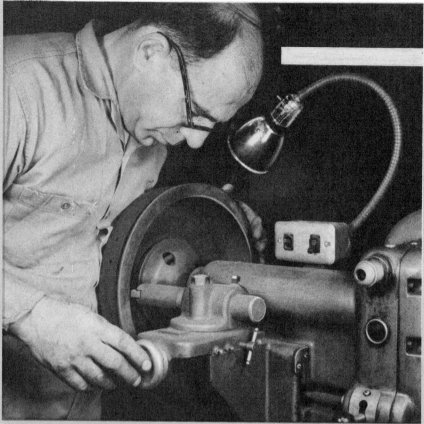

A brake job should always involve a light cut inside each drum surface to remove any high spots or rough areas that don't show up in a visual check

*give brakes a break, continued*

ilar to that already described for the master cylinder. Again, you'll want a rebuild kit. After disassembling the cylinder (see photo, lower right on p. 380), hone the bore and be sure the piston-to-cylinder wall clearance is .005 in. or less.

There's one more point to keep in mind when installing new parts from a rebuild kit in either a master or a wheel cylinder. Since you never know whether the parts are clean, wash each one in alcohol or a non-oil-base cleaning fluid before installation. Dirt on any part can score a cylinder wall. Also, soak the rubber parts in clean brake fluid. If installed dry, they may score and start to leak the first time you run the car.

Parts of a brake system that do require the most careful, highly skilled attention are linings, drums, springs and seals.

Too often when an accident occurs because of brake failure, the cause is said to be *"sudden brake failure."* But such a thing is quite rare.

Brakes usually give plenty of advance warning—in the form of a spongy pedal, hard stops or the like—before breaking down completely.

Furthermore, too many drivers put price ahead of quality. The car owner who believes he can get quality and save money at the same time by buying brake shoes selling for 25 percent less, or having the brake drums turned down once too often, or having the brakes adjusted just one more time before rebuilding them, is creating safety in his mind only—not in his car.

Another thing you can't skimp on is workmanship. Let only the most skilled, conscientious mechanic you can find work on your brakes. If you've had experience and know what you're doing and have access to the proper equipment, you can do it yourself. But there are some catches to this approach. For one thing, brakes now vary so widely from car to car that you must have *full* information about your particular model. Overlooking just one important fact could lead to a

Cutting too much metal from drum is dangerous. Pros mike inside diameters

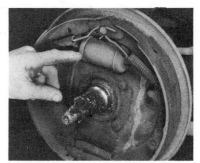
Most experts advise new or rebuilt wheel cylinders at relining time

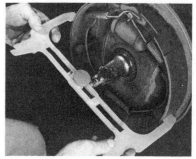
After relining, set shoe-drum spacing to specifications to avoid brake drag

serious accident. Therefore, it's probably best that you use the following information as a basis for evaluating a brake job, rather than doing one.

Remember that a *thorough* brake job starts at the master cylinder. When it comes to other parts —the "stopping parts"—a quality overhaul should guarantee:

• Trueness of the brake-drum surfaces and assurance that the drums have sufficient thickness to withstand the heat and forces of braking.

• Trueness of the brake shoes.

• Proper matching of brake shoe thicknesses to brake drum diameters.

• Assurance that anchor-pin holes of the brake shoes are not worn.

• Replacement of hold-down springs that no longer have sufficient tension.

• Smoothness and cleanliness of shoe platforms on the backing plates, and that they're of equal height and lightly lubricated before shoes are installed.

• Installation of new grease seals *every time* the brakes are relined.

• Correct adjustment of brake shoe-to-drum clearance and of anchor pins.

When you come right down to it, the most critical parts of a brake, and the parts which take the most punishment, are the drums and linings. Both, therefore, need particular attention.

Every time you make a stop, the friction between the brake linings and the drums generates heat. Normal temperature on the drums is considered to be about 220 deg. F. to 260 deg. F. However, the faster the stop, the higher this temperature goes. If something's amiss in the system, temperatures could reach 1400 deg!

Beside providing the surface which creates the necessary friction, the drums must also absorb about 90 percent of this heat and dissipate it. In doing so, they can become scored, roughened,

distorted, bell-mouthed, barrel-shaped or out-of-round. Any one of these conditions leads, of course, to erratic and unsafe braking. If extreme, they can lead to brake failure. Yet, when brakes are overhauled, the drums seldom get sufficient attention.

After 10,000, 20,000 or 30,000 miles of use, one cannot simply look at the drums, nod contentedly on finding nothing and press them back into service. Although rough or scored spots might not be visible readily, they can still be there. Furthermore, the drum can be slightly out of round without your noticing it.

Many experts say, therefore, that the drums should receive a light cut on a drum-turning lathe every time the brakes are overhauled.

But suppose you've had the drums turned down in the past. How much more metal can you safely remove, and what can happen if you remove too much?

This question can often be vividly answered by visiting a brake repair shop and just observing. No doubt a driver will pull in to have his brakes adjusted—maybe he has a low pedal.

The mechanic may adjust the first three wheels in the usual manner without trouble. But when he gets to the fourth wheel and turns the adjuster (star wheel) to where the wheel should start to drag, nothing happens.

A closer examination may reveal a malfunction, such as separation of the brake drum from the web. If so, the web has been rotating when the car is braked, but the drum stayed still. In other words, there would be absolutely no braking action on that wheel.

Another close look may reveal a crack in the drum in a direction parallel to the axle shaft. Thus, tightening the star wheel would no nothing but widen the crack.

Under these circumstances, the careful mechanic will take a micrometer reading of the drum. Perhaps it will show only ⅟₁₆ in. of metal remaining at the cracked point. Yet, a casual look at the drum will usually show nothing wrong—no crack, nothing!

Imagine what could happen if the driver had to make a panic stop.

Let's carry the hypothesis one step further. You question the driver and learn that he had the car to other shops before for brake work. And each time the drums had been turned, but the mechanics had failed to mike them to make sure enough metal was left.

In other words, taking too much metal off a drum weakens it and doesn't leave enough strength to absorb and dissipate heat. This results in cracking of the metal.

So, always be sure the drums are miked *before and after* turning to make sure no more than 0.060 in. of metal has been removed from the original thickness of the drum walls, as specified by the manufacturer of your car. Authorities stress the 0.060-in. figure is the *absolute maximum*.

Here's another critical point: In matching new linings to a drum that's been turned, make sure the lining is not too thin for the drum, or it won't make full contact. Usually, if less than 0.030 in. of metal has been turned off the drum thickness, standard linings (those specified as "standard" for your car) can be used. If, however, 0.030 to 0.060 in. has been removed, get shimmed or oversized linings.

### cleanliness is important

A word now about cleanliness. It's important. Whether you press old brake drums back into service or install new ones, they should be cleaned to minimize brake squeal problems. To clean old drums, remove small nicks and scratches with fine emery cloth and blow away dust and dirt with an air hose. Then clean with high-pressure steam or a non-oily solvent. With new drums, a cleaning with high pressure steam or solvent is sufficient.

In selecting new brake linings, keep one word in mind: quality! Whether you prefer bonded linings or the riveted type, buying anything less than the best is only cheating yourself, especially since the difference in price between the best and the cheapest is comparatively little.

What about bonded vs. riveted linings? Despite all the noise, it's a matter of personal choice. Some people say a riveted lining is less likely to come loose from the shoe when over-

heated and is less likely to squeal. Others argue that a bonded lining provides more uniform contact with the drum. The fact is either type gives fine service if well made and installed.

Here are some points to keep in mind when having new linings installed:

● Replace all linings, even if only one needs replacement. Assuming normal wear, if one or two linings are worn out, it can't be too long before the others reach the same point. So you might as well do the whole job at once. Besides, it's tough to get the correct adjustment and the proper braking distribution unless all linings are uniform.

● You just don't slap in new linings. Because it's imperative to have the correct lining-to-drum contact, today's re-lining jobs should all be "custom," with each lining being ground to the proper diameter to fit each individual brake drum. Otherwise, you're asking for brake chatter, uneven application, brake drag and a hard pedal.

● Backing plates must be absolutely clean, free of nicks and burrs, and lubricated.

● With new linings installed, they must be adjusted just right in relation to the drums to avoid rubbing, premature wear.

### check the old linings

Examining old brake linings can tell you much about the overall condition of the brake system. For example, if a lining is thicker on one side of a shoe than the other, it means the drum is bellmouthed or the shoe platform isn't at right angles to the web. Similarly, if the lining is thicker at both ends than in the center, the shoe arc wasn't correct.

Among the most neglected parts of a brake system are the return springs. Truckers claim they've found weak springs to be the primary cause of brake trouble with their rigs. And, believe it or not, weak springs can cause every known braking problem, including pulling, diving, excessive wear and drum scoring.

So, examine the springs carefully, feel them for tension and replace any that seem the least bit damaged or worn.

After the brakes have been rebuilt, of course, they must be adjusted and bled in the usual manner.

Now, when you begin driving with your newly rebuilt brakes, remember that new linings require about 250 miles of breaking-in. During this period, avoid high speed and panic stops.

**See also:** auto repair; driving, snow; steering, auto; tires; wheel alignment, auto.